Reclaiming the Salient

Resurrecting the Great War Battlegrounds of Flanders Fields

Roger Steward

Helion & Company Limited
Unit 8 Amherst Business Centre
Budbrooke Road
Warwick
CV34 5WE
England
Tel. 01926 499 619
Email: info@helion.co.uk
Website: www.helion.co.uk
Twitter: @helionbooks
Visit our blog at blog.helion.co.uk

Published by Helion & Company 2023
Designed and typeset by Mary Woolley (www.battlefield-design.co.uk)
Cover designed by Paul Hewitt, Battlefield Design (www.battlefield-design.co.uk)

Text © Roger Steward 2023
Images © as individually credited

Every reasonable effort has been made to trace copyright holders and to obtain their permission for the use of copyright material. The author and publisher apologise for any errors or omissions in this work and would be grateful if notified of any corrections that should be incorporated in future reprints or editions of this book.

ISBN 978-1-1915113-67-2

British Library Cataloguing-in-Publication Data.
A catalogue record for this book is available from the British Library.

All rights reserved. No part of this publication may be reproduced, stored in a retrieval system, or transmitted, in any form, or by any means, electronic, mechanical, photocopying, recording or otherwise, without the express written consent of Helion & Company Limited.

For details of other military history titles published by Helion & Company Limited contact the above address, or visit our website: http://www.helion.co.uk.

We always welcome receiving book proposals from prospective authors.

Dedication

This book is dedicated to all the hidden victims of war, in particular to all those who have fallen victim to the Great War since its end in 1919. The Great War is still claiming victims today.

Contents

Acknowledgements	v
Abbreviations and Glossary of Terms	vii
Foreword	ix
Author's Note	xi
Part I: The Iron Harvest	12
Introduction	13
1 An Insatiable Beast	23
2 Military Labour in the Salient	31
3 The Iron Harvest	36
4 Danger UXB	48
5 *Pericula Non Timeo* (I Do Not Fear the Dangers)	72
6 At the Sharp End: The Evolution of DOVO Poelkapelle	82
7 DOVO Today: A Day Out with DOVO	88
Part II: Recovering the Fallen	104
Introduction	105
8 An Extraordinary Englishman: Sir Fabian Ware and the Creation of the War Graves Organisations	108
9 Here Dead We Lie	114
10 Post-War Body Recoveries	121
11 Captain Crawford and the 68th Labour Company: 'The Pioneer Company in Work of this Kind'	128
12 Hooge Crater Cemetery Enquiry: Burial Discrepancies and Misidentification	145
13 The Lost Army: Abandoning the Search	157
14 The Recovery Restarts: The IWGC Takes Up the Torch	167
15 Bringing the Boys Home?: The Question of Repatriation	172
16 The Business of Death: Body Snatching and Illegal Exhumations in the Ypres Salient	182
17 The Reaper Returns: The Second World War and Post-War Era	206
18 Another Time, A Different Philosophy	213
19 Finding Lance Corporal Cook	222
Bibliography	230
Index	235

Acknowledgements

It is only when you research and write a publication, be it large or small, that you realise how tight knit and supportive the community of First World War historians and enthusiasts really is. I am deeply indebted to this community for their willingness to share information and images with the aim of continuing the story of the Great War. My research for this book has, amongst others, led me to contact notable historians and authors, international archival sources, members of the MOD, forensic investigation experts and the Belgian armed forces. Without exception, all have been very happy to help by providing extensive information and answering what must have seemed like an endless bombardment of questions and queries. In fact, many went beyond the 'call of duty' in providing me with the answers I needed. To everybody whom I contacted and, in return, helped me with the research for this book, I thank you. Without you, this project would not have been possible.

In addition to those already credited in the book, I would like to thank the following archival sources: Dr Dominiek Dendooven and all of the research team of the In Flanders Fields Museum (Ypres), Andrew Featherstone and Micheal Greet and the archives team of the CWGC, Wouter Moyaert of the Stadsarchief Poperinge, Wouter De Witte Kenniscentrum of the Memorial Museum Passchendaele, J. Jeffrey O'Brien, MAS Saskatoon City archive, Lindsay A. Stokalko (BA, MA), University of Saskatchewan archive and the National Library of New Zealand.

For granting me access to the operations of the Belgian bomb-disposal service, DOVO, I would like to thank Philippe De Cock, military commander of the Belgian Province West Flanders, and Jacques Callebaut, *adjudant-majoor* (Air) from DOVO – SEDEE.

My gratitude also goes to the organisations that explained to me their roles and procedures in body recovery and identification – including Rosie Barron and the team at the JCCC of the MOD, Dr Michael Walbank (forensic scientist at Cellmark Forensic Services), Steve Arnold of the CWGC (France) for his advice on body recovery procedure, Simon Verdegem of the Skylarcs archaeology group and Rob Troubleyn for their in-depth knowledge and experience of body recoveries in Belgium and Major Ret'd Peter Williamson MBE of the Essex Regiment Museum for his information regarding the identification of Lance Corporal Robert Cook.

In addition to the official organisations, I would like to thank the following historians, authors and experts in their own fields for having the patience to answer my emails, texts and calls without complaint, often giving me more information than I requested: Nele Bille, Professor Mark Connelly, Daisy Debacker, Wilfried Deryck, Jeremy Gordon-Smith, Peter E. Hodgkinson, Steven de Meulenaere, Martin Pegler, Paul Reed, Pete Smith, Daan Verfaillie and Bart Zino.

Finally, I would like to thank Duncan Rogers and Dr Michael LoCicero of Helion and Company for their faith in this project and their willingness to give a relatively new author this opportunity.

Abbreviations and Glossary of Terms

AGS	Australian Graves Services
AIF	Australian Imperial Force
ASD	Army Salvage Department
BDM	Body Density Map
BEF	British Expeditionary Force
BWGA	British War Graves Association
BWHI	Belgian War Heritage Institute
CC	Civilian Cemetery
CCTV	Closed-Circuit Television
CDC	Controlled Demolition Chamber
CEF	Canadian Expeditionary Force
CGS	Chief of General Staff
Clark I	Diphenylchloroarsine
Clark II	Diphenylcyanoarsine
COY	Company
CWGC	Commonwealth War Graves Commission
CWGD	Canadian War Graves Detachment
DADGR&E	Deputy Assistant Director of Graves Registrations and Enquiries
DGR&E	Directorate of Graves Registration & Enquiries
DNA	Deoxyribonucleic Acid
DOVO	Service for Clearance and Disposal of Explosive Ordnance (Belgium)
DOVOO	Service for Clearance and Disposal of Explosive Ordnance and Obstacles (Belgium)
EOD	Explosive Ordnance Disposal
FHA	Flanders Heritage Agency
GHQ	General Headquarters
GRC	Graves Registration Commission
GRU	Graves Registration Unit
GS	General Service
HDC	Hot Destruction/Detonation Chamber

IWGC	Imperial War Graves Commission
JCCC	Joint Casualty and Compassionate Centre
KIA	Killed in Action
LOC	Line of Communication
MOD	Ministry of Defence
NBC	Nuclear, Biological, and Chemical
NCO	Non-Commissioned Officer
OC	Officer Commanding
OP	Observation Post
OR	Other Rank
PINS	Portable Isotopic Neutron Spectroscopy
POW	Prisoner of War
PPCLI	Princess Patricia's Canadian Light Infantry
PTE	Private
QMG	Quartermaster General
RFA	Royal Field Artillery
SAA	Small Arms Ammunition
SDC	Static Demolition Chamber
SDM	Service for the Destruction of Munitions (Belgium)
SGD	Signed
SRD	Service of the Devastated Regions (Belgium)
UBS	Unknown British Soldier
UXB	Unexploded Bomb

Foreword

As the In Flanders Fields Museum rightly reminds visitors, the landscape is the last true witness of the Great War. Nature and human activity have done much to heal the wounds of war over the last hundred years, but the scar tissues remain. As anyone who has walked the battlefields in the winter months, and particularly after the ploughing season, knows, the marks of war on the landscape become vivid. On the chalky soils of the Somme, it remains easy to trace the runs of trenches; in the thick, claggy clay of the Salient, the gentle ripples that make up the ridges show the ebb and flow of the almost ceaseless flow of battle in the region. Among these marks of war, two reminders of the conflict stand out most starkly: unexploded ammunition and the cemeteries and memorials.

The amount of unexploded ammunition the rich soils of Flanders give up every year is quite remarkable. Sometimes, it is possible to spot the remnants of shell casings sticking out of a plough furrow, or small mounds of rusted iron scraps might be glimpsed in a farm courtyard. More dramatic is the sight of shells neatly stacked on the roadside awaiting the arrival of the specialist military engineering teams. To see whole shells looking not unlike the many wartime photographs of ammunition dumps is a truly arresting sight. They inspire strange, contradictory sensations. At one and the same time they appal as their lethal potential is calculated, and yet they are fascinating. Despite the dangers, it is impossible to not stand stock-still and stare at them as ancient peoples do in the visual representations of the discovery of fire. I have often found myself overcome by something like a sensation of shame as I realise that I am fascinated by the appeal of the utterly utilitarian and accidental aesthetic of these most dreadful aspects of industrial design and output. Here, in solid, metallic form, is the impact of the war, the footprint of the war, still starkly visible in the present.

The other obvious remnant of the conflict is one that inspires a different response. If the shells are the brutal, crude, almost insolent revenants of the war, the cemeteries and memorial are its elegiac, bardic witness. Most clearly seen in the stunningly beautiful neo-classical aesthetic of the Imperial (now Commonwealth) War Graves Commission, the commemorative landscape is the most poignant and haunting of visible traces. In the leafless environment of mid-winter when sightlines open up, particularly from those sanguine ridges around Ieper, the white Portland and Euville crosses of sacrifice create battlefield trig points across the landscape: 'Here Stood the Armies of the British Empire', as it states on the Menin Gate.

In this book, the hugely knowledgeable and experienced battlefield guide, Roger Steward, takes us on a journey across the salient. He interrogates these remaining witnesses in an insightful, careful and sensitive manner. In exploring the processes of ammunition expenditure, its subsequent recovery and the burial and commemoration of the dead, he picks up on the quotidian aspects of the war as it was fought and the war as it remains in the Flanders landscape today. Legacies of violence and legacies of heartfelt commemoration intertwine in this landscape. As Roger's work shows, the past is with us, and on the battlefields of the Western Front, its traces remain fresh, vivid and, in some cases, lethal.

Mark Connelly
Canterbury, December 2021.

Author's Note

In an effort to maintain historical continuity with regards to weights and measures, both pre- and post-decimalisation, I have decided to use the weights and measures in use at the time with regards to the relevant passages, resulting in both imperial and metric measurements being used in this publication. Please accept my apologies for any confusion this may cause.

Part I

The Iron Harvest

A local family photographed with several large, unexploded shells recovered from their land. (Photographer unknown. *De Poperinghenaar*, 21 March 1939. Courtesy of Stadsarchief Poperinge and John Desreumaux.)

Introduction

The Dreaded Salient

> *At the beginning of the First World War, popular opinion was that it would not last more than four months, that the science of modern warfare would take such a ghastly toll of human life that mankind would demand cessation of such barbarism. But we were mistaken. We were caught in an avalanche of mad destruction and brutal slaughter that went on for four years to the bewilderment of humanity. We had started a haemorrhage of world proportion, and we could not stop it.*
>
> Charles Chaplin.[1]

When the guns finally fell silent across the Western Front, the tumult of war had already departed the Ypres Salient. The battles of 1918 became the final instalments of a four-year chapter of death and destruction in the battlefields around Ypres. By the end of 1914, the war had stagnated, and the initial war of movement had turned into a war of attrition, where every inch of ground was hard fought over in a never-ending cycle of death and destruction. During the residency of the Great War in Belgium, the Ypres Salient had suffered every horror that modern warfare of the day could hurl at it. The year of 1914 witnessed the First Battle of Ypres and the halting of the German juggernaut as it powered its way through Belgium in an attempt to take the channel ports and knock Great Britain out of the war. Desperately outnumbered and outgunned, the BEF (British Expeditionary Force), with the help of their Belgian and French allies, managed to stop the German armies' advance at the outskirts of Ypres. The fighting was desperate, brutal and costly: an estimated 300,000 casualties were

---

1   Charles Chaplin, *My Autobiography* (New York: Simon and Schuster, 1964), p.213.

incurred across all sides during the approximate four weeks of fighting.[2] This level of carnage was to set the tone for the rest of the war in the Ypres Salient. Both armies dug in for the winter, with an eye to renewing the conflict in earnest the following year. Defensive positions protected by barbed-wire belts and well-placed machine guns were constructed, making the breaching of these systems virtually impossible in view of the limited technology available. The winter of 1914 and early 1915 passed with no more major offensives, but the Salient more than proved its lethality with over 7,000 Allied soldiers being killed in Belgium between the First and Second Battles of Ypres, a large proportion of them losing their lives in the dreaded Salient.[3]

The spring of 1915 saw the launch of the Second Battle of Ypres (22 April to 25 May 1915). In an attempt to break through the Allied defences, the Germans initiated a major offensive at 5:00 p.m. on 22 April 1915 with the launching of a poison gas attack in the Langemark sector of the Ypres Salient. That evening, the Germans released an estimated 168 tonnes of chlorine gas from around 6,000 cannisters, all of which had been brought up in secret to the front line and installed in the German trenches.[4] When the wind direction and strength was favourable, the Germans opened the valves on the cannisters and released the gas, creating a wall of noxious fumes an estimated four miles wide and at least 10 feet high. The gas drifted towards the French armies' positions and quickly enveloped them in a deadly cloud, creating death and panic whilst opening a four-mile gap in the front line. The Germans, however, failed to exploit the panic and confusion as they themselves were surprised by the success of the gas and some of their front-line infantrymen were reluctant to advance too quickly since they had witnessed the terrible effect of the gas on its victims.

Willi Siebert, who was a part of the German units responsible for releasing the gas on that fateful day in 1915, wrote of the attack:

> Finally, we decided to release the gas. The weatherman was right. It was a beautiful day; the sun was shining. Where there was grass, it was blazing green. We should have been going on a picnic, not doing what we were going to do … We sent the infantry back and opened the valves with the strings. About supper time, the gas started toward the French; everything was stone quiet. We all wondered what was going to happen. As this great cloud of green, grey gas was forming in front of us, we suddenly heard the French yelling. In less than a minute they started with the most rifle and machine gun fire that I had ever

---

2   The term 'casualty' includes the statistics for killed, wounded, missing and POWs (prisoners of war). Ian F. W. Beckett, *Ypres: The First Battle 1914* (London: Routledge, 2013), pp.225–26.
3   'Find War Dead', *Commonwealth War Graves Commission*, <http:www.cwgc.org/find-records/find-war-dead>, accessed 21 Jan. 2021.
4   Jean Pascal Zanders, 'The Destruction of Old Chemical Weapons in Belgium', in Thomas Stock and Karlheinz Lohs (eds), *The Challenge of Old Chemical Munitions and Toxic Armament Wastes* (Oxford: Oxford University Press, 1997), p.197.

heard. Every field artillery gun, every machine gun, every rifle that the French had, must have been firing. I had never heard such a noise. The hail of bullets going over our heads was unbelievable, but it was not stopping the gas. The wind kept moving the gas towards the French lines. We heard the cows bawling, and the horses screaming. The French kept on shooting. They couldn't possibly see what they were shooting at. In about 15 minutes the gun fire started to quit. After a half hour, only occasional shots. Then everything was quiet again. In a while it had cleared, and we walked past the empty gas bottles. What we saw was total death. Nothing was alive. All of the animals had come out of their holes to die. Dead rabbits, moles, and rats and mice were everywhere. The smell of the gas was still in the air. It hung on the few bushes which were left. When we got to the French lines the trenches were empty but in a half mile the bodies of French soldiers were everywhere. It was unbelievable. Then we saw there were some English. You could see where men had clawed at their faces, and throats, trying to get breath. Some had shot themselves. The horses, still in the stables, cows, chickens, everything, all were dead. Everything, even the insects were dead.[5]

A French soldier killed during the gas attacks of 22 April 1915. (Photographer unknown. Courtesy of the In Flanders Fields Museum.)

5   Willi Siebert, *Journal* (Ypres: In Flanders Fields Museum, 1915).

By the time the Germans had realised their error, the opportunity of breakthrough was gone. The Allied forces quickly regrouped and plugged up the gaps in the line, and battered battalions and individual stragglers were quickly reorganised into a composite brigade commanded by Colonel A. D. Geddes, whose initial task was to plug the hole between the French and Canadian units on the French right flank and then to 'fire fight' as and where needed. The Canadians, in particular, are famed for their last-ditch actions at Kitchener's Wood on the night of 22 April and in the coming days at St. Julien. The Second Battle of Ypres was to rage on until 25 May, and, at its conclusion, the Germans had advanced around two to three miles but ultimately failed in their goal of breaking out of the Salient. The casualty rate was high, with an estimated 116,000 casualties in four weeks across all sides. The gas attacks on 22 April 1915 were the first of a recorded 14 German gas attacks launched during the period of the Second Battle of Ypres.[6] The Salient had seen the first recorded use of poison gas on the Western Front, a momentous occasion but for all the wrong reasons. The next example of German 'frightfulness' was seen on 30 July 1915, when flamethrowers were deployed by the Germans against the British troops at Hooge. Another grim milestone had been reached at the Salient.

The interval between the Second and Third Battles of Ypres was just over two years, but the ferocity of the fighting in the Salient continued unabated. The Allied forces were surrounded on three sides and were overlooked from the high ground by German artillery spotters eagerly looking for their next target. Any visible movement attracted salvoes of German artillery shells as they attempted to wear down the British forces – they were, in effect, sniping with artillery. The geographical situation, the smaller but significant actions of 1916 at St. Eloi and Mount Sorrell and the hugely important and successful Battle of the Messines Ridge in June 1917 – coupled with the continuous cycles of trench raids, artillery fire, sniping and day-to-day trench warfare – equated to an average weekly Allied death toll in the Salient of around 600 men. In this war of attrition, the High Commands had an acceptance of daily losses or 'wastage', but it had risen to an unsustainable level in the Salient, and something needed to be done.

The weekly death toll was one of the many factors in the planning and reasoning for the Third Battle of Ypres. This death toll equated to three full-strength army divisions of 20,000 men being annihilated in two years for no gain. Overlooked by the Germans on the high ground and being fired at from three sides, the Ypres Salient had become a place of death and fear for the men of the British Army, who had named it 'The Dreaded Salient'. The other reasons for the implementation of the Third Battle of Ypres (or 'Passchendaele' as it became known) are well documented in the many books written on the subject, as is the debate on its outcome: was it a success or a disaster? There are arguments for both sides, and military historians still argue on this subject to this day. One thing that is for sure is that thousands of men fought and died in the most terrible of conditions. The casualty figures are still being

---

6   Zanders, 'Destruction of Old Chemical Weapons', pp.223–30.

updated and revised today, with the German figures in particular being in contention. According to the CWGC's (Commonwealth War Graves Commission) statistics, the armies of the British Empire lost around 78,000 men killed during the Third Battle of Ypres.[7] Robert. A. Perry quotes an estimated 250,000 to 270,000 casualties for the British Empire and around 238,000 to 270,000 German casualties, both sides losing roughly the same number.[8] The Third Battle of Ypres was brought to an official end in November 1917, although actions continued well into December.

The year of 1918 is thought to have been the deadliest year of the war. The spring of that year saw the great German spring offensive across France and Belgium. In the Ypres Salient, in the face of Operation Georgette, the British Army retired from the Passchendaele Ridge, relinquishing their hard-fought and costly gains of 1917, to shorten their defensive line in an attempt to halt the German onslaught. The Battle of the Lys (or the Fourth Battle of Ypres) was fought between 7–29 April 1918 and would cost all sides an estimated 228,000 casualties. In the face of extreme and sustained pressure, the Allied forces repelled the attacks and held the Germans on a line that passed through 'Hellfire Corner', barely two miles from the ruined belfry of the Cloth Hall in the centre of Ypres. The German offensive ground to a halt. Hindered by a lack of supplies and manpower, the German forces faced an enemy now bolstered by the arrival of thousands of fresh American troops – this was a war that was now impossible for the Germans to win. The Allied counterattacks known as the 'Hundred Days Offensive' began on 8 August 1918 and ended on 11 November 1918 with a decisive Allied victory. Fighting had resumed in earnest around Ypres on 28 September 1918 when the Allies launched an attack to finally break out of the chokehold that the Salient had over the Allied forces. The Fifth Battle of Ypres was fought between 28 September and 2 October 1918, and, in those few short days, the Allies gained more ground than they had in the previous three years. Another 9,000 Allied casualties and an unknown number of German casualties had been added to the butcher's bill of the Ypres Salient. On 11 November 1918, peace finally returned to the Western Front and the Ypres Salient. It was now the time to regroup, look forward and regenerate.

The twenty-first-century Flanders is a very different Flanders to that of 1918. Today, as you travel through its flat landscape of open fields and farmland, you could be forgiven for overlooking the fact that one of history's largest and destructive conflicts took place around you. Today's military cemeteries, monuments and remaining bunkers are a testament to the industrialised slaughter and carnage that gripped the fields of Flanders in the war of 1914–1918. By the end of the Great War, the 100 square miles of the Ypres Salient had witnessed death and destruction on an incomprehensible

---

7   'Find War Dead', <http:www.cwgc.org/find-records/find-war-dead>, accessed 21 Jan. 2021.
8   Robert A. Perry, *To Play a Giant's Part: The Role of the British Army at Passchendaele* (Uckfield: Naval & Military Press, 2014), p.569.

The devastated Ypres Salient. (Photographer unknown. Courtesy of the In Flanders Fields Museum.)

The devastation at Chateau Wood Hooge on the outskirts of Ypres. (Photo by Frank Hurley. Australian War Memorial (AWM). Public Domain.)

scale. The battlefield areas had witnessed almost complete extinction, not a building, tree or even a blade of grass existed in the old battlegrounds by 1919. The wildlife had been devasted, and ground-dwelling animals were eradicated by the constant artillery fire or by the insidious gas attacks. The only animals that seemed to thrive were the rats – the numerous rotten corpses that littered the battlefields of the Ypres Salient had provided them with an easy food source. Cities, towns and villages had been obliterated by the relentless artillery fire, with some in the most extreme cases reduced to a pile of rubble in the sea of mud.

The great city of Ypres was reduced to ruins as the German artillery pounded its buildings from 18 November 1914 right through to 1918. Huge 42cm-calibre German shells fired from a distance of 6 miles rained down on the city and reduced its cathedral to rubble and the belfry of the mighty Cloth Hall to no more than a brick stump. Such was the level of destruction, and it was said that, in 1919, a man on horseback could see right across Ypres from one corner to the other. Virtually no buildings in Ypres were left untouched by the end of the Great War. The destructive power of the artillery took a terrible toll not only on the infrastructure of the area but also on the bodies of the men and women who fought and lived in the Ypres Salient. It is estimated that 500,000 service men and women from all sides lost their lives in the Salient, with hundreds of thousands of their bodies unaccounted for, atomised by the artillery or lost forever in the seemingly bottomless mud of the Ypres Salient.[9] Figures on the losses of the civilian population are less easy to assess due to the movement of the population as the war approached and the loss of records, but the In Flanders Fields Museum in Ypres currently estimates the figure as in excess of 25,000 men, women and children.[10]

Artillery was king in the Ypres Salient. During the early days of the Great War, the British artillery had fired so many shells that they quickly outstripped their reserves and rate of production and so became handicapped by their lack of ammunition, leading to the rationing of shells. In early 1915, the British field artillery were limited to firing six rounds per day per gun and no more than two rounds per day for each heavy howitzer.[11] The 'shell scandal' of 1915 led to the reorganisation of the British munitions production and the formation of the Ministry of Munitions on 5 June 1915, which increased capacity to such an extent that, in the run up to the Third Battle of Ypres in 1917, the British artillery were able to amass over 2,000 artillery pieces of all calibres, which in turn fired an incredible 4.25 million artillery shells in just two weeks.[12] The hundreds of millions of artillery shells that bombarded the roughly 100 square miles of the Ypres Salient devastated the cities, towns, villages and the surrounding countryside. The fields of Flanders consist of a heavy impermeable

9   Dr Dominiek Dendooven, In Flanders Fields Museum, Ypres.
10 Dr Dominiek Dendooven, In Flanders Fields Museum, Ypres.
11 Lyn Macdonald, *1915: The Death of Innocence* (London: Penguin, 1997), p.64.
12 Perry, *To Play a Giant's Part*, p.100.

Ground Zero. The ruined city of Ypres. (Photographer unknown. Courtesy of the In Flanders Fields Museum.)

Ypresian clay soil and has a high water table, making the construction of drainage systems essential. The artillery fire quickly destroyed the drainage systems and broke the banks of the rivers and streams, leading to widespread flooding.

In the years of 1915 and 1917, Flanders also suffered two of the wettest summers and autumns in living memory. August of 1917 had seen 127mm of rainfall, which was a significant increase of the average figure expected at that time of the year.[13] All these factors combined and turned the Ypres Salient into a lethal swamp. The veterans of the Salient described the mud as a sucking glue that, once you were in, was nigh on impossible to escape unaided from. The seemingly bottomless mud consumed horses, artillery pieces, artillery shells and, of course, the men themselves. Lieutenant J. W. Naylor, Royal Artillery:

13 Perry, *To Play a Giant's Part*, p.573.

I came to hate the Salient. Absolutely loathed it … It wore you down. The weather, the lack of rations, everything seemed to be against you … We were wet through for days on end. We never thought we would get out alive. You couldn't see the cloud with the silver lining. There wasn't one. We had an awful time getting the guns up the plank road on to Westhoek Ridge … It was just sheets of water coming down. It's difficult to get across that it's a sea of mud. Literally a sea. It was my job to see that they got the wagons unloaded at the dump and to arrange carrying parties to take the shells and rations up to the battery. Oddly enough it was a quiet afternoon, but they must have seen some movement on the road because just as the wagon came up a heavy shell came over and burst very close. There were six horses pulling that wagon and they took fright at the explosion, veered right off the road and down they went into the mud. We had no possible way of getting them out. In any event they sank so fast that we had no chance even to cut them loose from the heavy wagon. We formed a chain and stretched out our arms and managed to get the drivers off, but the poor horses sank faster and faster and drowned before our eyes. The wagon and horses disappeared in a matter of minutes. One of the drivers was absolutely incoherent with terror. It was the thought of being drowned in that awful stuff. It's a horrible thought. Anyone would rather be shot and know nothing about it.[14]

The gas attacks of 1915 heralded the beginning of chemical warfare in the Ypres Salient, an event that would eventually lead to the involvement of all the protagonists. The first British gas attack in the Salient is believed to have taken place on 13 June 1916 when 300 cylinders containing chlorine gas were discharged along the front of the British 20th Division.[15] The first use of gas by the Belgian Army was recorded at the end of October 1917.[16] Tactically, the Belgian Army had chosen to use gas on a retaliation basis only, but, by September 1918, aided by French supplies of mustard gas, the Belgian Army changed tactics and was to use it as a weapon of offence. In total, the Salient suffered over 140 recorded chemical weapon attacks during the Great War, with the year of 1917 gaining notoriety for large-scale attacks and the general switch from canisters to projectiles as a delivery method for the gas.[17] This switch was to have a dramatic effect not only in the immediate aftermath of the war but also right up until the present day.

The returning refugees in the early 1920s faced an alien landscape that they quickly labelled as the 'devastated regions'. The landscape was almost lunar, a shell torn

---

14 Lyn Macdonald, *They Called It Passchendaele: The Story of the Third Battle of Ypres and of the Men who Fought in It* (London: Penguin, 1993), p.194.
15 Zanders, 'Destruction of Old Chemical Weapons', pp.223–30.
16 Zanders, 'Destruction of Old Chemical Weapons', pp.223–30.
17 Zanders, 'Destruction of Old Chemical Weapons', pp.223–30.

The appalling conditions of the Western Front. (Photographer unknown. Courtesy of the In Flanders Fields Museum.)

panorama of millions of interlocking water-filled craters linked by hundreds of miles of trenches. Bodies lay everywhere: some buried in shallow graves, some tipped into the foul water of the shell holes and some still on the surface close to where they had fallen, exposed to the elements and in various states of decomposition. Add to this equation the millions of unexploded artillery shells that littered the landscape, and you come to a vision of apocalypse. The Ypres Salient truly was the original ground zero. In order to return the Salient to some semblance of normality, a massive clean-up operation was needed on a scale seldom witnessed before. After four years of warfare, when the front lines had advanced back and forth over an area of no more than a few miles, the Salient was littered with millions of tons of debris of war left behind by the warring factions. Something needed to be done, and it needed to be done fast.

This is the story of how the Ypres Salient was, and still is, being reclaimed from the grip of the Great War of 1914–1918.

1

An Insatiable Beast

Four years of warfare on the Western Front had scarred the Belgian and French landscape to almost beyond recognition. The First World War had been the first of its kind, a truly global conflict of massive proportions. The days of small mobile armies clashing on a battlefield of limited size had passed; the armies of the Great War fought battles across frontages of several miles, involving millions of men across all sides, with the resulting casualty rates being dictated by economies of scale. The tried and tested tactics of hundreds of years of European conflict suddenly became obsolete as the technology of the new industrial world dominated the battlefield. Cavalry was no longer king, as the armies of the great empires got bogged down and slogged it out across the roughly 440-mile front line of the Western Front. This was a war of artillery.

The munition statistics of the 'war to end all wars' are truly staggering. It is thought that an estimated 1.5 billion artillery shells were fired on the Western Front; it has also been claimed that approximately one ton of high explosives fell on every square metre of the approximate 440-mile front line, which ran from the Belgian coast to the Swiss border.[1] In general, it is supposed that, on average, in excess of 20 percent of all shells fired were faulty (i.e., 'duds') and failed to explode, burying themselves deep into the ground or simply lying on the surface where they had landed.[2] Of the total amount of shells fired, seemingly up to five percent were chemical weapons, gas shells containing noxious substances that many of which were lethal.[3]

In terms of the Ypres Salient, the figures are just as dramatic. The Salient was approximately 25 miles long and four miles deep. The armies of the Great War fought desperately over this strip of land, going backwards and forwards as the war

---

1   Augustin M. Prentiss, *Chemicals in War: A Treatise on Chemical Warfare* (New York and London: McGraw Hill, 1937), p.658.
2   Hew Strachan, *The First World War* (Oxford: Oxford University Press, 2001), vol. 1: To Arms, p.1085.
3   Prentiss, *Chemicals in War*, p.658.

progressed. At the end of the war, the approximate 100 square miles of the Salient had claimed the lives of an estimated 500,000 soldiers from all sides, with anything up to 60 percent of them being killed by artillery fire. It is thought that approximately 300 million artillery shells were fired in the Ypres Salient during the Great War, of which an estimated 15 million were chemical weapons. As a result, and working on the general averages of faulty ammunition, we can take an educated estimate of 75 million unexploded artillery shells littering the landscape of the Ypres Salient in the immediate years after the Great War, with roughly 3.7 million of those being unexploded chemical weapons.

We can, however, get a more accurate assessment from the figures published by the British government. The statistics of the British Army and its Empire in the Great War were meticulously recorded and published by the War Office in 1922. The figures highlight the true scale of the conflict from the standpoint of the British Empire only, and do not include French, Belgian and German statistics. The British artillery expended 182 million rounds across all fronts during the Great War; however, this figure was out stripped by the French and Germans, who fired 350 million and 518 million artillery rounds, respectively, across all fronts.[4] On the Western Front alone, the artillery of the British Empire armies fired 170,385,295 artillery shells during the course of the war, of which over 99 million were 18-pdr shells for the field artillery, with shrapnel shells making up a high percentage of those.[5] Between 9 August 1914 and 10 November 1918, the British war machine manufactured a massive 5,253,338 tons of ammunition and produced 25,000 artillery pieces, the majority of which were shipped to the Western Front.[6] By 1917, it was generally accepted that a six-hour artillery bombardment would require approximately 68,000 shells of different calibres for every mile of front, with the same amount in reserve.[7]

The shell expenditure statistics for the Ypres Salient are more difficult to gauge, as the official statistics do not always differentiate between France and Belgium. By 1917, British munition production was at its height, churning out that year over 172 million filled and empty shells.[8] This record production rate was crucial since the Ypres Salient was to witness shell expenditure of epic proportions in 1917 with the Battle of Messines Ridge (7–14 June 1917) and the Third Battle of Ypres (31 July to 10 November 1917).

The Battle of Messines Ridge can be argued as being the most successful British battle to date in the First World War. Allied tunnelling companies had driven shafts deep beneath the German lines in complete silence at depths of up to 30 metres

---

4 Prentiss, *Chemicals in War*, p.658.
5 War Office, *Statistics of the Military Effort of the British Empire during the Great War, 1914–1920* (London: HMSO, 1922), pp.185, 485.
6 War Office, *Statistics*, p.485.
7 Philip J. Haythornthwaite, *The World War One Source Book* (London: Brockhampton Press, 2000), p.89.
8 Haythornthwaite, *World War One Source Book*, p.477.

below the surface. At zero hour, 3:10 a.m., 19 huge explosive charges were detonated in quick succession beneath the German lines. The combined total of just under one million pounds of high explosives detonated below key German strong points proved to be a decisive action at the beginning of the battle. Messines, however, was also a textbook battle from the artillery standpoint. Using modern sound ranging techniques and the Royal Flying Corps to spot muzzle flashes, the British artillery were able to neutralise the majority of the German artillery batteries in advance of the attack. That, and the effective use of the creeping barrage during the attack led to most of the objectives being gained in the first few hours of the attack. Commander General Plumer had amassed an artillery force of unparalleled numbers and power. A documented 2,266 British artillery pieces stood virtually wheel to wheel across a nine-mile front.[9] Between 26 May and 6 June 1917, an incredible 3,561,530 British artillery rounds rained down on the German positions.[10] The battle raged on until its official conclusion on 14 June 1917, by which time the British artillery had fired over 5 million artillery shells, equating to just over three shells per second every day for 19 days.[11] By the end of the battle, an estimated 1.25 million unexploded British shells littered the battlefield, with tens of thousands of them being gas shells. Of course, none of these figures include the German artillery duds.

The Third Battle of Ypres quickly followed and officially started on 31 July and ended on 10 November 1917, during which the expenditure of artillery ammunition would far outstrip any British statistics to that date in the war. The average weekly expenditure of artillery rounds during that period is thought to have exceeded 3.2 million.[12] The preliminary bombardment alone, between 17–30 July 1917, accounted for an incredible 4,283,550 rounds of ammunition.[13] By extrapolating these figures, it is estimated that the British artillery fired in excess of 53 million shells between 17 July to 10 November, equating to approximately five shells per second every day for 116 days, far outstripping the Battle of Messines. Working on an average of around 25 percent of shells being duds, we can estimate a phenomenal 13.25 million unexploded artillery shells laying in the battlefields after the conclusion of the Third Battle of Ypres, with approximately 662,500 of them containing poison gas. Add in the figures from the Battle of Messines, and you come to a figure of approximately 14.5 million unexploded shells laying in the battlefields of the Ypres Salient.

It was not only the weapons of destruction that were to leave their mark on the Ypres Salient. By the end of the war, over 8.7 million men had passed through the ranks of the British and Empire armies, of which just over 5.4 million saw service

---

9   Ian Passingham, *Pillars of Fire: The Battle of Messines Ridge, 1917* (Stroud: Spellmount, 2012), p.47.
10 Passingham, *Pillars of Fire*, p.47.
11 Haythornthwaite, *World War One Source Book*, p.89.
12 James E. Edmonds, *Military Operations: France and Belgium, 1917* (London: Battery Press, 1940), vol. II, p.239.
13 Edmonds, *Military Operations*, p.138.

on the Western Front.¹⁴ All of these men needed to be fed, clothed and equipped in order to perform the tasks demanded of them. The recorded shipments of stores to the Western Front during the Great War tell the story of a colossal logistical task on an unprecedented scale. Some of the stores shipped were consumables, food for example, which would leave no long-term traces on the battlefields. Huge amounts, however, were nonconsumable equipment and stores all needed by the troops in order to complete their allotted tasks and objectives, some of which would ultimately end up as scrap on the battlefield. For example, in the year of 1918 alone, the army had ordered from its suppliers 7.78 million petrol cans, 3.782 million water bottles, 3.63 million mess tins, 565,000 miles of barbed wire, 5.5 million entrenching tools, 9 million screw pickets, 5.4 million clasp knives and 9.6 million knives and forks, and this is just a small snapshot of the stores ordered.[15] In total, from 9 August 1914 to 10 November 1918, the British Army shipped 25,497,151 tons of stores to the Western Front, including 3,240,948 tons of food and 842,759 tons of timber.[16] The incredible rate of consumption and its associated costs hit hard across all sides on the Western Front, leading to shortages and the rationing of raw materials. With this in mind, the salvage of those raw materials from the battlefield took on a massive importance.

In an effort to efficiently organise the mammoth task of salvaging supplies at the end of 1917, the army created the ASD (Army Salvage Department). Prior to the formation of the ASD, the armies on the Western Front had put into place their own salvage and recycling policies. Under the original army salvage plan of 1915, brigade salvage officers were appointed, and divisional salvage companies were formed, which in turn were to be supported by corps salvage companies.[17] The 20th Division Salvage Company was formed on 7 August 1915 under the command of Captain A.J.B. Weare and consisted initially of one officer, two sergeants and 69 individuals of other ranks.[18] These early units tended to be uncoordinated and fragmented, as the main priority of the British Army was to halt the German advance and ultimately win the war, not battlefield salvage. Other units would also detail their men for battlefield clearance, and manpower was selected from whatever units happened to be in the area at the time, with tasks then being designated to those units. Once the fighting had passed through an area of battlefield, these units would comb through the recently fought over ground looking for bodies to bury and scrap to salvage. Roadside salvage

14 'Some British Army Statistics of the Great War', *The Long, Long Trail*, <https://www.longlongtrail.co.uk/army/some-british-army-statistics-of-the-great-war/>, accessed 10 February 2021.
15 War Office, *Statistics*, pp.527–528.
16 War Office, *Statistics*, p.485.
17 Robert Mckie, 'NZ Divisional Salvage Unit 1941-1942', *RNZAOC* (2018), <https://rnzaoc.com/2018/11/22/nz-divisional-salvage-unit-1941-1942>, accessed 11 February 2021.
18 The National Archives (TNA) WO-95-2110: War Diary of 20th Divisional Troops, Division Salvage Company.

dumping points quickly sprang up, areas where troops and labour units could drop off any collected salvage. Huge dumps of brass shell casings were commonplace, as the expended shell cases could be recycled for reuse. Signs were also placed to remind the troops to pick up any scrap they could carry on their way back from the front line and drop them off at these roadside dumps. The consumption of brass by the munitions industry for artillery rounds was huge, with the British artillery firing over 170 million artillery rounds on the Western Front alone during the course of the war – most of which required a brass shell case – and thus the collection, recycling and reuse of the shell cases was essential. Between 1 January 1917 to 24 April 1918, the British Army collected and shipped back to Great Britain 241,917 tons of ammunition empties, mainly from 18-pdrs and 4.5-inch howitzers. Once the shell cases had been collected and shipped back to Great Britain, they were refilled and tested in the munition factories, ready for reuse by the artillery.

A salvage sign encouraging soldiers to bring back items to be salved from the front line. (Photo by Ernest Brooks. AWM. Public Domain.)

A roadside salvage dump for spent artillery shell cases. (Photographer unknown. Courtesy of the In Flanders Fields Museum.)

The creation of the Labour Corps and the ASD in 1917 was to lead to a more efficient and targeted organisation. One of the tasks allocated to the Labour Corps was battlefield clearance. Each unit had to record their salvage figures, which was then passed up the chain of command. The recording of these figures not only gave the army and the relevant war departments an idea of what was being salvaged and in what amounts (this was incredibly important as they would factor these figures into their purchasing and production forecasting) but would also engender in the labour units a sense of pride in their work to such an extent that unit rivalry was not uncommon: 'The salvage system proved to be a success with statistical records published of what each unit had recovered, with competition between units not uncommon. To outdo the New Zealand Division, one of the Australian Divisions went to the effort of stealing copper appliances and hardware from a derelict brewery to accrue additional credits'.[19] The materials collected by the labour and salvage units from 1 April 1917 to 1 May 1918 equated to a monumental 1,647,330 tons – including 24,544 tons of scrap metal, 241,917 tons of ammunition empties and 30,418 tons of railway sleepers and pit props.[20] In the four weeks ending on 28 September 1918, it is recorded that the labour and salvage units retrieved 20,969 screw pickets, 12,780 pick heads, 53,513 steel helmets, 28,806 water bottles, 122,364 horseshoes, 61,016 rifles, 32,700 bayonets and 635 miles of telegraph and telephone wire.[21]

To maintain the level of salvage recovery, a sizeable force was required. The average monthly strength of the Labour Corps from June 1917 until the end of December 1918 was 310,722 individuals of all ranks.[22] Although sizeable, the strength of the Labour Corps was never enough to efficiently complete all of the tasks required of them. Therefore, in an effort to bolster the ranks, men were sourced from all corners of the Empire and the globe: units were being raised from Egypt, India, the British West Indies, China, South Africa and Russia, to name a few. The relaxing of the regulations in mid-1916 regarding the use of POWs as dictated by the Hague Convention of 1907, which stated that 'The state may utilise the labour of prisoners of war according to their rank and aptitude, officers excepted. The tasks shall not be excessive and shall have no connection with the operations of war', released thousands of German POWs to be shipped back to the Western Front to help clear the battlefields, although initially they were prohibited from handling ammunition.[23]

The system of salvage was tightly controlled and regulated. Agreements had been put into place with France regarding the sale of recovered materials from the British to the French state to help counter the shortages of raw materials that France was experiencing during the war. The agreements also covered what could and could not be recovered by the British as salvage. The British had the right to recover anything considered to be of the origins of the armies of the British Empire and also anything considered to be from the opposing forces in their sector. Anything deemed to be of French origin was deemed to be the property of the French state and should be returned as such. The policy seems to have been strictly adhered to, as the 1918 Controller of Salvage, Brigadier General Gibb, wrote in his war diary, 'Among other items dealt with in this way were two ecclesiastical brass candlesticks which were received at the ordnance depot, Calais. Arrangements were made for their return to the proper owners'.[24]

19 Arthur Forbes, *A History of the Army Ordnance Services* (London: Medici Society Ltd., 1929), vol. 3, p.76.
20 War Office, *Statistics*, p.525.
21 The National Archives (TNA) WO-95-82-5-017: War Diary of Controller of Salvage 3 Dec. 1918, p.5.
22 War Office, *Statistics*, p.220.
23 *Hague Convention of 1907*, Chapter 2, Article 6.
24 The National Archives (TNA) WO-95-82-5-025: War Diary of Controller of Salvage 3 Dec. 1918, p.25.

The British were also concerned about theft from the many and often unsecured roadside dumps that the labour units had formed as collection points. The British Army Controller of Salvage reported in 1918 that 'Suggested to QMG [quartermaster general] that in view of the large amount of pilfering from salvage small dumps which could not be guarded, French authorities be asked to issue fresh proclamations concerning illegality of civilians being in possession of British government property'.[25]

Whilst the process of salvage had proceeded rapidly in France, particularly after the Battle of the Somme in 1916, the same could not have been said for the rate of salvage in Belgium. The reason for the contrasting rates of recovery is quite simple: it was just too dangerous to perform such tasks on a grand scale on the battlefields of the Ypres Salient. Though the recovery of salvage was performed behind the front line, the actual areas of fighting had remained virtually static since the end of May 1915, with the whole of the Salient overlooked by German artillery observers, thus making it very difficult to salvage any items. All this was to change towards the end of 1918. On 9 November 1918, the British High Command announced the removal of restrictions on the salvage of trenches west of the line Ypres – La Bassee – Lens – St. Quentin; the trenches in this area could be dismantled and the area cleared with the 1st, 3rd and 5th Armies undertaking the salvage in the devastated areas.[26]

On 15 December 1918, the British 5th Army received a copy of a letter dated two days earlier from the CGS (Chief of General Staff) stating, 'The Belgians had agreed to our salving British materials in areas taken over by them. Arrangements to do this to be made, any Belgian material found to be set aside and notified to them. Light railway track not required for salvage operations to be offered to Belgians at a valuation or pulled up if not desired by them'.[27]

The race to reclaim the Ypres Salient was about to begin in earnest.

---

25 TNA: WO-95-82-5-025: War Diary of Controller of Salvage 3 Dec. 1918, pp.4–5.
26 The National Archives (TNA) WO-95-82-5-036: War Diary of Controller of Salvage 3 Dec. 1918, p.36.
27 The National Archives (TNA) WO-95-82-5-033: War Diary of Controller of Salvage 3 Dec. 1918, p.33.

2

Military Labour in the Salient

The clearing of the battlefields of Belgium now became a race against time. The war was over, and, once demobilisation commenced, manpower would be rapidly reduced as would the resources required to help in battlefield clearance. It was not only the men who were going home but the various forms of transport as well. On 16 November 1918, there was a recorded 26,809 serviceable British Army lorries in France and Belgium, and this figure had reduced dramatically by 1 November 1919 to 3,073 serviceable lorries and again by 1 April 1920 to only 957 lorries.[1] The lack of transport was clearly an important issue to the units tasked with battlefield clearance as highlighted in the war diary of the Controller of Salvage in September 1918. Describing the 3rd and 4th Army salvage areas, Brigadier General Gibb stated:

> The transport question has been less satisfactory, no special allotment having been possible. The total transport employed on 28 September was as follows: -
> Mechanical Transport – Nil.
> Horse Transport – 50 Blind Horses.
> G. S. [general service] Wagons – 7.
> Light Railway – 1 Locomotive.
> Trucks – 6.
> As a result of the shortage of transport it has been impossible to convey most of the material collected to the main dumps that have been established, and owing to the impossibility of guarding all of the numerous roadside dumps that were thus left, pilfering cannot be wholly prevented.[2]

The lack of transport was a sign of things to come and was to severely hinder the efficient clearing of the battlefields.

---

1   War Office, *Statistics*, pp.595–98.
2   War Office, *Statistics*, p.20.

The decline in manpower was equally dramatic within the labour units. The strength of the Labour Corps in December 1918 was 393,058 individuals of all ranks, in December 1919 it was 48,757, and in March 1920 it had been reduced to 23,092. The rapid decline of manpower due to demobilisation resulted in a recruitment drive in the UK for men who wished to re-enlist and in an increase of manpower from POW units and colonial labour units.

Initially, the use of POWs for manual labour was tightly controlled by the Hague Convention of 1907, banning their use for any purpose with connection to the 'operation of war'. This changed on 24 November 1918 when it was agreed that, as the war had ended, POWs could be used to handle war material, including ammunition.[3] Originally, they were barred from handling German ammunition at the collection depots in case of attempted sabotage. The change of policy on 24 November 1918 signalled the intentions of an intensive salvage policy on the Western Front and a huge increase in the use of German POWs in clearing the battlefields of France and Belgium. The guidelines of what was to be salvaged was set out in November 1918: 'Collection should follow the principle that everything safe to salve should be salved. It would be impossible, even for experts, to foretell what materials would be of value in the near future and what would not'.[4] By late November 1918, there was a documented 20,903 POWs working on the Western Front, which rose rapidly on 1 June 1919 to 198,652 POWs working in France and Belgium who were mostly employed in the battlefield clearance of scrap and ammunition and the exhumations of bodies and their reburial.[5] The war diary of the LOC (Line of Communication) commandant of the Ypres area recorded 13 POW companies of around 550 men per company arriving in the Ypres area between 3–28 May 1919.[6] This mass influx of prisoner labour was short lived since, under the terms of the armistice, the German POWs would have to be repatriated. This process was to start in September 1919 and was virtually complete by the start of November 1919, when only a handful of POWs remained on the Western Front.

The use of 'colonial' or 'coloured' units for labour started long before the armistice.[7] It had become clear to the High Command early in the war that a large labour force was needed to supply the armies on the Western Front. The armies were short not only on manpower for labour but also on fit, healthy men to serve at the sharp end. Every fit man employed in labour was a fit man who could have been sent to the front.

---

3   John Starling and Ivor Lee, *No Labour, No Battle: Military Labour during the First World War* (Stroud: Spellmount, 2014), p.156.
4   The National Archives (TNA) WO-95-82-5: BEF France and Flanders GHQ Controller of Salvage July 1917 to Jan 1919, p.41.
5   War Office, *Statistics*, pp.161, 636.
6   The National Archives (TNA) WO-95-40-48-09: War Diary of L of C Ypres Area Commandant April 1919–June 1919, p.4.
7   Please note these are not the author's terms but rather the terms that were in use at that point in history, as outlined in numerous documents.

With this in mind, the High Command raised labour units from across the Empire and beyond in an effort to release men for front-line action. Of all the colonial units to serve in the Ypres Salient, the Chinese Labour Corps are the ones that were featured the heaviest. First arriving on the Western Front in April 1917, by 23 November 1918, a documented 92,129 Chinese labourers were in the employ of the British Army.[8] By the beginning of 1919, there was an estimated 12,000 members of the Chinese Labour Corps serving in Belgium. The Chinese were tasked with the general labour duties concerning the clearing of battlefields and the clearing and handling of ammunition. Between the years of 1917 and 1919, when the involvement of the Chinese Labour Corps was at its height, it is thought 85 members of the Chinese Labour Corps lost their lives in Belgium, some from the influenza pandemic but many due to accidents resulting from battlefield clearance.[9] By March 1920, most of the Chinese had left for home, with only 70 left behind engaged in the work of engraving the headstones of their fallen comrades.[10]

Men of the Chinese Labour Corps at work engraving the headstones of their fallen comrades. (Photographer unknown. Courtesy of the In Flanders Fields Museum.)

8 War Office, *Statistics*, p.140.
9 'Find War Dead', <http:www.cwgc.org/find-records/find-war-dead>, accessed 15 Feb. 2021.
10 Dominiek Dendooven, *Asia in Flanders Fields: A Transnational History of Indians and Chinese on the Western Front, 1914-1920*. 2018. University of Kent, PhD, p.181.

Pekin Camp, home of the 101 Chinese Labour Company at Mont Kemmel in the Ypres Salient. (Photographer unknown. Courtesy of the In Flanders Fields Museum.)

The lack of available labour and methods of transport due to demobilisation was to lead to a shift in focus on what was to be salvaged. The British Army was running out of time to complete the salvage operation, so urgent decisions needed to be made. In March 1919, the British authorities informed the French and Belgian governments that the men of the Labour Corps would no longer be engaged in road repairs in the areas around the ports where salvage was stored and then shipped back to the UK. From that date onwards, the men of the Labour Corps were told to focus on battlefield clearance and the construction of the cemeteries. The original motivation for the battlefield clearance and the salvage work was twofold: first, to clear the land so the local people could return and get on with their daily lives and, second, to recover all the material that could be reused or sold at a profit without further danger to human life. During May 1919, the QMG issued new instructions stating that the only reason for keeping British forces in France and Belgium was to salvage materials and stores that were useful for reconstruction or could be sold. There was no obligation to the French or to the Belgians to collect stores, remove dugouts, fill in shell holes and trenches or remove barbed wire and damaged corrugated iron.[11] Both dud and unexploded shells were not to be collected, as such work was 'fait du guerre and the responsibility of the owner of the soil'.[12] From that point onwards, the main focus was on the creation of cemeteries and the locating and reburials of the dead.

At the conclusion of 1919, the number of labour companies on the Western Front had shrunk from 198 at the start of the year to 41, nearly all of whom were engaged in the task of body recoveries. The switch in focus from material salvage to body recovery in 1919 was driven by the fact that, whilst military manpower was rapidly decreasing, the recovery of the bodies of the fallen was increasing, as was the requirement for the construction of the new cemeteries in which to accommodate them. As a result, on 29 October 1919, it was reported in the Belgian press that the British government had given up its legal claim to all war materials that remained in their areas of operation.[13] The British had handed over all salvage responsibility, including the disposal of ammunition, to the Belgian state and focussed on the task of body recoveries until the last British Army units left Belgium in 1921. Although the task was far from complete at its conclusion, the salvage statistics make for interesting reading. Between 1 January 1917 and 1 May 1920, the salvage units had recovered 21,196 tons of scrap metal, 51,174 tons of ammunition, 218,075 tons of guns and carriages and 10,892 tons of medical stores, to name a few. In total, 827,667 tons of salvage was recovered from the battlefields, with a further 811,680 tons of returned stores making a total of 1,647,330 tons, saving the country millions of pounds in the process.

---

11 The failure to remove the corrugated iron is still in evidence today, with a lot of it still in use on farmland.
12 Starling and Lee, *No Labour, No Battle*, p.158.
13 John Desreumaux, *Land van schroot en knoken: Slachtoffers van ontploffingen in de frontstreek 1918 - heden* (Leuven: Davidsfonds Uitgeverij, 2011), p.11.

3

The Iron Harvest

From late 1918 to late 1919, the labour units of the British Army had been working as fast as they could to clear the battlefields around Ypres. Hampered by dwindling amounts of labour and a lack of transport, these units did their best to clear the area not only of general scrap materials but also of the millions of unexploded artillery shells and other items of ordnance that littered the Ypres Salient. The problem, however, was much greater than the unexploded shells: ammunition dumps lay everywhere, hidden in dugouts, bunkers, trenches and in the cellars of the ruined buildings. In their hurried retreat of late 1918, the German Army had buried caches of shells in the fields in an effort to deny their usage to the Allied forces, booby trapping some of them in the process. SAA (small arms ammunition) lay in abundance on the battlefields, as did hand grenades, trench mortar rounds and all manner of different explosives. Some of the ammunition was unfired and so was in a relatively stable condition. A large proportion, however, were duds, shells which had been fired but for whatever reason had failed to go off, due to a faulty fuse for example. Most of the shells probably would have never detonated, but a few would, the problem being that it was impossible to identify the dangerous ones by examining them. The German duds were particularly dangerous, and the Allied clearance teams were extremely wary of them since, due to shortages of raw materials, the Germans were using poor-quality shell casings and unstable explosives by the end of the war.

Another major problem facing the clearance teams was the sheer volume of chemical weapons used in the Ypres Salient by all sides. During the course of the war, the Ypres Salient was in the unenviable position of being the site where chemical 'firsts' took place – for example, the first use of chlorine gas on the Western Front in April 1915, the first use of phosgene gas on the Western Front in December 1915 and the first use of mustard gas in July 1917, when, in the space of 24 hours, the Germans fired an estimated 50,000 mustard gas shells in the Ypres Salient.[1] All of this material was

---

1 Zanders, 'Destruction of Old Chemical Weapons', p.225.

designed for a single purpose, that purpose being to kill or injure. Clearly, the task of clearing the ammunition was not going to be an easy one.

The original policy of the British Army during the war was to ship British munitions back to the UK so that they could be recycled and reused. If they were not in a condition where reuse was possible, they were to be dismantled and the components salvaged. German ammunition was to be dismantled in France and Belgium, and their components used for salvage. Large ammunition collection dumps were set up specifically for this task, the ammunition depot at Zeneghem near Calais being a good example. From these depots, the munitions would be deactivated and then transported to the ports to be loaded onto ships to be taken to the UK. The port of Antwerp in Belgium, in particular, handled large amounts of munitions. The relaxation of the rules concerning the use of POWs in November 1919 resulted in German POWs being authorised to work in the ammunition depots at Zeneghem and Audruicq, where British ammunition was being processed and loaded to be sent back to Great Britain, thus releasing the Chinese Labour Corps who were working there for other duties. The German POWs were not allowed, however, to work in the ammunition depot at Bourbourg, where German ammunition was being processed, for fear of sabotage.[2] The main day-to-day clearance work on the battlefields was performed by members of the Labour Corps, whose ranks included the Chinese Labour Corps. Non-POW labour was to collect all remaining trench ammunition, including the dud artillery shells. In the course of a single week in October 1918, in the 5th Army Area, three platoons of a labour company salved 31,419 rounds of gun ammunition of various natures and located a further 23,642 rounds. To take another example, 16,200 rounds of gun ammunition were salved in four days by one Chinese labour company.[3]

On 1 December 1918, it was decided to end shipments of munitions from France and Belgium back to the UK, as they were no longer needed. Instead, all ammunition – British and German – was to be dismantled in France and Belgium, and the reusable parts salvaged.[4] In 1918, the British in the Ypres Salient had set up a camp for the destruction of all types of munitions on the sidings of the Ypres–Kortemark railway at Poelkapelle, staffed by approximately 300 workers. The site dismantled conventional and chemical weapons and disposed of the toxic residues by incineration. The camp remained in use by the British until 1924, when it was being used as a base by the grave exhumation units, the dismantling of weapons at the site having ceased by 1920.

With the mass demobilisation of British labour companies and the repatriation of POWs, the task of ammunition collection fell on the shoulders of the Chinese Labour Corps until they also departed from France and Belgium in March 1920. The work of

---

2   Starling and Lee, *No Labour, No Battle*, p.156.
3   The National Archives (TNA) WO-95-82-5: BEF France and Flanders GHQ Controller of Salvage July 1917 to Jan 1919, p.52.
4   The National Archives (TNA) WO-95-82-5: BEF France and Flanders GHQ Controller of Salvage July 1917 to Jan 1919, p.102.

GRU (Graves Registration Unit) clearing munitions at Hooge c. 1919. (Photo by Corporal Ivan Bawtree. Courtesy of Jeremy Gordon-Smith.)

The seven graves of the men of the 48th Labour Company killed in the accident of 20 October 1919. Poelcapelle British Cemetery. (Photo by Patsy Mahieu.)

the various Labour Corps during this period was physically demanding and extremely dangerous. Between 1 January 1919 and 31 August 1920, 147 members of the various Labour Corps and men attached to Labour Corps lost their lives in Belgium. One of the deadliest incidents took place on 20 October 1919 at the site of the British camp previously mentioned at Poelkapelle, where men of the 48th Labour Company were preparing a midday meal for the rest of the unit, who were out searching for graves in the area. In preparation of the meal, a fire was lit. Unfortunately, the fire had been built unwittingly on top of a buried, unexploded shell, which then detonated and killed seven men and wounded a further three.[5]

The decision taken by the British government in May 1919 to effectively cease recovering ammunition, and in October 1919 when it gave up all rights on scrap war materials in its sectors, passed the problem onto the Belgian authorities – a problem that, not only had its drawbacks but, as it turned out, had some benefits as well.

From late 1918, small numbers of refugees started to return to the Ypres Salient. Some were the original home and landowners looking to rebuild their properties and their lives, whilst others saw the opportunity to benefit financially by relocating to the area. They had heard the stories of the devastation of the old battlefields surrounding Ypres, but nothing could prepare them for the reality that they faced upon returning to their lands. The old battlefields around Ypres quickly attained a new name – the locals called it the '*verwoeste gewesten*' or the 'devastated regions'. The destruction was total. Every town and village had been destroyed, and the water source was contaminated by chemicals from the millions of explosive and gas shells that still littered the Salient. The once fertile and well-nurtured farmland was now a moonscape of millions of interlocking shell holes filled with rancid water that concealed untold horrors beneath its surface. The soil was contaminated with heavy metals, billions of lead shrapnel balls littered the battlefields, zinc, iron, copper and brass lay all around. The wreckage of four years of conflict went on as far as the eye could see. Wrecked tanks, crashed aircraft, destroyed artillery pieces, helmets, rifles bayonets and barbed wire all lay in abundance in and on the once fertile ground of Flanders. For the refugees returning to the Salient, what was on the face of it, a devasted and contaminated wasteland, was actually a potential source of income. The scrap metals that lay all around had value, and it was there for the taking. At the end of October 1919, all war materials abandoned in the devastated regions had become the property of the Belgian state, and the unauthorised removal of this material became illegal and subject to large fines. The Belgian government wanted to discourage the illegal collection of scrap material not only for financial reasons but also because of the risk of serious injury and death to those engaging in these practices. However, many of the returning refugees were destitute, and so, in order to support their families, in some men's eyes, this was a risk worth taking.

---

5   Starling and Lee, *No Labour, No Battle*, p.156.

The process of clearing the Salient of the remaining war materials by the Belgians can be split under two headings: first, the official clearing efforts organised by the Belgian state and, second, the unofficial and often illegal actions of local people to sell their recoveries for profit.

From as early as July 1919, the Belgian authorities were putting plans in place to deal with the unexploded ordnance. In order to have some sort of structure to the clearance process, they prioritised areas that were to be cleared first. Numbered one to four, with one being the highest priority, they were 1. bridges/roads/railways, 2. municipal buildings, 3. local economy and 4. devastated regions. This policy meant that it would be some time before the official clearing process would start in earnest in the so-called 'devastated regions', a time gap that illegal scrap collectors would take full advantage of. In 1920, the Belgian SDM (Service for the Destruction of Munitions) was created.[6] This organisation was a military munitions disposal unit and was the forerunner of DOVO (the *Dienst voor Opruiming en Vernietiging van Ontploffingstuigen* (Service for Clearance and Disposal of Explosive Ordnance)), the modern Belgian Army equivalent. The task of the SDM was to locate, retrieve and destroy ammunition in their own purpose-built destruction sites. In West Flanders, which the Ypres Salient was a part of, the SDM was assisted by the SRD (Service of the Devastated Regions), which was created solely to operate in the regions of the old front lines.[7] Between them, they started on the task of clearing ammunition, taking into account the previously outlined priorities, starting with the bridges, roads and railways. The immediate problem facing the Belgian government and the SDM was the scale of the task, the lack of manpower to complete the task and the timescale involved. Every day, more and more refugees were returning to their former homes in and around the devastated regions, only to find them surrounded by dangerous munitions. In order to speed up the process, the Belgian government had to look further afield.

The business of munitions disposal was not only a specialist one but also one that could prove to be very lucrative. In 1919, it was reported that an Anglo–French engineering firm, F. N. Pickett et Fils, had purchased from the British government the whole of the remaining surplus of British ammunition in France at the cost of £2 million. It was also reported that they had entered into negotiations for a similar deal with the Belgian government as well, the firm believing that there were still an estimated 50 million British shells that needed to be dismantled in France and Flanders.[8] The company's proprietor was Francis Norman Pickett (1887–1957), who was responsible for the running of the company from 1918 to 1931. Pickett was aided in his operations by James Herbert Bingham, who was the factory superintendent and

---

6   The official name for the SDM was '*Service de Destruction des Munitions*'.
7   The official name of the SRD was '*Service des Régions Dévastées*'. Zanders, 'Destruction of Old Chemical Weapons', p.201.
8   'Ammunition Deal', *Kings Country Chronicle*, 21 September 1920, Issue 1422.

then subsequently the production superintendent for Pickett's operations in France and Belgium between 1920 and 1922.[9] Although not a huge amount is known about the company and its operations today, at the time, it was a major contractor citing its head office as being located in Wimereux, France, with other offices being recorded in Brussels, New York, Paris, Warsaw and London. The company was officially described as 'Dismantlers of Toxic and Explosive Munitions'.[10] Though it was not the only private company in France or Belgium involved in this practice, F. N. Pickett et Fils seems to have been one of the forerunners in its field, having been credited with developing safe techniques for the disposal of chemical weapons and their contents. F. N. Pickett wrote:

> We have accepted a great challenge by burning and emptying the German chemical shells, in particular those that contain arsenic. The German sneeze-provoking poison could not be eliminated in any other way. However, combustion was not always complete. One of the favourite tricks of the foreman of our burning site is to lower the intensity of the fire just before the arrival of visitors, so that they get a small taste of what is 'arsenic gas'. One of the gentlemen who inspected our plant in Belgium, at the injunction of the court intending a process, got so close to burning shells that he started sneezing so violently that his false teeth sprang from his mouth into the fire, where they slowly disappeared.[11]

In France, Pickett had at least 14 specialized plants, starting operations in 1920 and ending in 1928.[12] Included in the 14 sites were the British Army ammunition disposal sites at Audruicy, Dannes-Camiers, Saigneville, Fressenville and Blargies. It had also taken over all of the infrastructure in France from the British Army in relation to these sites, including the huts and temporary buildings, machinery, plant, stores, rail track, eight locomotives and 200 trucks.[13] On 24 April 1921, F. N. Pickett et Fils signed a contract with the Belgian government 'to dismantle ammunition of all calibres, their components and any gas apparatus used in the trenches'.[14] They set up site next to the British Army camp in Vrijbos Poelkapelle, taking over the ammunition destruction facility put in place by the British Army in 1918. Several other ammunition collection and destruction points were set up in the area, some of which contained small disposal

---

9   'James Herbert Bingham', *Grace's Guide*, <https://www.gracesguide.co.uk/James_Herbert_Bingham>, accessed 17 Feb. 2021.
10 Zanders, 'Destruction of Old Chemical Weapons', p.202.
11 D. Hubé, 'Industrial-Scale Destruction of Old Chemical Ammunition near Verdun: A Forgotten Chapter of the Great War', *First World War Studies*, 8/2–3 (2017), DOI: 10.1080/19475020.2017.1393347, p.18.
12 Hubé, 'Industrial-Scale Destruction', pp.205–34.
13 'Ammunition Deal'.
14 'Ammunition Deal'.

areas for the incineration of ammunition. These collection points were served by the ammunition workers, officially employed staff whose task it was to search for and collect any ordnance they could locate and then transport and deposit it at the collection points. The ammunition would then be transported from the dumps to a designated dismantling/destruction facility – for example, F. N. Pickett et Fils or the Belgian SDM sites situated at Polygone or Poelkapelle – or, if they were deemed to be too dangerous, incinerated in burning pits on or near the collection points.

Upon arrival at F. N. Pickett et Fils, the ammunition would be manually dismantled and broken down. When the shell had been emptied, the cordite was then burned. From the explosives, ammonium nitrate was extracted for sale to the fertiliser industry. Any steel recovered would be sent away to a steelmaker to be melted down, brass shell cases were crushed and sold to the brass founders, resin derived from the shrapnel shells was recovered and sold, and the black powder from the gun cartridges was recovered and sold for use in sporting cartridges. F. N. Pickett et Fils also developed a system for disarming and removing the charge from the brass fuses so that they also could be sold. In fact, the only thing that went to waste from an explosive shell was the cordite.

Potentially, this was a very lucrative business for F. N. Pickett et Fils. The first contract the company signed with the Belgian government required the Belgians to send Pickett a minimum of 1,000 tons of ammunition per month for a total maximum of 16,000 tons in the first 10 months. The first 15,000 tons were given to F. N. Pickett et Fils in compensation for the costs that the company had incurred in constructing a direct rail line into the compound in order to deliver the ammunition safely. Anything over and above the initial 15,000 tons was charged to Pickett at 13.5 francs per tonne. The salvaged materials then became the property of Pickett, who then sold it at a profit. The contract, of course, put in place safety precautions and gave provision for a permanent presence on site for the Belgian authorities to monitor the process. A second contract was signed with Pickett on 21 April 1921, concluding on 21 September 1922. It is recorded that, between 31 May 1920 and 21 September 1922, when the operation closed, Pickett had dismantled and processed 27,930 tons of ammunition.

As a result of the company's experiences in France with the development of its specialised facility in Dannes, F. N. Pickett et Fils was also tasked by the Belgian government with the destruction of the chemical munitions in the Ypres Salient. Millions of unexploded chemical shells littered the Salient, with large numbers containing chlorine, phosgene and mustard gas. By the end of the war, both sides were also routinely using chemical incendiaries such as thermite and white phosphorous, the latter also being highly toxic. All of these had to be dismantled, and their toxic contents disposed of accordingly.

The destruction process was tightly controlled by the Belgian authorities, who had put in place a strict set of safety and destruction procedures for Pickett to adhere to. Article IX of the contract with Pickett stated that 'The liquid, corrosive and toxic compounds must be destroyed on-site, removed, transformed into harmless products, or disposed of in a borehole with a depth of 2.50 metres after they have been neutralized. The holes will be filled and closed by the Pickett company, at its expense, to the complete satisfaction of the Belgian authorities'.[15]

In May 1920, Pickett had at least one furnace in use for the destruction of chemicals, with a second in the planning. All employees in the factory were issued gas masks that, depending on the area in which they worked, had to be worn at all times or have them ready to use. By 1 September 1922, Pickett had destroyed just under 7,000 tons of chemical weapons, with a further 2,500 tons in stock waiting to be disposed of. How closely Pickett adhered to the enforced procedures is questionable, with some gases being dealt with initially by trial and error. There are some claims that, in the early days, the company was disposing of the chemicals by simply pouring them straight into the soil and thus creating areas on the site that were devoid of all vegetation. Even today, if you visit the site of the old Pickett facility, you will find completely barren areas. This 'rotten place', as a local farmer calls it, is still strewn with the broken green glass of the German Clark bottles that were used to contain the chemicals within the shell and stopping it from mixing with the explosives. The existence of these areas and the broken glass seems to give credence to the claim that not all of the procedures were being strictly adhered to.

The work that Pickett performed was, by definition, extremely dangerous, with the mix of cheap and sometimes inexperienced labour and volatile explosives adding to the risks. During the course of the company's operation in Belgium, at least five of its operatives were killed on site whilst performing their tasks, and many more off site whilst involved in the recovery and transportation of the munitions. These losses ultimately led to the Picketts closing down their facility in 1922. With F. N. Pickett et Fils gone, the Belgian munitions organisations now found themselves solely responsible for the unenviable task of dealing with the conventional and chemical weapons that remained in the devastated regions.

Whilst the destruction of conventional artillery shells was (although dangerous) relatively straight forward, the destruction of chemical munitions was more of a problem for the Belgian authorities, with each chemical needing to be identified and then destroyed according to its type. Local people who lived near the destruction sites complained of the chemical smell, and some even claimed that livestock had been poisoned by the fumes emitting from the furnaces. As a result, it was decided to incinerate chemicals at certain times of the day and when the wind direction was favourable. Eventually, though, the Belgian military opted for a simpler solution, which was to dump it all at sea. It is estimated that, in 1920, the Belgian armed forces dumped around 35,000 tonnes of munitions from the battlefields of Flanders in the North Sea just off the coast at Zeebrugge. Most of it was thought to be of German origin, with around 11,600 tonnes of the total thought to contain mustard gas. The dumping area still exists today near to Zeebrugge and is marked on charts as the *Paardenmarkt* (Horse Market). The ammunition dump is approximately four square

---

15   Zanders, 'Destruction of Old Chemical Weapons', p.203.

Rare pictures of a Belgian labour gang at work destroying a British bunker near Brielen, on the outskirts of Ypres. The labour gangs involved in the destruction of concreted defensive positions had a somewhat novel, if not unhealthy, method of dealing with such structures, namely by packing the bunkers with unexploded artillery shells, lighting a fire beneath them and retiring as quickly as possible! (Photographer unknown. Courtesy of the In Flanders Fields Museum.)

kilometres in area and sits at a minimum sea depth of about five metres during low tide. It also sits around two kilometres from Knokke, an exclusive and affluent seaside resort. Although having been debated many times, it has been decided that the shells are best left undisturbed where they are. They are enclosed in crates that are now covered by substantial amounts of silt. As they are underwater, they are not exposed to air, so corrosion of the shells does not seem to be a problem. It is thought that the risk is too great in trying to salvage them.[16] The Belgian armed forces resumed sea dumping again in the years between 1954 and 1972 when they routinely dumped chemical munitions in the Bay of Biscay and for the last time in 1980 as a one-off large dumping operation.

Running in parallel with the official clearing operation in the Ypres Salient was the unofficial and often illegal clearing by local organisations, building contractors and individuals. The task of reclaiming the Salient was immense, millions of shell holes needed to be filled in, the ground levelled, concrete defensive positions removed, trenches filled in and toxic and explosive substances removed. The huge amount of salvageable material that still lay out in the devastated regions attracted people from a wide radius in an effort to earn some money. Although the departing armies had salvaged as much as they could, potentially valuable material was everywhere. Of particular interest was lead, copper, brass and steel – all of which were contained in the unexploded artillery shells.

It is thought that, between the years of 1920 and 1921, an estimated 30,000 people were engaged in battlefield clearance in Flanders, some of whom were authorised but many were not.[17] Even as late as 1926, it is estimated that 200 men per day were arriving in the area to search the battlefields for scrap metal.[18] Some of these people were engaged by farmers to clear the land and were paid in scrap metal, which they could then sell to the scrap dealers. Quite simply, the more they collected, the more they were paid. Others were in the employ of housing contractors who needed land cleared and levelled before any building could start. Many were individuals illegally scavenging for scrap in order to sell it at a profit. John Gabriel lived in Ypres between the wars and, as a child, would scavenge on the old battlefields:

> We used to go in old dugouts and find live ammunition and take it apart – take the cordite out of live bullets and put it into a long line and set fire to it, like a fuze. We used to follow the plough and all the little round lead shot came up – the size of a marble and they were what filled the shells. There were thousands

---

16 Zanders, 'Destruction of Old Chemical Weapons', pp.208–09.
17 Yannick Van Hollebeeke, Karen Derycke, Annemie Morisse, Franky Bostyn, and Steven Reynaert, *1917: Total War in Flanders* (Brugge: Stefaan Gheysen, 2017), p.139.
18 Desreumaux, *Land van schroot en knoken*, p.16.

and thousands of those – you could pick up bagfuls of them. We used to take them to scrap merchants and get a few francs.[19]

As the discarded war materials were technically property of the Belgian state, laws were put in place to attempt to control the illegal activity and also to try and stop the inevitable accidents that would occur. The Belgian government required everyone who was in possession of war materials to register it at their local government office by the end of December 1920; if you were caught after that date in possession of unregistered material, you were subject to heavy fines. The problem with the legislation was that it was virtually unenforceable. The ownership of the discarded war materials was not made clear due to the lack of published government information, and so many people had started to collect war materials long before the government had tried to regulate it and assumed it was theirs for the taking. Another important factor was that the devastated regions resembled the Wild West, with little to no law enforcement in the area and scrap collectors often fighting each other over their spoils. When law enforcement did make an appearance, it was often a game of cat and mouse between them and the '*Ijzerzoekers*' ('iron seekers').

The battlefield 'scavengers' employed crude methods to dismantle ammunition in order to salvage its components. Armed with a chisel and hammer, they would prise the copper drive band off the exterior of the shell and then try to loosen the fuse with a few 'taps' of the hammer so that it could be removed. The more experienced of them rejected the German shells of 1917 and 1918, as they were too unstable and, to make matters worse, had little scrap value because of the inferior materials used. The British shells were the most sought after since they were safer to handle and were composed of many valuable raw materials, such as lead, copper and brass. It comes to no surprise that many were killed whilst performing this task. It was not just these '*obuskloppers*' ('shell knockers') being killed on a regular basis, but also anyone with a task related to working in the old battlefields was at risk. Many people had secured official or unofficial employment helping landowners clear the land so that they, in turn, could resume farming. These 'front workers' filled in trenches and shell holes, removed barbed wire and other scrap materials, destroyed concrete defensive positions and of course moved ammunition. Initially, the front workers were paid in cash, but that policy changed to them being paid in scrap metal, which cost the landowner nothing and drove these men to work as hard as possible in order to collect enough scrap to make it worth their while. This, of course, led to men cutting corners and taking risks with the inevitable consequences of regular accidents, which often led to injury or death. The following incident was reported in the local press at the time:

---

19   Sue Elliot and James Fox, *The Children Who Fought Hitler: A British Outpost in Europe* (London: John Murray, 2010), p.65.

On 1 August 1921 between 3:00 p.m. and 4:00 p.m. three workmen tragically lost their lives and two were injured whilst clearing the rubble of a destroyed house near Hooge on the outskirts of Ypres. The men were working with picks and shovels when one of the men hit a concealed artillery shell which then detonated. One of the workmen, a 37 year old father of four, took the full force of the blast as he was closest to its detonation point, although he suffered terrible injuries, he was to live for another 45 minutes before passing away, this was his first, and tragically his last, day working as a front worker. His two work mates, a 28 year old father of one and a 60 year old man suffered terrible injuries and died on site roughly 10 minutes after the detonation. Two more of their work mates survived the blast, one suffered stomach and head injuries whilst the other was lightly wounded and managed to help carry his comrades to a farm roughly 100 metres away. The Red Cross ambulance took 45 minutes to arrive and transported the dead and injured to hospital in Ypres. All three of the deceased came from the village of Maldegem roughly 100 km from Ypres and had come into the area to help clear the farmland on behalf of an agricultural organisation called the Boerenbond.[20]

Make no mistake, the recovery of war materials in the Ypres Salient was a big business. Some enterprising families amassed personal fortunes from scrap metal trading, and, on a much smaller scale, individuals could easily earn enough money from scavenging the battlefields to pay for their winter heating fuel, for example. There were even cases of churches encouraging the children in their congregation to go out and collect scrap so that it could be sold and the proceeds be donated back to the churches. To give you an idea of the scale of the materials discarded by the armies, in 1926 (18 years after the armistice), a documented 10.221 million kilograms of scrap metal collected that year alone in the Salient had been transported out of Ypres to be recycled; that same year, there were a registered 39 explosions related to unexploded ordnance in the Ypres area, resulting in 34 civilian deaths.[21]

---

20 Desreumaux, *Land van schroot en knoken*, pp.85–86.
21 'The Names List', *In Flanders Fields Museum*, <https://namenlijst.org/>, accessed 4 Feb. 2021.

4

Danger UXB

> *There was a young girl of the Somme*
> *Who sat on a number five bomb*
> *She thought 'twas a dud 'un*
> *But it went off sudden –*
> *Her exit she made with aplomb!*[1]

The danger of unexploded ammunition was highlighted by this example of trench humour in 1916, written by a British soldier during the Battle of the Somme, when an estimated 30 percent of British shells fired during the preliminary bombardment were duds, landing harmlessly in the battlefield. The legacy of the Great War in Belgium is still very much in evidence today. Since the end of the First World War in West Flanders, over 360 people have been killed and over 535 wounded from a total of over 600 recorded explosions concerning ammunition from this war.[2] The Iron Harvest of the First World War does not discriminate: it has killed people of all races and religions, babies and old men, civilians and military personnel. Some of these incidents were pure accidents; some were caused by bad luck. Each death is equally tragic, devastating the families and friends of those involved.

Because of the sensitivities of this subject, when describing these incidents in the following pages, I have decided to use the initials of the deceased and not their full names, as many of their families still live in the area of the Ypres Salient. I must prewarn you that some of the descriptions to come are quite graphic in relation to the injuries caused by exploding ammunition. I make no apology for this for two reasons: first, this was how it was reported at the time – some newspapers being incredibly graphic when describing the incidents – and, second, unfortunately, there is still a need to highlight to visitors and locals in the area how deceptively dangerous rusting ammunition still is, even over 100 years since the end of the war.

---

1   Patrick Beaver (ed.), *The Wipers Times* (London: Peter Davies, 1973), p.116.
2   These figures increase annually and will have no doubt increased by publication.

A poster produced to warn of the dangers of live ammunition. (Designed by Joe English. Courtesy of the In Flanders Fields Museum.)

DANGER DES ENGINS EXPLOSIFS
GEVAAR DER ONTPLOFBARE VOORWERPEN

FATALE IMPRUDENCE · NOODLOTTIGE ONVOORZICHTIGHEID

From as early as 1918, just after the declaration of the armistice, there were recorded explosive incidents, both fatal and nonfatal, concerning unexploded ordnance in the Ypres Salient. The first full year of records started in 1919 with a registered 31 explosive-related incidents involving death or injury, rising to a peak of 73 incidents in the year of 1926. Between the years of 1919 and 1930, the annual incident level remained in the double figures, the 1920s being particularly bad as this was the height of the battlefield clearance period. Post-1930 to the present day, annual incidents have remined in the single figures, with the last fatalities to date occurring in 2014. Clearly, certain occupations would put you at more risk of being killed and injured by unexploded ordnance than others, the most obvious being the official bomb-disposal units and their civilian employees, agricultural workers and of course the *obuskloppers* who were engaged in the unofficial business of dismantling artillery shells in order to sell the components for scrap.

Since the creation of the Belgian bomb-disposal units in 1920, over 100 military personnel and associated workers have been killed by unexploded ordnance in West Flanders and the surrounding areas, with the modern-day Belgian Army bomb-disposal units, DOVO, recording 23 deaths since 1944, with the most recent deaths recorded in 1986. The nature of the work performed by these units is inherently dangerous and carries a high risk of multiple fatalities should something go wrong. On 13 June 1921, C. E., a married father with one child from Roeselaere, was working near Passchendaele, filling up deep pits or '*springputten*' with unexploded ordnance ready to be detonated later in the day. At around 3:00 p.m., a large explosion was heard, and nearby workers rushed to the site. The body of C. E. was found nearby terribly mutilated, and he died within one minute of the explosion. C. E. was in the employ of the government with the task of clearing ammunition from the front-line areas. He was 23 years old.[3]

Although terrible, these stories of individual accidents are all too commonplace, with many similar stories being recorded. The year of 1922 was a particularly bad year in terms of fatalities, with multiple deaths being recorded in two major incidents. On 2 February of that year, a major explosion took place on the beach at Lombardsijde, West Flanders, where the Belgian Army was engaged in the destruction of chemical weapons. The resulting casualty rate was high, with six men being killed on site and a seventh dying in hospital shortly afterwards.

Worse, however, was to come a few months later on Saturday, 24 June 1922. At around 1:30 p.m., the people of Ypres heard several explosions in the distance coming from the direction of Wytschaete, a village roughly six miles south of Ypres. By 3:00 p.m., news had reached Ypres of a major explosion that had taken place involving men from the Belgian Munitions Service at an ammunition dump halfway between the Kemmel Vierstraat and Wytschaete. The men had been clearing unexploded ordnance left behind by the German Army in an attempt to sabotage bridges in the area during their retreat in 1918. The workers had filled a cart with the explosives to take it to the ammunition dump about 15 minutes away. On arrival at the ammunition dump, the cart accidently tipped over, causing a massive explosion with devastating consequences. Upon hearing the explosion, local people nearby rushed to the scene to help as best they could. The scene that confronted them can only be described as carnage. Eleven horrifically mutilated men lay in an unrecognisable bloody mass in a large pool of blood, many of them partially naked since the force of the explosion had blown the clothes off their bodies. Some of the victims were missing parts of their faces and had lost their limbs, which were found several metres away from the explosion site. Nine men died instantly whilst three had some signs of life, two of whom died shortly afterwards. Only one man survived the incident. As the news of the disaster started to circulate around Ypres, worried family members and friends started to gather outside the hospital and were present when the dead and injured started to arrive in motor vehicles. It soon became apparent that 10 of the 11 victims were 'Yperlings' (i.e., originally from or currently residing in Ypres), a fact which caused great sorrow and grief to the inhabitants. On Monday, 26 June, it was

---

3 'The Names List', <https://namenlijst.org/>, accessed 4 Feb. 2021.

announced that a public funeral would take place the following day and that everyone was invited to take part in the funeral procession and attend the funeral service. On the day of the funeral, Tuesday, 27 June, all flags were flown at half-mast in the city of Ypres, and black sashes were hung from windows. From 8:00 a.m., crowds started to gather at the hospital to pay their last respects to the victims and to join the funeral procession. At 9:00 a.m., the procession departed from the hospital, being led by the cross from St. Maartens church. Behind the cross was the Ypriana band, who played Chopin's funeral march. They, in turn, were followed by veterans' organisations and priests. The coffins of the deceased were carried by two large motor vehicles that had been dressed as hearses in black. Behind the coffins came the town officials and then the families and friends of the deceased. The streets were lined with mourners as the procession made its way to the site of the partially rebuilt St. Maartens church for the service. By 10:45 a.m., the service had finished, and the procession made its way to the town cemetery for the burial of the victims. At the cemetery, the Burgemeester of Ypres and other dignitaries made speeches, many of whom blamed the Germans for the disaster, which was seen as a direct result of their invasion and occupation. The news of the disaster had spread quickly. The Belgian Queen Elizabeth had sent a condolence telegram to the town Burgemeester, followed by a wreath of roses from herself and her husband, King Albert.

The families of the victims received financial compensation for their losses, as the deceased were classed as victims of war. Each widow received 500 Belgian Francs, and each child under the age of 16 received 100 Belgian Francs. The citizens of Ypres quickly formed a fundraising committee to help the families, and, on Sunday, 23 July, a fundraising fair was held in the Grote Markt, which eventually raised 20,000 Belgian Francs for the families. The events of 24 June had been another dark day in the history of Ypres.[4]

The year of 1922 finished on a low point for the workers of the munition's clearance service when two young lads were killed in an accident close to the Belgian Army bomb-disposal site at Polygoonveld near Zonnebeke. R. M. and H. E. from Ypres – aged 19 and 18, respectively – were both killed instantly when a German 77mm howitzer shell they were carrying exploded. R. M. had all of his clothes blown off, whilst H. E. was completely mutilated with one of his legs being found 70 metres away.[5] By the time that the year had ended, at least 42 deaths had been recorded as the result of unexploded ammunition in the Ypres Salient and surrounding area, an unsurpassed total.

A large proportion of the fatalities concerning unexploded ordnance amongst the civilian population post-1919 resulted from the illegal dismantling of artillery shells for financial gain. Armed with hammers and chisels, the *obuskloppers* would try to dismantle artillery shells in order to salvage their valuable scrap material. These

---

4   Desreumaux, *Land van schroot en knoken*, pp.107–14.
5   'The Names List', <https://namenlijst.org/>, accessed 4 Feb. 2021.

individuals were called 'shell knockers' for a good reason. In normal circumstances, the brass fuse (nose cone) of the shell should unscrew and be removed relatively easily. However, once the shell has been fired and has lain undetected in the ground for some time, the fuses would often become impossible to unscrew by hand. To loosen the fuse, the shell knockers would give it a few well-placed hits with a hammer in an effort to free it up. Considering that the fuse is the thing that sets the shell off, the act of hitting it with a hammer is not the best idea in the world and neither is it a long-term career move!

Unsurprisingly, there are a lot of recorded accidents and fatalities concerning these 'enterprising' individuals spanning from 1919 right up to the present day. The dangers of this occupation become very apparent upon reading a selection of the incidents recorded in the local press at the time. In fact, accidents and fatalities were so frequent that many newspapers had a regular column dedicated to them, reporting under the title of '*De Ontploffingen*' ('the explosions').[6] The descriptions of the injuries to the victims were often printed in graphic detail, partly in an effort to warn people of the potential dangers of tampering with unexploded shells. The effects of an explosion on the body from close proximity are devasting, and the newspapers regularly described the injuries with terminology such as 'arms and legs blown off', 'clothes were disintegrated', 'the body was disembowelled with the innards still hanging out', 'there was blood and brains everywhere' and 'the head was unrecognisable'. These descriptions of the injuries form a common thread when reading the details of individual cases.[7]

F. V., P. G., T. S., M. A., M. L. and M. V. were all killed in the same incident on 1 June 1920 near St. Eloi, south of Ypres. It seems that three of the group were dismantling shells with hammers and chisels when a huge explosion occurred, killing the six and wounding many others. Witnesses describe hearing the explosion from some distance away and finding the victims' bodies terribly mutilated and laying in pools of blood. Three of the victims were females who had happened to be in the vicinity and were taking no part in the shell dismantling, all three being killed by flying pieces of metal.

H. D. died on 2 May 1922 after a shell he was dismantling blew up. Parts of his body were found several metres away whilst his hammer was blown 800 metres from the explosion site.

A. S. died on 1 February 1922. It was reported that his head and legs were blown off, he was disembowelled and his torso was a lump of bloody flesh.

P. Z. died on 26 September 1923 whilst dismantling a shell indoors. His remains were scattered over the walls and ceiling of the room he was working in.

H. M. and C. M. both died in the same incident on 26 April 1924 when they were trying to release a copper fuse from a shell. The official description of their injuries

---

6 *De Poperinghenaar*, the newspaper of the area of Poperinghe, was one such newspaper.
7 Desreumaux, *Land van schroot en knoken*, pp.50–382.

is 'mutilated'.⁸ H. M. was found on fire, which proved very difficult to extinguish, probably as a result of the shell containing thermite or phosphorous. Both men died on their way to hospital.

L. W. died on 16 March 1924 when a shell exploded as he was trying to remove its copper drive band. When rescuers got to the site, all that was left of L. W. was a few lumps of flesh that were being eaten by his pet dog.

A. M. died on 8 November 1925 whilst trying to dismantle a shell in a field. Upon hearing the explosion, rescuers rushed to the scene to find a smoking shell crater with bits of flesh scattered around it. The arms, legs and head had been destroyed by the explosion. His official injuries were described as 'torn apart'.⁹

G. S. and his brother-in-law L. R. were both killed on 18 April 1926. G. S. was trying to knock the copper drive band off a large shell when it detonated. The blast threw G. S. into the air, and his body disintegrated. L. R. was standing close by and was killed by shell fragments. He also died on the spot.

R. P. was dismantling a shell at around 1:30 p.m. on 1 May 1925 when it went off. His body was found in pieces minus its head and feet; both feet were found over 100 metres away.

D. G. and J. V. both died in the same incident at Zillebeke on 22 April 1930 from an explosion whilst they were searching for copper. The head of D. G. was found to be crushed beyond recognition, and his hands were blown off. J. V. was disembowelled by shell fragments.

A. D. died at Voormezele on 5 July 1932 in an explosion concerning First World War ammunition. His body was found on fire and laying in a pool of blood, both legs were missing, and the body was disembowelled. A. D.'s shoes were found hanging in a tree nearby.

E. D. was 62 years of age when he died in an explosion whilst searching for copper on 9 February 1952. Rescuers found the disintegrated remains of his body blown into a bush, the only recognisable thing being a leg.

F. M. was killed on 6 July 1990 whilst dismantling a shell at home. It seems that F. M. was an experienced ammunition collector well versed in dismantling shells, but something went wrong in this instance, and the ensuing blast killed him instantly and destroyed much of his house.

S. Z. and J. P. were workers from Poland who were digging out a large pond on a farm on 27 September 2001. During the work, they came across a German artillery shell and then tried to remove its fuse with an angle grinder. The shell exploded, killing S. Z. and badly burning J. P., who ultimately survived his injuries.

R. A. was a retired stone mason and was killed in an explosion at home whilst working on a shell with an angle grinder. He died on 29 February 2008.¹⁰

---

8   'The Names List', <https://namenlijst.org/>, accessed 4 Feb. 2021.
9   'The Names List', <https://namenlijst.org/>, accessed 4 Feb. 2021.
10 Desreumaux, *Land van schroot en knoken*, pp.50–382.

In 2014, at the start of the centennial commemorations of the Great War, Ypres was shocked when two workmen were killed whilst working in the city. A. H. H., a worker from Turkey, and Y. N., a worker from Bulgaria, were killed in an explosion on 19 March of that year after tampering with a shell that they had recently dug up. Both men's remains were shipped back to their relevant countries for burial.

The last reported death to date (at the time of writing this book) occurred in 2018 when a 38-year-old man was killed whilst trying to dismantle a shell in his workshop at home.

Every single death is a tragedy for all those involved, none more so than the people who have been killed in explosions purely by accident. By that, I mean someone whose job or hobby was not linked to the removal or dismantling of ammunition as in the previous examples. There are many documented cases of individuals losing their lives as a result of being in the wrong place at the wrong time.

K. L. was 10 years old when he was tragically killed on 17 June 1919. At around 5:00 p.m., soldiers were busy destroying shells in an area that was cordoned off. K. L. was passing the site from about 400 metres away when he was hit by a flying shell fragment, which killed him instantly.

A. D., A. V., P. E. and A. V. were all killed as a result of the same incident on 1 September 1921. All four men were workmen who were transporting earth for a local road building project when a concealed shell exploded, ultimately killing all four of them.

M. D. died in a tragic accident on 6 September 1921 when he accidently set fire to a hedge whilst burning vegetation. Unknown to him, an unexploded shell was concealed in the hedge, which was detonated by the heat of the fire, severely wounding the unfortunate gentleman. M. D. died of his injuries the following day in hospital.

A whole family was devastated when a father and his two daughters were tragically killed on 24 February 1922. J. D. and his two daughters, E. D. and J. D., were working in a field when a cart loaded with ammunition passed by. Unfortunately, a shell fell from the back of the cart and detonated, killing all three family members on the spot.

J. G. was killed on 23 March 1926 whilst emptying rubbish from a bag. As he shook the bin bag to empty it, an explosion occurred, killing him instantly and severely wounding his wife.

The most tragic stories, of course, relate to the children who have lost their lives due to unexploded ammunition in the Ypres Salient. Since 1919, there have been at least 92 explosions in which children were involved, resulting in 124 children being seriously injured and at least 19 fatalities.[11] These are a few of their tragic stories.

E. V., aged 11 years old, and C. D., aged six, were both killed in an explosion on 24 August 1918 whilst playing in a ruined building. Upon hearing the explosion, bystanders rushed to help only to find both boys in a pool of blood. E. V. had died instantly whilst C. D. died later in hospital.

---

11   Desreumaux, *Land van schroot en knoken*, p.31.

O. W. and J. W. were two brothers aged eight and nine years old, respectively. On 20 October 1921, whilst their father was working in a field, the two boys lit a fire in the same field. Unbeknown to them, they had built the fire on top of a buried artillery shell, and a massive explosion followed. Both brothers were killed instantly.

L. C. (aged eight years old) was playing with her brothers, M. C. (aged four) and G. C. (aged three years), at home on 14 May 1922 when a shell exploded. L. C. lost both of her legs in the blast and died shortly afterwards; her two brothers were badly injured but survived. The family had only moved back to the area a few days earlier, and the children were unfamiliar with the dangers of unexploded ammunition.

J. G., aged 12, was playing with his sister and two friends on 3 March 1923 when an artillery shell they were playing with detonated. J. G. died instantly whilst his friend M. V., aged seven, died two days later in hospital.

Brothers H. L. and P. L. – aged 12 years old and 10 years old, respectively – were both killed on 26 April 1924 when a shell they were playing with exploded. The shell was so powerful that it partially demolished the building in which they were playing. Both boys were terribly injured and died later that night.

One of the worst incidents concerning children took place on 19 May 1929 in the village of Geluveld, a few miles on the outskirts of Ypres. A group of children were playing in the Waterstraat with unexploded shells that had been left for collection by the munitions service. One of the shells exploded, and three children, E. K. (aged six), A. W. (aged eight) and A. D. (aged seven), all died as a result of the explosion.[12]

It was instances such as these that prompted the Belgian government to instruct schoolteachers to educate children of the dangers of playing with live ammunition. The government also launched an advertising campaign, distributing posters warning of the dangers of discarded war materials, and, through law enforcement, pursued an aggressive policy of large fines for anyone caught in the illegal possession of such objects. The deaths and accidents concerning children still continue today and will continue until the Salient is fully cleared of ammunition.

On 6 July 1992, M. R. (aged eight) was enjoying sitting around a campfire with her fellow scouts. One of her friends picked up what he thought was a mouldy log and tossed it onto the fire. The log turned out to be an unexploded shell, which went off, severely injuring M. R. After spending two years in hospital and enduring 29 operations to save her badly injured leg, M. R. is now officially classed as a victim of the First World War.[13]

Farming can be a very dangerous occupation in the Ypres Salient, and there have been many incidents involving unexploded ordnance and farming reported over the years, with approximately 28 farmworkers killed and 37 farmworkers injured since the end of the First World War.[14] The unrelenting artillery fire had left the agricultural

---

12   Desreumaux, *Land van schroot en knoken*, pp.50–382.
13   Denzil Walton, 'The Iron Harvest', *Flanders Today*, 1 December 2010, p.5.
14   Desreumaux, *Land van schroot en knoken*, p.49.

An official Belgian poster warning children not to play with ammunition. (Courtesy of the In Flanders Fields Museum.)

ground around Ypres in poor condition. The ground had been churned up by explosion after explosion, which brought the underlying blue clay to the surface and destroyed the fertile topsoil. In addition, the ground had been poisoned by chemicals and the heavy metals. In the early days after the war, once farming recommenced in 1922, the farmers were only allowed to shallow plough because of the risk of accidents caused by the plough bringing artillery shells to the surface. However, because of poor crop yields, it was decided in the 1970s to resume deep ploughing in an effort to rotate the fertile soil back to the surface. This decision, however, resulted in mores shells being dragged up and, of course, increased the risk of accidents to those engaged in ploughing. The only reason there has not been more fatalities amongst the farming community is the fact that most farmers always plough in the same direction, unwittingly hitting the shells with glancing blows that pushes the fuse away from the plough and so reduces the chance of a detonation. However, there are accidents most years, resulting in damage to machinery or injury or death to the farmer. Between the years of 2000 to 2013, the Belgian government paid out approximately €140,000 in compensation to farmers for damage caused to farm machinery by First World War ordnance.[15]

15 Martin Fletcher, 'The Deadly Iron Harvest', *Daily Telegraph Magazine*, 12 July 2013, pp.1–4.

One of the earliest incidents resulting in the deaths of farmers occurred on 4 April 1923 concerning two brothers, C. V. and G. V. (aged 17 and 16 years of age, respectively). C. V. was ploughing with his brother when the plough hit a shell, which detonated. The explosion killed the horse and terribly wounded the two brothers, who both died shortly afterwards after being taken to hospital.

On 23 May 1983, local farmer Jacques Covemaeker (aged 35) was preparing his land for ploughing. There had been a sustained period of wet weather, and Jacques was determined to make use of the first sunny day for some time. At around 8:45 p.m., Jacques' rotary harrow hit an unexploded shell. Witness testimony describes the tractor as being engulfed momentarily in a flash of flame as the sound of the explosion rebounded off the surrounding hills. Rescuers rushed to the scene but found Jacques dead in his cab, having been hit by shrapnel. The following year, Jacques' wife, Magda, planted an oak tree on the spot where he was killed. Jacques left behind two children, aged five and seven years old. Ironically, one of those children, Fredrik Covemaeker, had a lucky escape himself when ploughing a field in October 2015 when he noticed plumes of yellow smoke rising from the ground behind his tractor. DOVO was called, and the incident was safely dealt with. In the space of one year, Fredrik has ploughed up over 40 shells in various conditions in his 18-hectare site.

In July 1983, author John Laffin penned a poem in honour of Jacques Covemaeker:

> Flanders' Harvest.
> (Loker, Flanders, April 1918)
>
> In a last mad fling
> of men and steel
> that desperate spring
> the Germans broke
> the British line
> and Messines and Neuve-Eglise
> and Bailleul and Loker
> and a score of other places
> fell to field grey.
> Shocked British infantry
> pulled back while
> gunners galloped
> on to the hills and
> through open sights
> flung frantic fire on the
> spreading German stain.
>
> 'Quick!' a sergeant ordered.
> 'Into action! We'll have
> that lot with shrapnel!

Aim two degrees right of the farm.'
And he pointed to a field.
'Fire!'
The British watched,
Counted the seconds – and then …
'Damn! Bloody shell's
a dud, gone into that
bloody mud.
Let's move, boys, before
Jerry gets our range
and strafes us.
The war's not over yet.'
'Bloody mud', a gunner grumbled.

The long winter over,
the soft and fertile Flemish fields,
stirring in the springtime warmth,
waited bride-eager for the plough
to let in light and air.
On soil enriched by concentrated war –
the bodies of men and horses,
the earth churned and turned –
two generations of farmers
had prospered on this land.
Jacques Covemaeker worked it
as a boy, learned the value
Of each field,
loved the green and yellow flax,
the honest-toil potato crop,
the rich-harvest sugar beet
in the field behind the cemetery
of British soldiers –
Lancashire lads who'd died
defending it.

The weather was benign at last,
the light was long
and there was much to do.
Jacques, proud with new tractor,
was drilling the beet field and
after a quick meal at the farm
climbed back into his seat.
'I'll work till dark',

he told his wife and kids,
and smiled. 'The harvest will
be rich this year.'

From the farm they saw
man and tractor silhouetted
as daylight slipped into dusk
and dusk to transparent twilight,
and they heard the drills
driving into the thick earth.
At nine o'clock
precisely
a drill found
the British shell …
As it exploded
the shrapnel balls
ripped through man and tractor.
Jacques lived a little –
long enough for his
wife to reach him.

'Bloody mud', the sergeant
growled, 'the war's not over yet.'

And the mud was bloody now,
And the war was still not over.
And the harvest is the same –
For these are Flanders fields.[16]

Anybody working on the land in the devastated regions was at risk of death or injury from the unexploded ordnance. This risk extended to the official units of the DGR&E (Directorate of Graves Registration & Enquiries), who were tasked by the British to search for graves and bodies in the old battlefield areas, and the gardeners and staff of the then IWGC (Imperial War Graves Commission), who were constructing the cemeteries at the time.[17] William Curtis was born in Hereford on 10 April 1880 and served as the rank of sapper in the Royal Engineers during the First World War. In 1921, Curtis applied to work for then IWGC, was duly appointed as a gardener on

---

16   John Laffin, 'Flanders Harvest' [poem], (20 July 1983), reprinted with the kind permission of Anny De Decker.
17   The IWGC (Imperial War Graves Commission) formally changed their name to the CWGC (Commonwealth War Graves Commission) in 1960.

15 June 1921 and then proceeded to France and Belgium.[18] On 26 June 1923, Curtis was severely injured in an explosion whilst at work in Zillebeke, on the outskirts of Ypres, and was taken to hospital. The hospital records state he was badly wounded in the throat and arm. Curtis succumbed to his injuries and died on 30 June 1923, and he was buried in Ypres town civilian cemetery. Not much is known of the circumstances of Curtis' accident, but a lady called Eve Dobers from London was admitted to hospital at the same time with injuries caused by the same explosion. Dobers had lost the index finger from her right hand as a result of the incident and was discharged from hospital on 8 July 1923. Prior to the explosion, Dobers had been staying in a guesthouse in Ypres, which leads to the possibility that she was a tourist. We can only surmise what happened on that fateful day: perhaps Dobers had found a hand grenade and was showing it to Curtis when it went off, or maybe Curtis was showing Dobers the ordnance thinking it was safe? Whatever the circumstance, this is a particularly tragic story. Curtis – having fought on the Western Front and, more than likely, in the Ypres Salient during the Great War – had felt the need to return after the war and

The grave of IWGC gardener William Curtis. (Author's photo.)

18   Commonwealth War Graves Commission Archive (CWGCA) CWGC/6/4/1/2/1572.

tend to the graves of his fallen comrades, only to be killed by a piece of ordnance left behind by the war that he had survived five years earlier.

There is, however, one piece of positivity concerning this tragic story. During the research for this book, it became apparent that William Curtis had been incorrectly listed on the official names list of the In Flanders Fields Museum and was recorded as 'William Cuattus' as a result from an administrative error in the old hospital records. After checking with the National Archive and the CWGC archives on the existence of William Cuattus, it became apparent that no such man existed in the employ of the IWGC at the time. A quick trip to Ypres Town Cemetery soon solved the mystery with the location of the grave of IWGC employee William Curtis, who died on 30 June 1923. The local authorities were informed, and Curtis is now correctly recorded in the town records.[19]

There are many modern-day incidents involving gardeners of the CWGC and unexploded ordnance, although, luckily, none of them have been as serious as the incident involving William Curtis. Many gardeners have stories to tell of finding hand grenades in compost, of digging up ammunition and of live shells being left at cemetery gates by members of the public who have no idea of the reporting procedure. In 2018, preparations for the burial of three soldiers in Tyne Cot Cemetery were halted after a large shell was discovered during the excavation of the graves. There are cases of patches of grass mysteriously turning yellow and dying in some cemeteries and, upon further investigation, the cause being found to be leaking chemical shells lying beneath the surface.

The CWGC of today has strict procedures in place for dealing with incidents of this nature. All of their workers are fully trained in the relevant health and safety laws, filling out a 'Near Miss' form for each incident. Upon the discovery of ammunition in a cemetery, all work must cease. In the case of the discovery of SAA, a five-metre area is cordoned off. For anything larger than a bullet, the cemetery is immediately closed to the general public and evacuated of all personnel. In both cases, the police are then informed and will attend the scene and take the process on to its next step.

The discovery of ammunition in cemeteries is not unusual, something that I have first-hand experience of. In 2013, a ditch was dug across the width of Tyne Cot Cemetery in preparation for the laying of irrigation drainage pipes. The ditch was a couple of feet deep and ran across the cemetery in front of the Cross of Sacrifice, which was, in turn, constructed over a large German defensive bunker that saw heavy fighting in October 1917 during the Third Battle of Ypres. I had been engaged by the assistant to the ambassador of Pakistan to show him around the cemetery in preparation for forthcoming ceremonies. As we strolled through the cemetery in the early evening, we walked along the edge of the drainage ditch. All along the inside wall of the ditch, you could see the tell-tale signs of corroding green metal of spent

---

19 Thanks to Dr Dominiek Dendooven of the In Flanders Fields Museum and Allison Cain of the Stadsarchief for their help.

and live rounds of SAA, such as .303 rounds from the Lee Enfield rifle. Several of them were intact and were in plain view.

The old battlefields around Ypres are far from being cleared of explosives. Every year, DOVO collects, on average, an incredible 250 tons of unexploded ammunition from the area. Some years, the grim tally will fall only to be surpassed again the following year. Most of the time, the shells are recovered individually, but, from time to time, large ammunition caches are discovered. In March 2014, a local farmer in the Passchendaele area ploughed up a few shells in his field and then some more and then some more. Worried by this turn of events, the farmer wisely called DOVO, who attended the scene and started to assess the situation. They realised quickly that this was an ammunition cache of a size rarely seen in Belgium. In order to deal with the threat, a cordon was put into place to keep the general public well away. DOVO then started to excavate the site. What they found was staggering. It turned out to be the largest single discovery of ammunition ever in Belgium since the end of the First World War to that date. It took the bomb-disposal units three weeks to excavate the site, during which they recovered an incredible 848 shells, of which 771 were chemical weapons. The shells were mainly German, but around 50 French shells were also recovered. In total, the cache was over seven tons in weight.[20]

The discovery of another large cache occurred three years later in November 2017 in the district of Heuvelland, a few miles south of Ypres. A local battlefield tour guide explained, 'In my corner of Belgium there is a man who spends much of his time searching the fields with a metal detector. He is the one who found the old depot, he told me that the total was 15 tons! One of the toxic shells was leaking and they had to secure it (onsite) with a plaster cast'.[21] Upon completion of the recovery, DOVO had taken away over 450 shells, 35 fuses and three hand grenades. Of the shells recovered, all were of British origin, with the exception of one German 77mm round. The majority of the cache was made up of 211 rounds of British 4.5-inch shells, 175 rounds of British 3-inch Stokes mortar shells and 59 British 18-pdr rounds. The find, although significant, is not particularly out of the ordinary, as DOVO operative Daan Verfaillie explained, 'It is by far not the biggest find; on the contrary this is a normal find for the region. I dare say that we have similar finds (between 150 and 400 pieces), as an average once a month between April and October'.[22] The discovery and recovery of field artillery rounds is particularly common in the Ypres Salient. Between the years of 2016 and 2020, DOVO recovered and destroyed 25,890 British 18-pdr shells and 11,473 German 77mm shells.[23]

---

20 DOVO (2021), 'Heuvelland November 2017'. E-mail (8 March 2021).
21 Carl Ooghe (2021), 'Roger'. E-mail (2 March 2021).
22 DOVO, 'Heuvelland November 2017'. (8 March 2021).
23 DOVO (2021), 'Heuvelland November 2017'. E-mail (11 May 2021).

A large discovery of artillery fuses and unexploded shells. (Image courtesy of DOVO, Belgian Armed Forces.)

The mixture of tourism and unexploded ammunition is one that has many potential pit falls. From as early as 1919, when the first tourists started to arrive in the Ypres Salient, visitors liked to be pictured standing next to unexploded ammunition, the photo being a souvenir of their visit to the battlefields around Ypres. Even today, visitors are fascinated by the rusting piles of ammunition that lie on the edges of fields or roadsides in the Ypres Salient. The huge annual recovery rate of munitions means that there is always a pile of rusting artillery shells somewhere for tourists to look at. The problem is, however, that the majority of visitors fail to recognise the dangers these objects still pose, either from explosion or from the leakage of deadly chemicals such as mustard gas. There are many tour guides in the Ypres Salient who, like me, constantly warn guests of the dangers involved in tampering with live ammunition, advice that some people heed and some do not. Many of my colleagues have stories to tell with regards to the potentially deadly mixture of tourists and ammunition. Over the years, my fellow guides have witnessed people taking unexploded shells away in their cars, individuals kicking shells by the side of the road and, in one instance of unbelievable stupidity, a coach stopping to allow the teacher to jump off, pick up an unexploded shell and take it back onto the coach to show it to the children on board. Two specific incidents relating to my own experiences immediately spring to mind:

In 2014, I was taking a tour group around the northern area of the Ypres Salient. Roughly halfway through the tour, as we approached the New Zealand Division memorial near the Grafenstafel ridge, I saw a rusty, but fully intact, British 18-pdr artillery shell laying by the side of the road. I had already talked about the Iron Harvest and its dangers earlier in the tour and so pulled the van over so that the clients could get a better look. As they wanted to take photos, we all got out of the van. I told them not to get too close and 'do not poke, kick or touch this thing as it could kill you'. Once the photographs had been taken, we started to get back in the van when I noticed a father and young son were missing. I turned around to see the father had picked up the shell and was pretending to throw it to his son!!! Using my best 'Anglo Saxon', I told the gentleman to put the thing down and do it gently. Luckily, the situation turned out okay, nobody was hurt apart from the guy's pride, who later apologised for his stupidity. He did, though, seem quite pleased that he had learnt a few new English words!

The second incident occurred in 2017, when I was taking two German guests on a private tour. The incident happened in Bellewaerde wood on the lip of one of the craters. I was explaining to my guests that, up until a few years before, this was private land and so unexploded ammunition was quite common, so they needed to be careful with what they touched. One of the guests stood on the lip of a mine crater, and I was a few feet below him at ground level. It was in the middle of summer, and so the clay soil had been baked hard by the sun. The guest on the crater lip saw a rusty piece of metal protruding from the ground and, before I could say anything, gave it an almighty kick. Out jumped a rusty Mills bomb, which bounced down the rock-hard side of the crater and landed squarely between my feet. Apparently, my complexion went from normal to sheet white and then to red as I recovered from the initial shock and realised the thing had not gone off!! Once again, I 'explained' in my best Anglo Saxon why kicking a hand grenade was not a good idea, and, when things had calmed down, I marked the grenade's position in the field and called the police so that they, in turn, would contact the bomb-disposal unit. We then completed the tour, and I dropped my guests off in the centre of Ypres and then went home. Later that night, I received a phone call from the local police asking if I would accompany an officer to the site so that he could locate the grenade easily. By the time they arrived at my house, it was getting dark, so I equipped myself with a torch and drove to the site followed by a police car with two policemen. The site itself is quite isolated, so I was surprised to see another car parked there on my arrival and was even more surprised to see that it had German number plates! The two police officers and I walked up the pathway towards the site where the grenade was. As we walked around the corner, we came across the two German guests from my tour earlier, who had obviously come back to retrieve the hand grenade as a souvenir. When questioned, they of course claimed they had come back to make sure the spot was marked correctly, a claim the police had no time for, so, after a stern warning, they were sent away with orders not to return to the site! I dread to think what would have happened if we had not shown up at that point.

It is not only local tour guides who have tales to tell. Hotel and bed and breakfast owners have stories of their own. Many have stories of guests returning after a hard-day's battlefield exploration proudly carrying some 'unusual' souvenirs. Muriel Bostyn was the owner of Cavell's Bed and Breakfast before it was sold in 2015 and has a story concerning a British guest and his Porsche:

In 2013 a British gentleman and his son checked in for a couple of nights to do a tour of the area. The gentleman was driving a nice Porsche and the plan was to tour the old battlefields in the Porsche with his son. The father and son checked in late afternoon after already doing some touring of the area having driven from the Somme in France. The father was a well presented, seemingly intelligent man who seemed to have been successful in his life. The following morning after breakfast the father and son left for another day's touring in the Porsche. Once they had departed, I went upstairs to service their room, only to find sitting on the windowsill of their room a large artillery shell. On their return I informed them of the potential danger, the guest refused to believe it was dangerous (it had no fuse) but took it out of the building and left it in the Porsche overnight. The following day they checked out and headed home via Eurotunnel in the Porsche with the shell packed with their luggage.[24]

24   Muriel Bostyn, Cavell's Bed and Breakfast, Ypres (March 2021).

A common scene in the Ypres Salient, unexploded ammunition awaiting collection, collectively known by the locals as the 'Iron Harvest'. (Author's photos.)

Souvenir collecting from the battlefields of France and Belgium became a major problem for the port authorities during the commemoration years of 2014–2018 and the massive increase of visitor numbers that followed. Of major concern was people bringing back live ammunition on the ferries, Eurotunnel and Eurostar. As a result, signs were erected at the major ports warning people to declare these objects before boarding. Failure to do so would lead to arrest and very heavy fines.

The casual attitude of the general public towards the dangers posed by unexploded munitions seems to be induced by over familiarity and the lack of warning signs or safety barriers around the piles of rusting shells that litter the landscape around Ypres. Here in Belgium, if a farmer ploughs up a First World War shell, he will pick it up and leave it by the roadside for collection often in full view of anyone passing by. The farmer will then call the police, who will then come out to assess the danger, and they will in turn inform the bomb-disposal unit. Modern-day society and its reliance on health and safety rules seems to have generated a lack of common sense amongst

Tourists posing for a picture by a large British shell. (Author's photo.)

some people, the belief being that, if it is not roped off and covered in warning signs, it cannot be dangerous. Nothing is further from the truth. In an effort to try and stem the growing problem of the public tampering with or taking away unexploded munitions, DOVO has started to request that the farmers leave the ammunition they have found out of sight and away from prying eyes – behind a hedge, for example.

Another misconception is that, since the ammunition is old, it is less likely to cause problems. Again, untrue. As the shell cases start to rust, deadly chemicals can leak, exposing anybody nearby to any variety of noxious gases or liquids. As time goes by, explosives become more and more unstable, and the vital components within a shell start to rust through, making accidental detonation more likely. A good example of this is the rusting of British hand grenades known as 'Mills bombs', which the Belgian Army bomb-disposal units are particularly wary of. Jacques Callebaut, *adjudant-majoor* (Air) from DOVO, explained that 'The mills grenades are notorious because the cocked striker is only held away from the primer with a small piece of metal, many of which are rusted away by now'.[25] The Mills bombs can be a particular problem to farmers in the area not only because of their instability but also because they come out of the ground caked in clay roughly the size and shape of a large potato. It is not unusual that, during the potato harvest, when the potatoes are being sorted and washed, that a Mills bomb will turn up amongst them, which the farmer will then pick out and leave for DOVO to collect. In February 2019, it was reported that a First World War German hand grenade had been found in a Hong Kong crisp factory in a consignment of potatoes that had recently arrived from France.[26] The German grenade is thought to have been used but had failed to explode, making it very unstable. Once the grenade had been retrieved, the Hong Kong bomb-disposal team detonated it in a drainage channel on site.

Even today, there is a lively trade in such items. Visitors to the area like nothing better than being able to bring a genuine souvenir from the First World War battlefields back home to show family and friends. Items of particular interest are shrapnel balls, cartridge cases, bullet heads and uniform buttons. Local farmers and collectors search the fields for these objects and bring them into Ypres to sell. The British Grenadier bookshop has been situated near the Menin Gate for nearly 20 years and has become the 'must visit' shop for anyone touring the area with the Great War in mind. The shop sells a wide range of genuine artifacts recovered from the local battlefields. The current proprietor, Mr. Steve Douglas, explained:

> It always fascinates me when I see an emotional and amazed response from people who have asked me if these items, on display in my shop, really came

---

[25] Interview with Jacques Callebaut, *adjudant-majoor* (Air), DOVO (2021).
[26] 'World War One Grenade among Potatoes at Hong Kong Crisp Factory', *BBC News* (3 February 2019), <https://www.bbc.com/news/world-asia-china-47107609>, accessed March 2021.

A rusty, potato-sized British Mills hand grenade. (Author's photo.)

from the battlefields. Many assume they are replicas. Once they realize that these bullet tips, fuses, buttons and such are authentic relics of WW1, their face lights up and they feel a visceral connection to the war. For many it is a real connection, especially if they have lost a relative in the area. Finding such things in my shop is cool enough but for others, finding items still in the ground is the best thing. I remember back when we first opened the shop, in 2003, two young Dutch boys of about 15 or 16 years of age came in. They had been in a day or two prior and we had chatted. This day they came back after cycling around the battlefields, all excited to tell me about the things they found in the fields. 'We found some shrapnel balls, a complete grenade, a bottle, part of a bayonet and …' 'Whoa, whoa' I interrupted, 'tell me about the grenade. What did you do with it?' 'Oh, it's right here in my backpack' said one of them. I took a deep breath as he dug it out from his pack. Sure enough, it was a complete British Mills bomb grenade and apparently, still very much live, still intact and very dangerous. I carefully took it from them after explaining the situation. I took it to the backyard and put it into a bucket of water and then called the police to arrange removal. They then call the Belgian Army bomb disposal team to come and get it. That was my first such experience with live ammo, but not my last. About five years ago a Canadian gentleman who was also cycling the battlefields on his fourth or fifth visit to the area, also came in with a slightly concerned look on his face. He too had found a Mills bomb but was unsure of its current status and wanted my 'professional' opinion on whether or not it was still live.

When he opened his backpack, he produced a complete grenade that, again, was live. This time he decided to take it with him and dispose of it into a nearby lake, which he did. I guess the moral of these two stories are that if you should come across a bomb or grenade that seems to be intact, leave it alone. Do not touch it or move it. They are very much alive even after more than 100 years. Some may be even more volatile now and getting worse all the time due to corrosion. The thing is that if a bomb never exploded, we will never know just how close it came to exploding and any disturbance could be enough to set it off given the effects of time and corrosion. Many local farmers are quite used to dealing with battlefield detritus from their fields and a few will gather up items they think I may buy from them and 'take them to market', so to speak. There is one retired old farmer of about 80 years who comes in on a regular basis. He wanders in looking like he has nothing to sell, but then pulls out a heavy brass fuse from one pocket, a rusty corroded old horseshoe from another. Then a broken piece of bayonet from his inside jacket pocket. Everything is wrapped in newsprint. Just when I think that's it, he bends over and unrolls his sock and pulls out a little package. A bit of newspaper wrapped packet and then the same comes from the other sock. At this point my anticipation grows that this must be something extra special only to find that he has just brough me a single bullet tip in each packet. What a let-down and what a laugh. He is paranoid that this is some sort of illegal activity and the police will catch him. 'Okay' I say. 'Just throw in into that box with the hundreds of others I have'.[27]

There are severe penalties in place to deter people from collecting war materials should they be found to be dangerous or illegal. In 2017, a 77-year-old man from Kortrijk Belgium was in court after having been caught in possession of a substantial amount of First World War weapons and explosives. The gentleman had been a collector of First World War artifacts for many years and was found to be in possession of items worth over €25,000. The items consisted of over 200 weapons and six artillery shells. DOVO attended and defused the shells at a cost of €7,500. The man faced six months in prison and a fine of €12,000.[28]

---

27 Steve Douglas, The British Grenadier Book Shop, Ypres (26 February 2021).
28 Ben Storme, 'Zes Mijnen en 200 Wapens Gevonden bij Zeventiger', *Focus WTV* (25 September 2017), <https://www.focus-wtv.be/nieuws/zes-mijnen-en-200-wapens-gevonden-bij-zeventiger>, accessed 5 March 2021.

5

Pericula Non Timeo
(I Do Not Fear the Dangers)

Created in 1920, first Belgian bomb-disposal service was tasked with the clearing and deactivating of munitions that lay scattered across the Belgian landscape at the end of the Great War. Known as the Belgian SDM and aided in the old battlefield areas by the SRD, the organisation operated very successfully and recovered so much ordnance that it led to some military and civil officials to claim that the job of battlefield clearance would be completed by 1922, and so they started to scale back the operation. The decision was reversed by 1923, when the existence of large German ammunition dumps came to light and it soon became clear that the job of munitions disposal was far from completed.

The German Army was soon to return, and, on 28 May 1940, in the face of overwhelming odds, Belgium capitulated to Germany, and the units of the Belgian

A DOVO badge. (Image courtesy of DOVO, Belgian Armed Forces.)

Army became POWs. The fighting in Belgium and the retreat to Dunkirk in May 1940 added to the already significant issue of problem munitions. The retreating armies had laid mine fields and booby traps in an effort to slow the advance of the German Army, and, now that the fighting had stopped, these had to be cleared. The Germans then pressed into service poorly trained units of Belgian Army POWs in order to recover and deactivate the abandoned munitions.

On 16 August 1941, DOVO was created. The unit was raised from imprisoned Belgian Army personnel who had been given the task of clearing unexploded ordnance by the German occupiers. The new organisation operated across the whole of Belgium and was officially responsible for recovering unexploded munitions from Allied air raids, the fighting of 1940 and munitions left over from the Great War. Many members of DOVO at the time saw this new role as an opportunity to help in the fight against the German occupying forces. Contact was made with resistance groups and with London. Members of the service secretly recovered and concealed explosives, handing them over to local resistance groups to be used in acts of sabotage against the Germans. More importantly, information was sent back to London concerning reasons why some Allied types of ordnance had failed to detonate – for example, faulty fuses on unexploded aerial bombs. This information was crucial to the Allies, as it would increase the reliability and ultimately the effectiveness of the Allied air raids. It was for this reason that the German occupiers would only allow DOVO to work on Allied ammunition and not their own, the fear being that sensitive information of the workings and failures of German ordnance would find its way to the resistance and ultimately back to London.

There were, of course, inherent dangers in participating in such actions. First Lieutenant Pierre Boveroux was a prime example. Boveroux had been taken prisoner on 8 May 1940 whilst serving in the 8th Battalion of the Engineers in the Belgian Army and imprisoned in Hasselt in the Limburg region of Belgium. Having been forced by the German occupiers to recover and dismantle unexploded mines and artillery shells, Boveroux saw it as an opportunity to help in the fight against the German occupation. Working closely with the resistance group LUC, he would pass to them explosives sourced from dismantled munitions and would use a small truck placed at his disposal by the Germans to recover explosives parachuted into Belgium by the Allies, distributing them to his resistance comrades. Boveroux was also in contact with London and would pass to them information on faulty Allied fuses and explosives. This was nearly to cost him his life when an explosion from a faulty shell severely injured him, putting him out of action until June 1942. It is possible that he then resumed his work but was betrayed to the Germans on 17 October 1942 when he was arrested and imprisoned by the Gestapo. After enduring weeks of terrible torture and mistreatment at the hands of the Gestapo, First Lieutenant Pierre Boveroux succumbed to his injuries and died on 6 December 1942 in the town of Saint Gilles.[1]

---

1 Jacques Callebaut (2021), 'Another Question'. E-mail (8 March 2021).

First Lieutenant Pierre Boveroux. (Image courtesy of DOVO, Belgian Armed Forces.)

This chapter in the history of DOVO is one that is often overlooked but deserves to be recognised.

On 16 October 1944, during the liberation of Belgium, the newly reformed Belgium army officially formed the *Dienst voor Opruiming en Vernietiging van Ontploffingstuigen en Obstakels* (Service for Clearance and Disposal of Explosive Ordnance and Obstacles) or 'DOVOO' for short. This was, in fact, the new official name for DOVO and had a strength of 300 personnel, including German POWs. DOVOO was again restructured in December 1945, being centralised under one command and reverting back to its previous title of 'DOVO'. For the next few years, the organisation underwent several changes in an effort to find the most efficient way of working and as a result of a decreasing workload. For these reasons, DOVO was reduced to a strength of 115 personnel in 1955. The following years again saw changes, with DOVO being dissolved and reinstated in the 1970s and all services' bomb-disposal units coming under one command structure in the year 2000. January 2011 saw all DOVO EOD (Explosive Ordnance Disposal) personnel move from the Logistic Corps to the Engineer units, enabling them to wear the Engineers' black beret with the insignia of their EOD units attached.

The strength of today's DOVO stands at 267 personnel who are distributed across three sites in Belgium: Meerdaal, Poelkapelle and Zeebrugge.[2] The increase in personnel is as a result of the Belgian Army's involvement in various areas around the world, the rise of international terrorism and of course the ongoing problem of wartime munitions, particularly in the region of West Flanders. Of the total personnel, 174 are EOD technicians, trained in the recovery and dismantling of unexploded munitions. For the purpose of this book, we will focus on the task DOVO has in clearing ordnance from the Great War in and around the Ypres Salient.

The depot tasked with the collection and disposal of First World War ammunition is situated in the Houthulst Forest in the region of Poelkapelle, West Flanders. The approximate 700-acre site has been in use since the end of the First World War and has facilities for storing and deactivating both conventional and chemical weapons. Staffed by 106 base personnel, including 65 EOD technicians, it is responsible for an area with its furthest point being 95 kilometres from Ypres. Within that area, they recover an average of 250 tons per year of unexploded munitions mainly from the Great War, of which 20 tons annually are termed as 'problem munitions'. Of the three DOVO bases in Belgium, Poelkapelle is the only one that has facilities to dismantle chemical weapons. As a result, not only all of Belgium's chemical weapons

A DOVO EOD team on site. (Image courtesy of DOVO, Belgian Armed Forces.)

2   Callebaut, 'Another Question'.

are sent there to be dismantled, but the Netherlands and Luxembourg's are also. The base despatches three mobile teams each day to respond to prearranged collections. In addition to the three teams, there is always one team on standby to respond to unforeseen and urgent incidents. The standby team must be ready to respond within 30 minutes of a request during office hours and within one hour outside of the normal working day. Each team of three EOD technicians handles around 13 call-outs per day, with spring and autumn being their busiest times since this is the time when the farmers are working on the land. In the year of 2020, DOVO was called out to nearly 2,400 incidents in West Flanders and around 4,000 times across the whole of Belgium.

A strict and well-documented procedure is in place for dealing with unexploded ammunition. Once DOVO has been contacted by the police, they will plan a collection of the ammunition depending upon where it is, how much there is and the type of weapon. Any explosives found near built-up areas, where they could cause serious harm, are prioritised as high risk and are collected as soon as possible. Training is essential, and each EOD technician has completed a one-year training course followed by an advanced four-month course after five years of experience in order to become an EOD team leader. All training is done in house and has a reputation of excellence, offering EOD courses to foreign operatives from around the world. The EOD technicians travel in a flatbed truck; most of the back is taken up by a large, shallow sandpit and a crate. Anything deemed to be of little danger is put into the crate, SAA for example, and anything larger and with risk, such as artillery shells, are carefully laid in the sand with the fuses facing away from each other in order to insulate them from the jolts and bumps in the road and avoid accidental detonation. Each van also contains protective chemical suits to be worn if any of the shells start to leak noxious substances. The scenario of chemical contamination is very real. As each year passes, shell casings become more and more unstable as they lie rusting in the ground. After 100 years since the end of the Great War, the chemical weapons that both sides hurled at each other still remain viable and will either kill or seriously injure if you come into close contact with them. Incidents involving these weapons occur most years, incidents such as workmen being gassed after accidently fracturing a shell whilst digging a hole, of a farmer found choking on phosgene gas after hitting a shell while laying irrigation pipes on his land (his life being saved by the quick actions of the DOVO team who were quickly on site) and of a workman suffering blisters on his hand and arm as he picked up a shell that was leaking a black oily liquid, which was mustard gas. These incidents serve as a warning that, no matter how harmless they look, each shell could well contain a hidden danger – a danger that the members of DOVO are well aware of and, as such, are equipped to deal with.

Réal Desmarets was an EOD technician for most of his working life, seeing active service around the world including the Bosnian conflict, where he and his colleagues cleared Serbian minefields along the embankments of the Danube and Drava rivers. On his return to Belgium, Desmarets was reassigned back to the DOVO unit at Poelkapelle:

Pericula Non Timeo 77

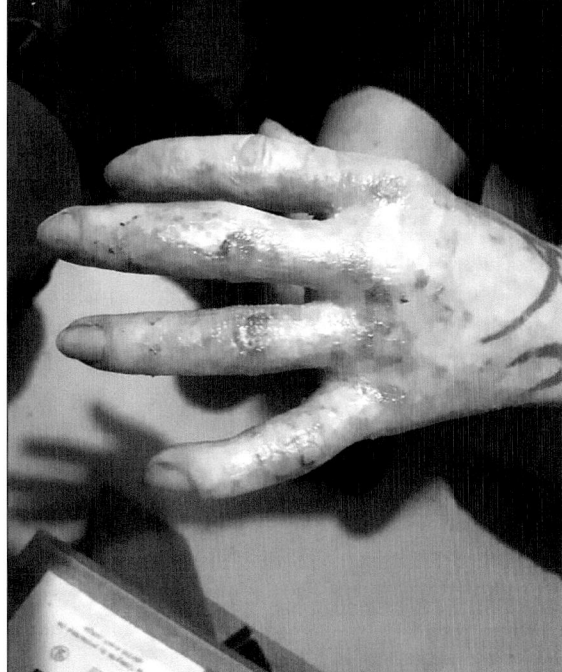

A leaking mustard gas shell and the subsequent burn injuries suffered by its unsuspecting victim. (Image courtesy of DOVO, Belgian Armed Forces.)

For twenty-seven years, I was a deminer in Belgium. I am passionate about the history of the First World War and the Second World War. Since a kid, I dreamed of working in the army. I passed the tests to become a para commando. But my wife didn't want me to: 'It's dangerous', (we'll see it later !!) So, I was posted to Germany with the 4th Chasseurs à Cheval (RECCE Regiment) Two children were born there. For the education of children, we wanted to return to Belgium. That's when a note came out 'EOD request.' In January 1990, I started the EOD training course and in November I was attached to Poelkapelle, to the Bomb Disposal, an organization which was created after the First World War. At that time, it was believed that the munitions clearance would only last a few months, but today, more than a hundred years later, 200 to 250 tonnes of ammunition are still found annually in Belgium. I worked on the yard platform; this is the platform where the shells are unloaded on arrival at the depot. When you arrive at the Poelkapelle barracks, you pass the war memorial. It is a Hermann Goering one ton WWII bomb placed vertically. On one side of it are the names of the EOD technicians killed in Flanders, at the coast is another monument for those killed in the exercise of their profession since 1944 and in Stavelot is the National monument for the fallen EOD technicians. When you read them, you hope that your name will never appear there. I remember the first time I handled a shell, I asked myself a lot of questions, I constantly had this doubt in my mind: Why didn't it explode at the time? What if it explodes now? But I'm trying to focus on what needs to be done. Remember the procedure. Keep calm.

Most of the time, shells are found in farmers' fields. Sometimes during the creation of an industrial zone or pipe work in a street. When we arrive at a call out, we secure the site to keep curious people away, especially the old, because they have become accustomed to unexploded munitions having grown up with it, their attitude being 'yeah, it's not dangerous!' If we listen to them, they all know about ammunition better than we do! Some have seen the Germans laying mines and the deminers removing them. Sometimes some shells are so heavy that two or three EOD technicians are needed to lift them. We have to place and carry the shell on a stretcher. If one of us does the wrong thing, he puts the other in danger. Everyone has the life of their colleague in their hands. Some shells weigh 120 kilos. If there are two of you, in a potato field with mounds of earth, it's not easy to walk. In winter, the shell is frozen in the ground, it is removed with a crowbar. When the deminers leave the site, people are relieved, some give us an appointment for the next discovery. The shells from 1914–1918 are still found in West Flanders along the old front line. In the region of Ploegsteert, Messines and Wytschaete for example, in June 1917, nineteen mines exploded, killing several thousand Germans in a matter of seconds. At that point, three mines had not been fired: the British command wanted to keep them in case the Germans counterattacked. It means that there are still about

60 tons of explosives beneath the fields. In 1955, one of the mines accidentally detonated after being hit by lightning in Warneton, luckily nobody was injured.

On a mission, fear sticks to the stomach. I spoke with deminers active in 1944–45. The war had just ended. They occasionally carried out one hundred to two hundred demining operations a day. Belgium is known for its EOD, with so much of it left here after two world wars. The armies of Germany, France, England, etc. fought here and as a result, we are internationally renowned for our land and naval demining expertise.

In June 2015, I was alone in the platform, the platform where the shells found in Belgium were brought back. It is 2:30 pm. With only a few hours left before we go home. At that time I checked a German shell from the First World War, an illuminating pot. It is an object shot over the battlefield at night. Equipped with a mini parachute, it burns up during the trajectory and illuminates the terrain. The pot falls. I want to pick it up. I squat down. It catches fire. Powerful flames erupt and are propelled over my knees, hands and face. Intense burning. I'm not panicking. I stay calm. I shake my hands. My gloves are falling. The flames enter by the sleeve against my right arm. A colleague runs up and sees my body on fire. He soaks me with water. I tell myself it's going to be fine, it's going to be fine. I look at my body: I see myself whole. My hands are normal. I say to myself: it's okay.

Before I was transferred to Ypres Civil Hospital, I called my wife to inform her: 'I had an accident, but it's okay'. A colleague comes to take my wife to the hospital. She remembers, 'They put on a silver blanket so he wouldn't get cold. He didn't seem to be in pain. He had no doubt been given something'. In the evening, an ambulance takes me to the burns centre of the military hospital in Brussels. Transport. Operating room. It's midnight when I come into the bedroom. Lying on the bed, I bend down and suddenly see my hands. They had swelled so much that I could not recognize them.

My wife is spending the day after in Brussels at the hospital with the children. There is a shock! Impossible to recognize me. My face is a rugby ball. Fortunately, I had seen it the same day. In fact, the skin is still burning three days after the accident.

In the hospital, I am well cared for. But the care is painful. They give me morphine, so I'm rambling. Colleagues pass by. My brother-in-law travelled a hundred and thirty kilometres to come and visit me. I don't recognize them. I have visions. I wait for a bus that I never see arriving. Then it's home revalidation. Care, physiotherapy. I wear compression gloves, made to measure, for eighteen months to flatten the scars. Eight hundred euros a pair, I had to put them on for twenty-three hours a day. I had three operations to be able to open my hand and pick up things.

Back home, I'm not the same man anymore. Something was wrong. It was broken. I didn't want to go out anymore, I stayed locked up. Normally I love animals, but I didn't want to walk the dog. I was psychologically assessed, one hour on the phone every week. Having that two years away from retirement hurts a bit, all the same. I would have liked to have had a full career without incident.

And then, I overcome these difficult times. I resume the routine and start working again. First in the administrative department. I train new teams of deminers, I make files. And then in the last months before my retirement, I returned to missions. Why? I didn't want to stay on a failure. I wanted to leave the profession by the front door. My last day, I was on a mission to bring ammunition back to the area. Back at base, when it was time to haul the last shell out of the van, I said to my colleague, 'This one is for me. It will be the last'. I took a good look at it for a moment. It was a German shell. I got it out of the van and put it on the sandbox.

Now it's over. I had carried thousands of shells. From now on, I could breathe. The next day, I was going to retire.

When I look back at all those years, I still feel proud in having cleaned up, handled this ammunition and in having destroyed it we may have saved lives.[3]

Whilst there is still ammunition to be recovered in the Ypres Salient, the bomb-disposal units of the Belgian Army will still be at risk of death or serious injury on a daily basis. The last fatalities within DOVO relating to First World War ammunition occurred on 7 May 1986 at around 1:20 p.m. when four members of the unit were killed at the bomb-disposal site at Poelkapelle. André Ronsmans (34), Jean Lebeke (33), Wilfried Vynckier (42) and Xavier Demoor (33) were all tragically killed whilst handling and sorting chemical shells. It is believed that a German 77mm shell exploded, with the shrapnel killing the four men.

We will remember them.

---

3   Réal Desmarets (2021), 'My Story'. E-mail (10 March 2021).

The DOVO Memorial.
(Author's photos.)

6

At the Sharp End
The Evolution of DOVO Poelkapelle

The average working day of an EOD technician in the old Ypres Salient is as varied as it is dangerous. For most of us, going to work is nothing more than a routine, something to be completed as quickly as possible in order to get home and enjoy the fruits of our labour. For the EOD technicians, every day they go to work could potentially be their last. Although some accidents cannot be avoided, as an element of bad lack can always be present, the risk can be reduced by extensive training and the adherence to strict procedure. No EOD technician takes anything for granted. Every shell and explosive are treated with the same skill and care in an effort to avoid death or serious injury not only to themselves but also to the wider population. The base at Poelkapelle is always on standby and sends out three teams of operatives a day, each team consisting of three members, of which one is a team leader. These teams cover prearranged collections only. A fourth team is on standby, ready to handle unforeseen and priority call-outs. In rarer cases, DOVO has a prearranged presence on sites where major works are taking place, particularly in areas known for heavy fighting during the Great War. In recent years, DOVO collected thousands of shells on site as a new gas pipeline was laid between the towns of Koekelare and Ploegsteert and in 2019 during the construction of the new Bellewaerde Aquapark, which was built on the front line of 1915, the scene of some of the most savage fighting in the Ypres Salient.

Between the years of 2001 and 2020, the DOVO team from Poelkapelle responded to over 65,000 registered call-outs in their operational area, equating to an average of over 3,000 calls per year. Some calls related to single shells being dug up by a builder, for example, or some related to finds of multiple tons by farmers busy ploughing their fields. In all, this totalled to an incredible 5,100 tons of munitions recovered during that period, which in turn equals an average of just over 250 tons per year of munitions recovered in the old Ypres Salient and surrounding area.

The facilities at the DOVO base at Poelkapelle have evolved from their pre-1980s operations to the sophisticated and high-tech operations that they are today. Post-First World War, the depot was underfunded and viewed as a backwater operation by the powers in Brussels. As the years progressed and the importance of Flanders increased, financial support was more forthcoming. Nobody could ignore the fact that the rate of recovery of Great War munitions was increasing rather than decreasing. Coupled with the regular accidents and sometimes fatalities related to the abandoned munitions, it was realised that this was an ongoing and long-term issue that needed to be dealt with.

A normal working day starts at 8:00 a.m. for the DOVO teams. Once they are allocated their munition collection tasks, they leave the depot in their flatbed vans to make their way to their first call. On arrival, if needed, the site is secured, the ammunition assessed by the EOD team leader and then collected by hand to be placed in the sand tray in the back of the collection vehicle. Once they have completed their designated tasks, they then carefully transport their cargo back to the depot at Poelkapelle for its destruction. On arrival, each shell has to be identified by type and by its contents. With a high proportion of deadly chemical weapons in the area, it is crucial that this identification process takes place since each type of shell has a different dismantling method. To get the identification wrong at this stage could easily lead to death and injury further down the line. The process of identification takes place on the identification platform. Historically, this process took place in a basic building where a technician would knock the clay and rust off the shell with a hammer and a wire brush, not a job for the faint-hearted!

In 1987, a new platform was constructed, quickly followed by a new building in 1988. The new building was to house an automatic Corund blasting machine. The machine was designed to blast the rust and clay off of shells using a nonmagnetic mineral, the idea being to clean the shell for identification with little or no risk to the DOVO technician. The machine had some success but, as a result of operating costs, was soon replaced by a blasting machine that used frozen CO_2 pellets to clean the shells. However, after some assessment and deliberation by the personnel involved, it was decided that none of the new methods were as effective as the old method of a hammer and wire brush, and so the old system was quickly reinstated. In 1993, a roof was built over the identification platform to protect the ammunition from the elements. This allowed the ammunition to dry out quickly, aided the cleaning procedure and, of course, kept the DOVO technician dry in the process!

More investment followed in 1998 when the identification platform had a fully enclosed building installed that was to house the depot's first fully automated munitions x-ray system. The new installation allowed the operator to identify chemical shells in complete safety, giving the operator not only an internal view of the shell but also the amount of chemical liquid contained within the shell. The x-ray process was again upgraded in 2002 with the installation of a second machine. Although the x-ray machines were great at distinguishing chemical shells from explosive shells, what they could not do was identify the actual chemical contained within the shell. The identification of the chemical was essential, as it would dictate how the chemical would be destroyed, so each shell had to be manually tested with the chemical being extracted from each shell and sent for analysis before it could be disposed of. The lead time between the extraction of the chemical and receiving the results of the analysis delayed the process and resulted in dangerous chemicals being stored until they could be dealt with. This problem was solved as new technology was developed, and, in 2003, the depot's first neutron analysis system was installed, allowing the operator to identify the chemical within the shell without the need for laboratory analysis. As technology advanced and systems improved, a new upgrade to this system took place in 2019. Once the munitions are identified, the chemical and conventional munitions are destroyed in separate processes. Each shell is labelled with a bar code for identification and stored until it can be disposed of.

The crates containing the explosive shells are then taken to the demolition field, which is situated in the forest within the confines of the base. The demolition field has been in use since the First World War. Originally, the shells were transported to the demolition field by a light railway track installed after the war; however, it was found to be more efficient to use tractors and trailers to transport the shells, and so, in 1983, the railway track was dismantled. At this point, however, the access leading to the demolition area was just a muddy track, which in bad weather would become boggy and difficult to negotiate. To solve the issue, major works were carried out on the base in the 1990s when roads and concrete platforms were laid, enabling the use of normal road vehicles to transport the munitions safely to the demolition field. The destruction of the conventional shells in the demolition field takes place twice a day, once in the morning and once in the afternoon from early spring to late autumn. There is a limit placed on the amounts destroyed at any one time to negate the risk of making the ground unstable and affecting the inhabitants of the villages in the vicinity of the base. No detonations take place in the winter, as the shock waves from the explosions are amplified by the wet ground, increasing the risk of damage to the surroundings. The method of destruction of the explosive shells has not changed greatly over the years, the only changes being the use of modern-day machinery to help with the manual labour.

Historically, the deactivation and dismantling of chemical shells or 'problem munitions' has been a major issue for the Belgian authorities, with DOVO estimating that 11 percent of the shells recovered in the Salient contain noxious substances. With tens of millions of unexploded chemical weapons littering the Ypres Salient at the end of the Great War and with no set procedures in place or technology available to deal with them, the bomb-disposal units of the Belgian Army have had to develop their own techniques in order to deal with this problem. Initially, the chemical shells were dealt with by F. N. Pickett et Fils, but, upon the closure of its factory in the 1920s, the burden fell on the shoulders of the Belgian authorities and the 'deminers' of the bomb-disposal units. The problem was initially dealt with by either blowing up the chemical shells or incinerating them. These two methods had inherent dangers of accidental release of toxic fumes either after a detonation or during the process of incineration. There are several documented cases of local people complaining about toxic fumes and farm animals being poisoned by said fumes.

It was also common practice for chemical munitions to be dumped at sea, either off the coast of Belgium or in the Bay of Biscay, where it is thought that the Belgian authorities dumped 810 tonnes of concrete encased munitions between 1954 and 1972.[1] This practice continued until the Oslo Convention of 1972 banned the dumping of ammunition at sea. The new legislation created a problem for DOVO in the Ypres Salient: they now had a much smaller capacity for the disposal of chemical shells and could not deal with them at the rate they were being recovered from the old battlefields around Ypres. The only solution was to stockpile them at the base until a viable solution could be found. Between the years of 1972 to 1980, the amount of rusting chemical shells stored at the base steadily increased by an average of about 20 tonnes per year, the shells being stored on the ground and stacked up in piles in the forest at the base.[2] As each year passed, the piles of shells increased and became more and more unstable as they were exposed to the elements. One explosion could have had disastrous consequences. In an effort to solve the problem, the Belgian Minister of the Environment and Public Health in 1980 invoked article nine of the Oslo Convention, which allowed for emergency sea dumping. A licence was issued allowing the dumping of 225 tonnes of chemical ammunition in the Bay of Biscay, although under strict regulation.[3] The munitions were encased in 850–1,250kg reinforced concrete blocks, increasing the gross weight of the cargo from 225 tonnes to 2,700 tonnes. The dumping mission was completed in November 1980 and was the last of its kind carried out by the Belgian authorities.

The retrieval of chemical weapons carried on in the Ypres Salient, and, inevitably, the stockpile started to grow again, resulting in 289 tonnes of chemical munitions in storage at the depot by 1996.[4] In an effort to try and create a more stable environment for the storage of the shells and negate the possibility of leakage into the ground, eight covered concrete platforms were constructed and used for shell storage from the mid-1980s onwards. Each concrete platform had a surface area of about 90 square metres and was separated by blast walls designed to contain an explosion in case of accidental detonation. The shells were stacked up in a pyramid fashion in metal frames each containing a maximum of 50 shells. The tragic accident of May 1986, which caused the deaths of four EOD technicians, forced a rethink with regards to storage methods, resulting in wooden crates being used to safely contain the shells and to ensure that there was no physical contact between them. Shells were stored with the fuses facing away from each other in attempt to stop a chain reaction of explosions should one shell partially detonate. The system using wooden crates for storage was soon improved upon by replacing the wooden crates with sturdy plastic crates, the idea being to contain any chemical spillage from leaking shells within the crate and therefore reduce the risk of cross contamination. By the mid-1990s, an incredible 24,000 explosive munitions of different types were in storage at the depot, leaving

1 Zanders, 'Destruction of Old Chemical Weapons', p.210.
2 Zanders, 'Destruction of Old Chemical Weapons', p.211.
3 Zanders, 'Destruction of Old Chemical Weapons', p.211.
4 Zanders, 'Destruction of Old Chemical Weapons', p.212.

only one of the eight platforms with capacity for storage, and it was estimated that it would take up to nine years to dispose of the backlog, with approximately 18,000 of those shells thought to be chemical munitions.

The accumulation of munitions was of course foreseen, and plans were put into place in 1993 to create a chemical disposal facility at the base. The facility finally came into operation in 1998 at the cost of over 500 million Belgian Francs, equating to over 12 million euros. The facility was designed to either dismantle or detonate chemical munitions on site depending on the type of chemical munition in question. In 2001, tests were carried out on a portable detonation chamber manufactured in the US. The detonation chamber, called the 'Donovan T10', allowed for specific chemical munitions of a 'fixed' payload to be detonated on site in a contained environment. The portable detonation chamber was very successful and processed over 1,000 chemical shells between the years of 2001 and 2004, and, as a result of its success, a new static detonation chamber named the 'Donovan T60' was purchased from the same American company and was installed in 2004, which during its operational lifetime processed over 3,700 chemical shells.

The success of the T60 and advancement in the processes of dismantling chemical weapons led to the purchase and installation of a new CDC (controlled demolition chamber) from a Japanese company in 2007. This process of rolling investment and upgrade proved to be very successful, with DOVO now being able to dispose of around 56 solid chemical shells per day in controlled circumstances with a greatly reduced risk to its technicians. Prior to the purchase of the CDCs, the method of disassembling both solid and liquid chemical shells consisted of a system involving drilling into the shell to access the liquid chemical fill for laboratory analysis and milling and sawing to remove the fuse and burster charge, the process being carried out in a sealed protective chamber with the work being performed by automatic robotic systems. The chamber was designed to be blast resistant and thus protected the operators from chemical contamination in the event of an accident. Depending on the chemical identification, the liquid chemicals from the shell were vacuum pumped into a container and then shipped to a civilian contractor for disposal, the exception to the rule being phosgene gas, which was too dangerous to transport and so was destroyed on site. The process of extraction and destruction of the chemical contents of the shell were arguably the most dangerous part of the process, as it could potentially expose the operators to deadly chemicals. The safety of the technicians during this process was paramount: each worker was required to wear a protective suit, with two types of chemical protective suits in use at the time. The standard suit in use will be familiar to anyone who has served in the armed forces, the NBC suit. Standing for 'nuclear, biological and chemical', the NBC suit was designed to protect its wearer from all chemical eventualities. The second suit was only used in the case of an incident or when the levels of chemical agents in the air had crossed the safety threshold. This protective suit was fully encapsulating, with the outer layer comprising of 14 layers of laminate, and the impermeable suit even consisted of chemical proof underwear! In addition to one of the suits, the technician also wore butyl rubber boots and gloves, with the face being covered by a breathing apparatus with oxygen supplied by a compressed tank worn on the technician's back. From 2001 onwards, the solid chemical shells were disposed of in the then new CDC, simplifying the process of the dismantling of Clark munitions.

Between the years of 2007 and 2012, DOVO had successfully dealt with over 8,000 chemical munitions in the new dismantling facility. However, disaster struck in 2012 when an incident forced the closure of the facility and stopped the destruction of chemical munitions on the site. The accident was caused by a 15cm German shell filled with two different types of high explosives. One of the two explosives had suffered some water intrusion as a result of the shell laying in the heavy clay soil of Flanders. Due to this water intrusion, a 'liquid level' in the shell was detected on the x-ray results. The PINS (Portable Isotopic Neutron Spectroscopy) neutron analysis machine also registered an incorrect result. Therefore, it was assumed that the shell was filled with liquid chemicals when actually it was filled with high explosives. When the process of opening the shell was applied, it exploded, resulting in the complete shutdown of the building. Luckily, there were no injuries to the personnel. The accident highlighted the importance of correct identification of the munitions and the potentially serious consequences that could occur in the event of a simple error.

Once again, chemical munitions were stockpiled at the facility until a new installation could be agreed upon and installed. In April 2017, a new multi-million-euro installation was inaugurated, built by the Swedish company Dynasafe. The new SDC (static demolition chamber) restarted the process of the deactivation and destruction of chemical weapons on site. Between the years of 2012 (when the incident occurred) and 2017 (when the chemical facility reopened), the recovery of chemical weapons in the Ypres Salient and surrounding area had continued at the average rate of about 20 tonnes per year. Thrown into the equation were some particularly large finds of chemical munitions – for example, at Passchendaele in March 2014 when 771 chemical shells were recovered in one incident alone. All of this added up to an estimated backlog of around 5,000 chemical shells, which were being added to on a daily basis. On 14 August 2018, a milestone was reached when it was reported that DOVO had destroyed its five-thousandth chemical shell in the new facility, thus, in effect, finally clearing the backlog that had accumulated between 2012 and 2017. Since that date, the rate of recovery has continued unabated, as does the work of the DOVO technicians.

7

DOVO Today
A Day Out with DOVO

The unrelenting recovery of First and Second World War munitions in Belgium has resulted in DOVO having a virtually unrivalled reputation in the field of deactivation and destruction of explosive and chemical weapons. The technical expertise of DOVO gives rise to regular visits of bomb-disposal operatives from various nations, who often visit the facilities at Poelkapelle in order to view the processes involved in the destruction of explosive and chemical munitions. In the spring of 2021, I was fortunate enough to be given permission to spend a day at the DOVO chemical and conventional weapons dismantling facility at Poelkapelle and spend a morning with the collection teams around the Langemark area, responding to prearranged call-outs. As a result of this access, and the cooperation of the Belgian Army, I am able to describe in detail the procedures in use today for ammunition recovery and destruction in the Ypres Salient. Some of the procedures have evolved over time, and some procedures have remained very similar from their inception to the present day.

Each morning, the three collection teams receive their confirmed call-outs for the day. Each collection demand has been generated by the local police and then sent across to DOVO. The procedure itself starts with the person who finds the munitions, the most common calls originating from farmers working their fields or workers on construction sites, but calls are sometimes received from other sources – somebody digging his garden, for example. Belgian law requires that all ammunition discoveries must be reported to the local police. The police will then attend the scene and write a brief report to be sent to DOVO. The report will contain location details, contact details for the location, how many units of munitions to be recovered and any special comments. The police will also prioritise the call depending on the size of the shell and its location. For example, if a shell is located near a public place such as a school, it will receive an urgent priority status and will be collected immediately by the standby collection team. All non-urgent calls will be attended by one of the three standard collection teams within three days of its registration, and any ammunition that is not collected in the timeframe is normally because it has not been reported by the person who found it. Whilst all police officers fill in what is required on the form, some officers with more experience in dealing with munitions (e.g., the Ypres police) will send unprompted extra information in the form of a digital photograph of the location and the munitions to be collected. This extra information is of great value to the DOVO technicians, as it helps them to assess the ammunition type and its condition and so prewarning them of any potential hazards prior to their arrival.

Once the information is received and collated by DOVO, each team leader will plan the route for collections before the team leaves the base and makes their way to the first collection. It must be stressed that, because of legal and insurance requirements, the DOVO teams only collect ammunition from prearranged call-outs and in the amounts recorded on the paperwork. They do not, as is often thought, tour the area looking for ammunition to collect. Upon arrival at the location, the munitions are initially approached by the team leader only, who will make a visual assessment to determine the safety and stability of the ammunition. It is only when the team leader is satisfied of the safety of the location that the rest of the team are allowed to approach. The team will also do a visual check on the ammunition and confer with the team leader on how to proceed. If any member of the team disagrees with the team leader's proposal, they have the option to contact the base and speak with a senior officer to discuss the proposal. This option, however, is rarely used. Once agreed, the team will then try to identify the shell by nationality, type, contents and whether it has been fired or not. An operative will then use a hammer to gently tap the shell around its base to remove the mud and rust in order to view a small section of the copper band at the base of the shell called a 'drive band'. If the drive band is grooved, it usually means the shell has been fired and so is armed. The experience of the team is such that they can identify most shells by nationality and calibre by a quick visual check; however, they cannot be sure what the shell contains until it is x-rayed back at the base. There are some telltale signs that point towards chemical contents – for example, if it is leaking a black oily liquid (i.e., mustard gas) or if, when picked up, a liquid can be felt moving inside the shell case. At this point, this visual identification is for the safety of the collection team only, as the shell and its contents need to be formally identified back at base. Once it is safe to do so, the shell is picked up by the operative and carefully placed in a tray of sand in the back of the collection vehicle. The team leader then completes the relevant paperwork for that location, and the vehicle and cargo move off to the next prearranged collection.

The collection vehicle itself is a small box van consisting of three compartments: the crew compartment, a smaller compartment to contain smaller items of munitions (e.g., SAA) and the larger rear compartment accessed via a tail lift and roller shutter and containing the large tray of sand. Depending on the size of the shells, the tray of sand will hold approximately 30 shells laid flat, with the axis of the shells facing across the width of the van. Therefore, if the van breaks suddenly, the ammunition will not keep travelling in the same direction of the van, which would increase the chance of a detonation by an impact on the fuse. The vehicles themselves are of a standard construction and have no armour plating fitted; the only additions are the blue lights

Shells safely stowed and ready for transportation back to base. (Courtesy of DOVO, Belgian Armed Forces.)

on top of the cab. Interestingly, the DOVO operatives themselves see no need for any extra protection since the immediate danger is from leaking chemical weapons as opposed to high explosives. However, they do not take anything for granted. Once the vehicle can carry no more munitions or it has completed its collections, it will return to the base at Poelkapelle to deposit its cargo.

Upon arrival at the base, the vehicle's cargo is offloaded by a forklift truck in an area known as the 'Afbikzone'. It is in this area that each shell is cleaned, identified and labelled before being sent for destruction. Even today, the cleaning process is done by hand: operators wearing protective clothing and breathing apparatus carefully chip off the mud and rust from the shells using a small hammer and a wire brush. The cubicles in which they work are enclosed by thick, concrete, blast-proof walls so that, if an accident were to happen, the explosion would be contained in that area only to reduce the risk of further casualties.

As the accident in 2012 highlighted, the correct identification of a shell and its contents is essential in order to dispose of the shell accordingly and, of course, to protect the technicians involved in the deactivation process. Once cleaned, the shell is x-rayed to ascertain its contents. The initial visual assessment may or may not confirm if the shell has a chemical filling. In order to aid with the identification process, the image of the shell is compared on screen to a database of shells recorded in the system. Sometimes, the image will reveal a bottle inside the shell, and this indicates the presence of a German chemical agent called 'Clark I' (i.e., diphenylchloroarsine) or 'Clark II' (i.e., diphenylcyanoarsine). Both chemicals were classed as irritants and were designed to permeate gas masks, making the wearer sneeze uncontrollably or vomit in the gas mask, and, as a result, the wearer would wrench off the mask and unwittingly expose himself to other deadly chemicals that may be present. Clark I and Clark II are not liquids but are chemical solids, white crystals that vaporise on contact with the air once the shell case and the bottle contained within have ruptured. As the war evolved, so did the chemical-warfare tactics, with many shells containing a mixture of chemicals designed to get the wearer to remove the gas mask and expose him to more dangerous chemicals. It is estimated that over 100 different types of toxic payloads were used by the combatants during the Great War.[1]

Another method used to ascertain if the shell contains a liquid chemical is to tilt the shell slightly, and the level of fill will then be clearly seen on the screen of the x-ray machine. If there is still doubt on the chemical composition of the shell, it can be then identified with the help of the PINS neutron analysis machine, which returns quick and accurate results. The identification will ultimately determine how the chemical is destroyed at the end of the process.

Offloading shells for identification. (Courtesy of DOVO, Belgian Armed Forces.)

1 DOVO Poelkapelle (23 April 2021).

Cleaning shells, not for the faint-hearted. (Courtesy of DOVO, Belgian Armed Forces.)

Identifying the contents of a shell. (Courtesy of DOVO, Belgian Armed Forces.)

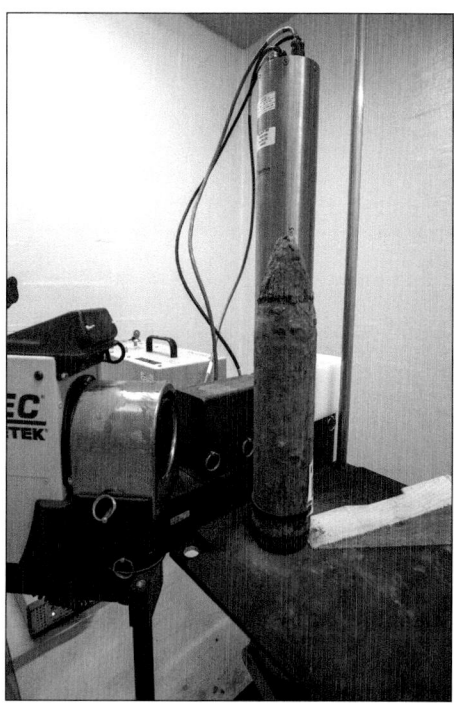

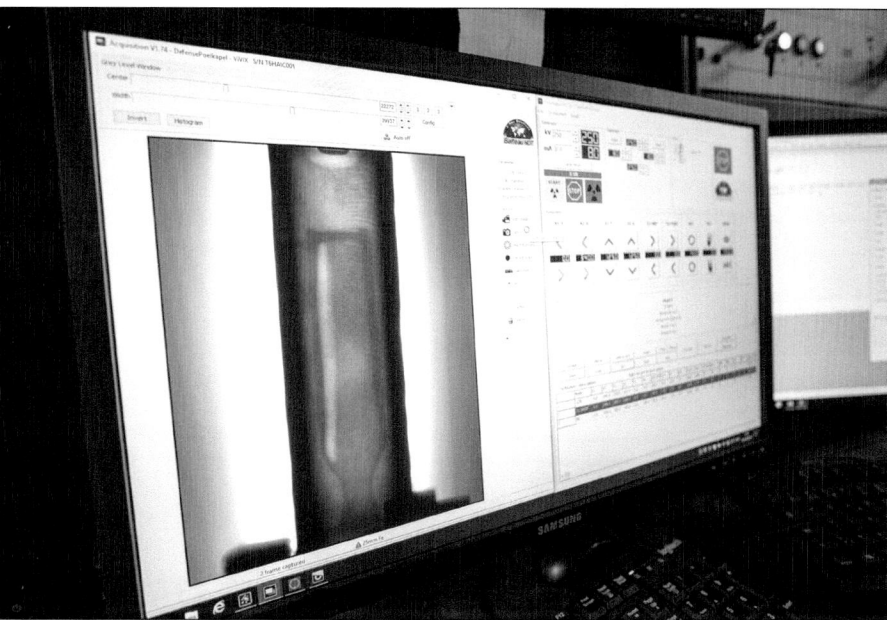

A scan clearly showing the presence of a German Clark bottle inside a shell, indicating that this is a chemical weapon. (Courtesy of DOVO, Belgian Armed Forces.)

Once the identification of a shell is confirmed, it is clearly labelled with a bar code and the details entered into a database. If the shell is found to contain explosives, it is then stored ready for destruction with the other shells of the same type. If the x-ray confirms the existence of a chemical solid (e.g., a Clark bottle), the shell is then stored ready for destruction at the CDC. If the x-ray and neutron analysis confirm the presence of a liquid chemical in the shell, it is sent to the SDC to be destroyed.

Identified shells labelled and ready for destruction. (Courtesy of DOVO, Belgian Armed Forces.)

To aid in the shell identification process, and to help train new technicians, DOVO has built an incredible physical library of munitions at the base at Poelkapelle. Started in the 1990s, the library contains at least one complete example of every type of munition recovered by DOVO and serves as an important tool of reference. The collection totals over 440 different types of munitions, ranging from hand grenades to artillery shells, the largest being a 15-inch-calibre British high-explosive shell and a German 38cm-calibre shell.

The next stage of the dismantling process depends on the type of shell and its contents, with shells being sent to one of the three available dismantling facilities: the SDC, the CDC and the demolition field. Shells identified as having a chemical liquid fill are sent to the SDC to be destroyed. The SDC was purchased in 2017 to replace the dismantling facility destroyed in the accident of 2012. The acquisition of the new SDC was a game changer in terms of operator safety and the rate at which toxic chemicals could be disposed of: at the end of its first year of operation, the SDC processed just under 2,500 shells. The system is virtually fully automated, with

The DOVO shell library. (Courtesy of DOVO, Belgian Armed Forces.)

minimal 'hands-on' human input, minimising the risks to the DOVO technicians with each stage of the shell-demolition process monitored from a safe distance via CCTV (closed-circuit television).

The SDC facility is split into several parts, the first being the loading area. It is here that munitions that have been preloaded into cardboard boxes are placed onto a conveyer belt. The conveyer belt takes the box of munitions to a small elevator that lifts the box to the top of the SDC structure, where it is pushed into a gas-tight chamber from where it then progresses into a second loading chamber ready for entrance to the detonation chamber where the munitions will be thermally destroyed. Consisting of an upper and lower part, with the upper part being approximately one-third of the chamber, the HDC (hot destruction/detonation chamber) resembles a large, armoured sphere on an axis that allows it to tilt to a certain point on requirement. The detonation chamber automatically rotates 90 degrees, which exposes an opening and allows the box of munitions to drop from the second loading chamber into the detonation chamber itself. The chamber then rotates back to its original position to seal the opening.

Inside the chamber, the munitions are exposed to temperatures of over 550 degrees Celsius. The temperature is constant and is driven by a fan-operated hot-air system. The temperatures inside the HDC are well above the auto-ignition temperatures of the chemicals contained in the shells and the burster charges in the detonation system of the shell. The shells are superheated, causing the burster charges in the shells to detonate, fracturing the shell cases and releasing the chemicals in the process. Upon their exposure to the heat, the chemicals are destroyed. This system is equally effective for chemical munitions that have no burster charges. The heat in the HDC heats the shells and their chemical contents to such a point that the chemicals vaporise, creating a pressure inside the shells that fractures the bursters well within the shell, allowing the escape of the chemical vapours, which are then destroyed by the high temperatures. Any agent contained within a munition cannot survive for more than 15 minutes at this extreme temperature.

Once the destruction is complete, the process is repeated until the HDC chamber reaches the point where it needs emptying of the scrap shell casings that lie in its bottom. This process is initiated at the beginning of each day's operations. At this point, the top and bottom of the chamber are isolated from each other, the top section being lifted slightly to allow the bottom section to tip slightly in order to empty the scrap shell casings onto a discharge conveyer belt for them to be removed and sent to a private company for destruction. The bottom and top sections of the HDC are then automatically reconnected, and the process starts again. The bottom section is never completely emptied of the hot scrap, as a certain amount always remains to retain the temperature inside the HDC, and this prolongs the life of the chamber since it is not then subject to the stresses caused by heating and cooling and also ensures maximum productivity since no break is needed in the destruction process while the chamber reheats to its required temperature. The temperature within the HDC is maintained at a constant 550 degrees Celsius even during weekends and nights when it is not in use.

The waste gases are then treated in the off-gas treatment section, where they are subject to temperatures up to 11,000 degrees Celsius to destroy any organics that may remain. The gas is quickly cooled, and any remaining dust is removed via the bag house filter. At this point, the gas is cooled further to enable it to pass through a chemical scrubbing system that removes any remaining acids or sulphur dioxide that may still be present in the off gas. The cleaned gas is then safe to release. The whole treatment process of the off gases is performed slightly below atmospheric temperature, making it impossible for any of the gas to be accidently released into the atmosphere before it is fully treated.

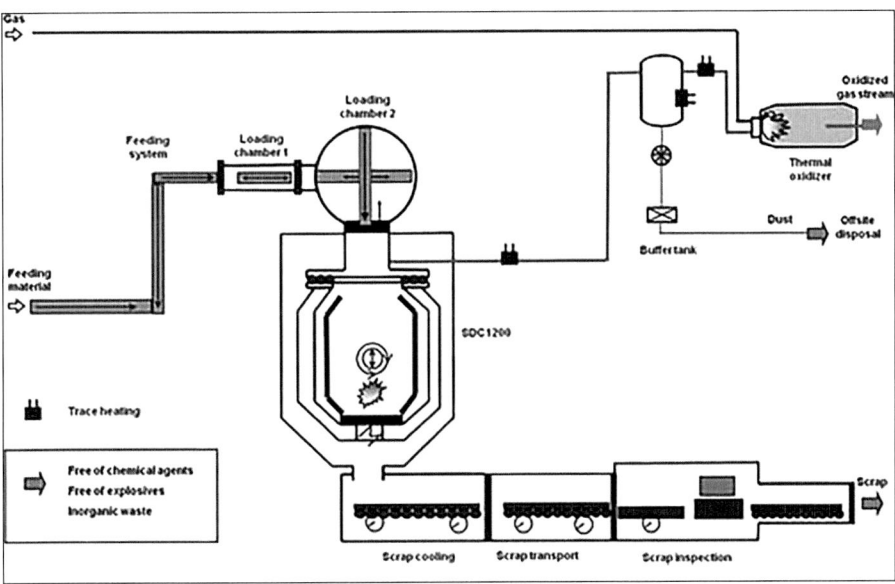

A diagram showing the stages of munition destruction in the SDC. (Courtesy of DOVO, Belgian Armed Forces.)

The second dismantling facility is the CDC. The latest CDC was purchased from Japan in 2007 in order to destroy solid chemical munitions (mainly of the Clark type) and German HE-R shells. These shells were primarily smoke rounds used by the German artillery to assess the accuracy of their fire; the chemical inside, however, contains a high level of arsenic and so needs to be destroyed accordingly. The CDC mainly deals with shells of 77mm, 10.5cm, 15cm and 21cm calibre and destroys them by controlled explosions that are contained in a sealed chamber that is capable of destroying a maximum of 56 shells per day depending upon their size. The CDC itself consists of the detonation chamber for the destruction of the munitions and the off-gas treatment process for the neutralising of any toxic waste carried in the waste gasses. The detonation chamber is manufactured by Kobe Steel and has a total weight of around 100 tons. The chamber consists of a double-shelled inner and outer chamber. The inner chamber's function is to limit the fragmentation effect of the shells caused by the destruction of the munitions within its walls. The inner chamber weighs around 38 tons and has a total thickness of 99mm, consisting of one layer of 75mm and four layers of 6mm, with the latter's role being to give the chamber a limited flexibility in order to reduce potential damage to the inner chamber. The inner chamber is removable so that it can be replaced when needed. Inside the chamber is a rail on which the munitions packs are hung prior to their destruction, an electric detonation system and an outlet for the off gasses produced as a result of the detonation. The outer chamber is a pressurised container whose function is to keep the whole process gas tight, stopping the possibility of an accidental release of toxic gas into the surroundings. The outer chamber has a total thickness of 75mm split between one layer of 12mm thickness and seven layers of 9mm thickness each. The total weight of the outer chamber is approximately 52 tons.

The CDC site is divided into three separate areas: the CDC unit itself, the control room and the personnel decontamination area. In order to reduce the risk to the personnel, a strict operating procedure is in place, which is adhered to rigidly at all times. The first part of the process involves the assembly of the ammunition packages that are to be destroyed in the CDC. The assembly of the ammunition packages takes place in a separate building from the main CDC. The building is split into two rooms: one room is used for the assembly of the detonators, and the second for the assembly of the ammunition packages. The detonators and the ammunition packages are kept isolated from each other until the very last minute. This part of the process is done by hand by a two-man team of operatives, one man being responsible for the assembly of the munition packages in one room whilst the other in a separate room is responsible for the assembly of the detonators. Each operative is fully protected by a chemical-resistant over and undersuit, rubber boots and gloves and a fully encapsulating face mask with an independent air supply attached to the operative's back.

The first part of the assembly process involves a final visual check of the ammunition to be destroyed. A check of the internal and external characteristics of the shell is completed in order to confirm that the munitions are of the Clark type or HE-R type. Once confirmed, the operators then can move to the next step of assembling the donor charges and the munition packages to be destroyed. The size of each package to be assembled depends on the size of the shells to be destroyed and is split between multiple packages and single packages. Multiple packages will consist of 77mm shells and 10.5cm shells, and each package will contain a maximum of three shells and a sausage-shaped donor charge of IREMITE explosive with a weight of 1.5kg for each shell. Each multiple shell package has two detonators arranged in a series. Single packages will consist of either one 15cm or one 21cm shell. The size of these shells requires four IREMITE donor charges per shell with a single detonator. The 15cm packages require a charge of 3.2kg whilst the 21cm packages require an IREMITE charge of 4kg. Each single package will also have 4.5kg of sheet explosive added to the package to ensure complete detonation and destruction. In addition to this, each

DOVO Today 99

The CDC. (Courtesy of DOVO, Belgian Armed Forces.)

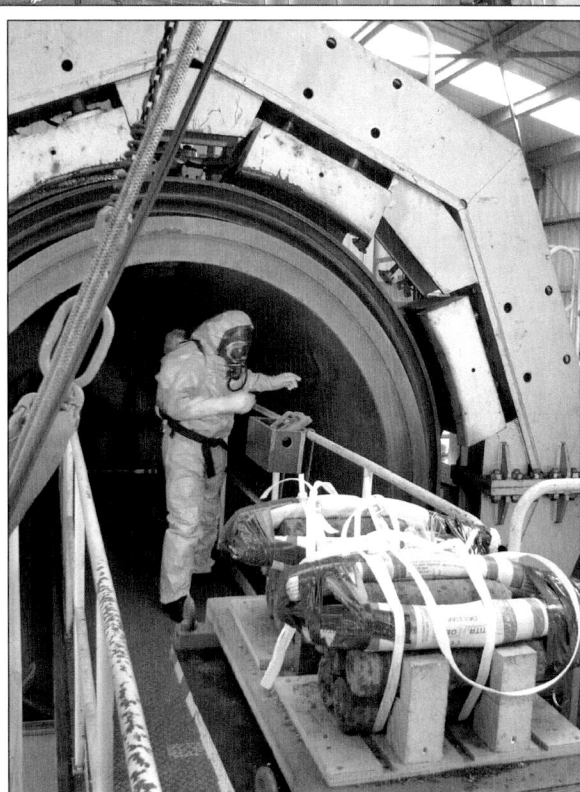

Loading the CDC with prepared ammunition packages. (Courtesy of DOVO, Belgian Armed Forces.)

package, whether multiple or single, will have added an extra booster of 35g of sheet explosive. Upon completion, the packages are labelled by date, number of shells and calibre and are then secured together with the IREMITE charges by straps. Hanging straps are also cut and measured so that the package can be hung from the rail in the CDC chamber as centrally as possible, ready for detonation. The packages are then loaded onto a trolley ready to be moved to the CDC when required.

The next step involves the opening of the blast-proof door of the CDC for inspection prior to the loading of the ammunition packages. This step is performed remotely from the main control room, with the air pressure being controlled to prevent any remaining gasses leaving the chamber, and is monitored by CCTV and warning sensors. Once it is confirmed that the previous detonations have been successful, the area is then declared safe for the operatives to enter the building where the detonation chamber is situated. The operators, wearing their protective clothing and independent breathing apparatus, then enter the room with the trolley of ammunition packages. At this point, the team leader takes over control of the room from the personnel in the control room, thus giving the team working in the CDC total responsibility for the process. The munition packages are then hung on the sliding rail with the help of a jib crane and then pushed into the detonation chamber; the operatives will also enter the chamber to remove any remnants of the previous detonation. It is at this point that the electric detonators are attached to the charges. The operatives then leave the detonation chamber and make their way to the decontamination facilities in a separate building. Upon their leaving of the CDC building, the control of the CDC is handed back to the control room. From the control room, the door of the CDC is closed and secured by hydraulic clamps, and the vacuum pump system is initiated. The vacuum pump drops the pressure in the CDC to '0' in the detonation chamber before the detonation of the munitions. The effect of the vacuum is to cause the munitions to implode rather than explode. The firing software is initiated, connecting the electric detonators, a warning of firing and a countdown is broadcast over the intercom system, and then the firing buttons are pressed. In the control room, a dull thud is heard as the munition packages detonate, and the automatic destruction of the toxic gasses within the CDC is then closely monitored by a system of sensors and CCTV. Once the munitions have been destroyed, waste gasses are extracted from the detonation chamber by a system of vacuum pumps and passed through the off-gas treatment process. The vacuum pump removes the gas from the chamber and pumps it through a system of oxidisers that remove and neutralise all toxins from the gas, enabling it to be safely released in line with the current regulations. The vacuum makes it impossible for gas to leak from the off-gas treatment process should a fault develop. Once completed, the process starts again with a maximum of four cycles per day.

Whilst the destruction process is being carried out, the loading operators enter the decontamination building where their chemical suits and equipment are removed and sent for destruction. All the protective equipment worn is single use only, with the exception of the breathing apparatus, which is decontaminated to be reused by the same team member each time. The protective undersuit can be reused up to 10 times

Shells are packed into crates, transported to the detonation field and then buried in a deep hole before detonation. (Courtesy of DOVO, Belgian Armed Forces.)

before it is also destroyed and a new suit is issued to the operator. Before and after missions in the CDC, each operator undergoes stringent medical tests, which monitor lung capacity and also heart rate. If the operator fails any of the tests, he is replaced by another team member until he is deemed fit to return to the task.

The third facility at the site for destroying ammunition is the demolition field. It is here that all conventional munitions are destroyed. Once the munitions have been identified as nonchemical, they are prepared for destruction in the demolition field. The conventional explosive shells are packed into wooden crates, each fully loaded crate weighing a maximum of 50kg. Each crate is primed with TNT and a single M6 anti-tank mine before being transported by a tractor unit and trailer to the demolition field. Upon arrival at the demolition area, the crates containing the shells are offloaded and lowered into pre-dug firing holes in the ground known locally as *'springputten'*. The firing holes have been dug by mechanical excavators and are around four metres deep, with each firing hole containing one individual wooden crate containing the munitions that are to be destroyed. The hole is then filled in by a bulldozer and a pile of earth is mounded on top. At two set daily times (11:30 a.m. and 4:00 p.m.) sirens sound, and, from a concrete shelter approximately 200 metres away, the crates are detonated in succession: six in the morning and six in the afternoon, with a maximum of 300kg of explosives being destroyed each time. The process then restarts the following day and runs from spring to the end of autumn each year.

So, it is with these three methods that the members of DOVO deal with the left behind ammunition of the Great War. Although safety is paramount, risks can only be reduced, not eliminated. As you have read, accidents can and do happen, sometimes resulting in fatalities. Ammunition collectors are a problem in the area. From time to time, one will be reported to the police, and DOVO will attend the collector's property and remove the munitions. In one recent instance, DOVO removed over 1,500 shells from a collector's house in Flanders. Unfortunately, accidents and fatalities still occur and are reported in the press. It is interesting to note that, after such incidences, the rate of call-outs to DOVO will increase for a short time as people start to become worried by the artillery shell sitting in the corner of the living room or the hand grenades on the mantlepiece left behind by grandad that they just assumed were safe but never really checked. After the terrible accident in 2014 when two builders were killed after tampering with a shell in Ypres, DOVO call-outs increased to a 20-year record of over 4,000 call-outs for the year! My advice to anyone touring the Ypres Salient is, if you come across live ammunition, fascinating though it is, leave it well alone and remember why it was manufactured in the first place – to kill people.

Part II

Recovering the Fallen

Clearing the battlefield of its victims' (Photographer unknown. Courtesy of the In Flanders Fields Museum.)

Introduction

Throughout the course of history, armies of all nations have been faced with the problem of how to deal with their dead. Often fighting in distant lands, and with no modern transport available, there were often very few options with regards to dealing with the mass fatalities of a major battle. Up to the Crimean War of 1853–1856, British soldiers were viewed by many as being disposable commodities who deserved no special treatment in death. That, coupled with the fact that large amounts of dead bodies lying on the battlefield posed a risk to health, meant that they were often disposed of by the quickest and most cost-effective methods, either by mass cremation or by burial in large pits. After the Battle of Waterloo in 1815, the bodies of Wellington's heroes were stripped of valuables by battlefield scavengers, and some had their teeth ripped from their mouths by opportunists to be made into dentures. These so-called 'Waterloo teeth' were sold by the dentists of the day to wealthy clients, who were quite happy to boast that their new teeth had come from the battlefields of Waterloo. Even the bones of the fallen were not sacred, allegedly exhumed and sent to the bone-grinding factories of Yorkshire to be ground down and sold to the agricultural industry as fertiliser. The following article was published in 1822:

> It is estimated that more than a million of bushels of human and inhuman bones were imported last year from the continent of Europe into the port of Hull. The neighbourhood of Leipsic, Austerlitz, Waterloo, and of all the places where, during the late bloody war, the principal battles were fought, have been swept alike of the bones of the hero and of the horse which he rode. Thus collected from every quarter, they have been shipped to the port of Hull, and thence forwarded to the Yorkshire bone grinders, who have erected steam-engines and powerful machinery, for the purpose of reducing them to a granular state. In this condition they are sent chiefly to Doncaster, one of the largest agricultural markets in that part of the country and are there sold to the farmers to manure their lands. The oily substance, gradually evolving as the bone calcines, makes a more substantial manure than almost any other substance, particularly human bones. It is now ascertained beyond a doubt, by actual experiment upon an extensive scale, that a dead soldier is a most valuable article of commerce; and, for ought known to the contrary, the good farmers of Yorkshire are, in a great

measure, indebted to the bones of their children for their daily bread. It is certainly a singular fact, that Great Britain should have sent out such multitudes of soldiers to fight the battles of this country upon the continent of Europe and should then import their bones as an article of commerce to fatten her soil![1]

By the time of the Crimean War, the British establishment's attitude towards its military dead was starting to change. With the advent of the telegraph, war correspondents were now able to report the realities of war on a daily basis, and, by 1855, their reports were reaching London within a few hours of being sent. The government no longer had complete control on what was being reported, and the British public were now fully informed of the realities of war and the treatment of their wounded and dead. The scale of the British Empire, and the lack of transport options at the time, meant that repatriation of war dead was virtually an impossible task, with only the bodies of senior ranks or of wealthy and influential families being returned home. The fate of the common soldier was to lie in the land where he had fallen and, by the Crimean War, in British military cemeteries set up around field hospitals and dressing stations. The new availability of information sent from the front by war correspondents, which included the introduction of battlefield photography, engendered in the British population a sense of empathy towards the soldiers fighting in Crimea. William Howard Russell's regular despatches to *The Times* newspaper were particularly influential, and it was his account of the Charge of the Light Brigade during the Battle of Balaclava in 1854 that inspired Alfred Tennyson to write his iconic poem of the same name. As a result of this newfound empathy, memorials to the fallen of the Crimean War started to materialise in the towns and cities of Great Britain at the war's end. At that point in history, war memorials were normally financed and placed by the state and so were reserved to highlight the glory of individual generals or battles and placed in areas of national importance. These new memorials were different. Funded by towns and villages, they were placed in honour of the rank-and-files and, in particular, to honour the sons and the husbands of the villages in which the memorials were placed. By the end of the Second Boer War of 1899–1902, war memorials in the UK were becoming more commonplace. The die was cast, and the British public would no longer accept its war dead as being treated as a disposable commodity.

There can be no doubt that the BEF of 1914 were ill prepared for dealing with their dead in the early days of the First World War. The lack of preparation and procedure can be explained by the fact that the authorities famously believed that this would be a short conflict of movement that would more than likely all be over by Christmas of that year. What the armies had failed to realise was that this was the first truly global industrialised war and that the size of the armies now opposing each other was on a

1   G. Robinson, W. Goodwin, A. Kippis, G. G. Robinson, and J. J. Robinson, *The New Annual Register, or, General Repository of History, Politics, Arts, Sciences, and Literature for the Year 1822* (London: Longman, Hurst, Rees, Orme, Brown, 1823), p.132.

scale never witnessed before. It was a watershed of military tactics and technology, where the old world of cavalry and movement clashed head on with the new world of modern artillery, machine guns, trenches and barbed wire. With nations fielding armies that numbered in the millions, economies of scale dictated casualty rates accordingly. In short, the BEF had not foreseen the terrible losses they were about to suffer during the next few years of the conflict.

Of course, as with everything in life, hindsight is a wonderful thing, and the main focus of the BEF in 1914 was to stop the German advance as it steamrollered through France and Belgium and to protect the channel ports that were the lifeline of the Empire. If Germany occupied the French and Belgian ports, it would pose a direct threat to the shores of Great Britain. In short, if the channel ports fell, Great Britain might also fall. Understandably, from the point of view of the BEF of 1914, the management of their dead was not a priority. Instead, not losing the war was their main concern.

8

An Extraordinary Englishman
Sir Fabian Ware and the Creation of the War Graves Organisations

In the chaos of the fighting of August and September 1914, many of the dead were left behind by the retreating BEF, either left lying where they had fallen or, where possible, hurriedly buried by their comrades in shallow graves marked by an improvised grave marker. The task of recording the locations of the burial sites was the responsibility of the unit chaplains, who quickly found out that this was virtually an impossible duty as not all of the graves were accessible due to the fighting still continuing around them. Many of the recorded grave sites were destined to fall victim to the all-pervading artillery fire, which destroyed any surface evidence of the location of graves. The shell fire would also disinter the bodies, often severely mutilating them in the process with the remains being strewn around the immediate area. Even the dead could not rest in peace. The fighting that was to come in the following months and years was to result in a sustained casualty rate never before experienced by the British Army. The main problem facing the army in terms of clearing the battlefields of its fallen was not the inaccessibility of the front line but the sheer number of bodies that needed to be located and registered. In short, the army had no organisation in place that could manage the treatment of its dead on such a scale.

All this was to change with the arrival of Fabian Ware on the Western Front in 1914. Ware was working on behalf of the Rio Tinto mining company at the outbreak of war and was the former editor of *The Morning Post*. At the age of 45, Ware was too old to enlist but, like many men of his generation, was desperate to get to the front and do his 'bit' for King and Country. This sense of duty drove Ware to explore other avenues as to how he could be useful in the war effort and so answered a call from the British government for motor vehicle owners to travel to France to help look for and transport stragglers from the retreat from Mons. On arrival in France, it soon became apparent that the locating of the stragglers was virtually an impossible task, with many of them now behind German lines, so Ware took it upon himself to locate the wounded and transport them back to dressing stations for treatment. As a result of this work, he came to the attention of the British Red Cross and soon found himself in charge of a Red Cross mobile unit in September 1914.[1]

Whilst collecting wounded soldiers, Ware and his team noticed that, despite army regulations that required the proper disposal of the dead, many men's graves were not being recorded and so were in danger of being lost forever. Determined that the location of these men's graves should be preserved, Ware and his team started to record the locations of every single isolated grave they came across. By the end of 1914, Ware's unit had expanded and was not only recording the position of graves but was also physically marking the position with a wooden cross, as per standard army procedure, on which was stencilled the casualties' details. This system would later be

Sir Fabian Ware (holding the white papers) with King George V during the King's Pilgrimage of 1922. The full list of men visible in the photograph is as follows (from left to right): Major W. B. Binnie (IWGC deputy director of works), Captain John Truelove (IWGC architect), Major General Sir Fabian Ware (IWGC vice chairman), Colonel Clive Wigram (King George V's private secretary), Field Marshal Sir Douglas Haig, Colonel Herbert Thomas Goodland (deputy controller, France and Belgium, IWGC) (his head can be seen between Sir Douglas Haig and the King), King George V and Mr. T. Elvidge (head gardener at Tyne Cot Cemetery). (Commonwealth War Graves Commission Archive (CWGCA), with permission.)

1   Commonwealth War Graves Commission (CWGC) – *Sir Fabian Ware. Founder of the Commonwealth War Graves Commission.*

fine-tuned by using stamped aluminium tags to replace the stencilled details on the cross. The work carried out by Ware and his team came to the attention of General Macready, the adjutant general of the BEF. Macready understood the importance of the work of Ware and his mobile unit, as the subject of the care of war graves in France and Belgium was already starting to capture media attention in Great Britain. On 2 March 1915, upon Ware's suggestion, Macready formalised the roles of Ware and his unit by creating the GRC (Graves Registration Commission) and awarded Ware the rank of honorary Major. The importance of public opinion with regards to dealing with the dead was a point clearly not lost on the higher echelons of the BEF at the time. Having received negative press regarding their treatment of their dead during the Second Boer War, the army was not about to make the same mistake. In March 1915, the then General Douglas Haig described in a report to the War Office the importance of the work of the GRC: 'It is fully recognised that the work of the organisation is of purely sentimental value, and that it does not directly contribute to the successful termination of the war. It has, however, an extraordinary moral value to the troops as well as to the relatives and friends at home'.[2] The care of the dead was already becoming a political issue.

That same month, the first GRU (Graves Registration Unit) was created within the GRC, and two more quickly followed. The new GRUs were put to work searching areas of battlefield in order to locate and record the position of isolated graves so that army burial parties' armies could locate, exhume and then recover the remains back to a predetermined burial ground, a deeply unpleasant and morale-sapping task for those army units allotted to the task. Once the remains were buried, it was then the responsibility of the GRUs to erect an official grave marker on the grave.

From early on in the war, the authorities were receiving correspondence from grieving relatives requesting information detailing the location and condition of the graves of their loved ones, some relatives resolving to travel to the Western Front in order to find the graves of their missing loved ones themselves. This situation had the potential to become a major headache for the British Army. The last thing it needed was British civilians, and often wealthy ones from families of standing and influence, roaming the battlefields and taking up the army's valuable time and resources. The obvious danger to life was one concern but so was the reality of the battlefields, as the dead still remained on the surface, in many cases weeks and months after the fighting had left the area, a situation that would not be favourably viewed back at home. In an effort to negate these potential problems, the army banned civilians from visiting the areas of operation, and, in order to appease the families, a photographic unit was created within the GRC whose role it was to send photographs of graves to grieving families upon their request in order to allay their fears on the conditions of the burial of their loved ones. The service offered by the photographic department proved to be

---

2   T.A. Edwin Gibson and G. Kingsley Ward, *Courage Remembered* (London: HMSO, 1989), p.45.

The reality of battlefield burials on the Western Front. (Photographer unknown. Courtesy of the In Flanders Fields Museum.)

very successful in giving comfort to the grieving families and in delaying any potential grave visits to after the cessation of hostilities. By 1917, 12,000 photographs had been sent to the relatives of soldiers KIA (killed in action).[3]

Almost immediately, the work of the GRC started to pay dividends. In September 1915 of that year, the now Major Ware received a letter from the Duchess of Beaufort asking for assurances that the grave of her son, Captain Maurice Arthur de Tuyll of the 10th Hussars, had been registered and was safe from further actions. As a direct result of the work done by the GRUs, Major Ware was able to send the Duchess the following letter dated 3 October 1915:

> Major Fabian Ware, O.C. [officer commanding], Graves Registration Commission, presents his compliments to the Duchess of Beaufort and begs to state the position of the grave of Capt. Maurice de Tuyll has been carefully registered. The burial grounds near the front are under the care of the military

---

3   Commonwealth War Graves Commission (CWGC) – *A History of the Commonwealth War Graves Commission*.

authorities who are doing everything which is possible. All that can be done at the moment is to secure that the position is carefully marked and the cemetery as a whole is under proper supervision. He suggests, therefore, that the Duchess of Beaufort should delay any further action till the cessation of military operations in this area.[4]

This letter not only appeased the Duchess and negated the possibility of negative press in Great Britain from a woman of influence but, more importantly, also gave peace of mind to a woman who, when it came to her son, was no different to any other grieving mother in Great Britain. From all angles, the importance of such work and correspondence cannot be underestimated. Nothing was heard from the Duchess until the end of the war when she again enquired of the condition of her son's grave. A regular flow of correspondence ensued, with the last letter being sent in 1944; the subject of the correspondence varied from the condition of the grave, the siting of the grave, and later return of a brass plaque on the grave, the planting on the grave of the Duchess' favourite Gladioli, the installation of the permanent headstone, her niece's and hers visit to the grave in 1923 and 1928, respectively, and the condition of the grave after the occupation during the Second World War. Captain Maurice de Tuyll is buried in plot one, row A, grave 10 of Potijze Chateau Grounds Cemetery on the

The grave of Captain Maurice Arthur de Tuyll. (Author's photo.)

4   Commonwealth War Graves Commission Archive (CWGCA) CWGC/8/1/4/1/2/46 (CCM 15034).

outskirts of Ypres. His mother, the then Dowager Duchess of Beaufort, died on 11 October 1945 at the age of 81.

In October 1915, the GRC was officially incorporated into the army, giving it access to all the relevant resources the army could provide, including extra personnel and vehicles. By mid-1916, the GRC was replaced by the DGR&E, with Ware appointed as its director general. The role of the DGR&E was again to locate, verify and register the graves of soldiers in all theatres of the war. It was still the job of the army to exhume the bodies once the location was confirmed. The DGR&E was further expanded in May 1917, Ware was promoted to temporary lieutenant colonel, and his main office was moved to 32 Baker Street London with an expanded staff of over 700 members. GRUs were then allocated to each of the five armies' headquarters and the LOCs, with each headquarters' GRU comprising of one surveyor, three clerks, two draughtsmen and a photographer.

In the field were 23 units of the GRU, and each unit consisted of one lieutenant, one corporal, 26 cemetery men, one cook and one batman. Each unit was given an assigned area of operation, with the battlefields around Ypres and northern France being identified as 'DGR&E Area no. 5'. This geographical area encompassed Ypres, Ploegsteert, Vlamertinghe and Poperinghe in Belgium and Bailleul and Estaires in France, with GRU no. 1 originally operating in the area from 1915/1916. By 1919, there were 10 GRUs operating in DGR&E Area no. 5 alone. In May 1917, the IWGC was established by royal charter, and – because of his excellent work to date and supported by the Prince of Wales – Fabian Ware became its vice chairman. The task of the then IWGC was to acquire permanent ground for cemeteries, design and lay them out and care for the graves within. It was not the task of the IWGC to search, locate, record and exhume the bodies, as this was the responsibility of the GRUs and other attached units.

In May 1916, Ware had initiated negotiation with the Belgian government in order to secure land on a permanent basis to create military cemeteries in which to bury the fallen. The initial agreement was signed on 20 July 1917, with a more comprehensive agreement being signed on 13 June 1919. The Belgian government had, as the French had done before them, agreed to gift the land in perpetuity to the British authorities for the creation of the cemeteries needed in which to bury their war dead. The agreement stated that the cemeteries should be used for military burials only and that the Belgian rule of law should preside over the burial grounds. The signing of the agreement meant that body recoveries and reburials could now proceed at pace, safe in the knowledge that, once concentrated into a specifically formed cemetery, the bodies would not have to be moved again.

The achievements of Sir Fabian Ware and his colleagues during this period cannot be underestimated. In three years, mainly under Ware's direction, the British authorities had gone from having a very limited system in place for the management of their fallen to a system of grave registration, recovery and reburial that was fit for purpose and that would ultimately evolve into the CWGC of today.

9

Here Dead We Lie

> *Here dead we lie because we did not choose*
> *To live and shame the land from which we sprung.*
> *Life, to be sure, is nothing to lose;*
> *But young men think it is, and we were young.*

A. E. Housman.[1]

Throughout the conflict, and up to the point when mass demobilisation prohibited the practice, it was the army's responsibility to provide men to perform the task of burying and exhuming the dead. It is fair to say that the scale of the task was underestimated by the army in the early days of the war; many first-hand accounts exist from veterans describing the dead that littered the battlefield and how they lived side by side with the dead on a daily basis. The Bluff was an area of British-held high ground close to Hill 60 in the Ypres Salient. Like Hill 60, it was subject to fierce fighting throughout the war and had a terrible reputation amongst the troops:

> I never knew a place like the Bluff for corpses. During the battle last month, the troops, suffered heavily and were too tired to bury their dead. Many of them were merely trampled into the floor of the trench, where they were soon lost in the mud and water. We have been out a lot of these trenches again, and are constantly coming upon the corpses. They are pretty well decomposed, but a pickaxe brings up chips of bones and rags of clothing. The rest is putrid grey matter. It makes me sick. At other times, they scooped out hollows in the rear face of the trench, or in traverses, and stuffed their corpses into them. There was part of a hat sticking of the back of one trench, the head inside which still seemed to be bleeding after at least a fortnight. One often sees hands or boots

---

1 Brian Gardner (ed.), *Up the Line to Death: The War Poets 1914–1918* (London: Methuen, 1976), p.149.

sticking out. In a disused dugout behind the old front line, half a man's head was sticking out. It had been largely eaten by rats.[2]

The sight of unburied corpses was commonplace for the soldiers of the Western Front, and, although it had become an accepted part of reality for troops in the front line, large numbers of unburied corpses created problems for the British Army. First and foremost, it was unhygienic and posed a serious health risk to the soldiers at the front. Rotten and bloated corpses attracted flies and rats that potentially could spread disease. In the summer, the stench of death became almost unbearable for the soldiers in the front line as the bodies decomposed in the hot Flanders sun. It is said that, in the summer of 1917, at the height of the Third Battle of Ypres, if the wind direction was correct, soldiers could smell the stench of death four miles from the front lines. Not only did vast amounts of rotting corpses prove to be a health risk, but it was also bad for morale. The sight of decomposing bodies was particularly difficult for the troops to deal with, especially when it was the bodies of men from their own units or

The ignominy of death in the Ypres Salient. (Photographer unknown. Courtesy of the In Flanders Fields Museum.)

2   *Diary of 2nd Lieutenant John Glubb M.C. RE 7th Field Company* (7 March 1916).

close friends and family members. For the soldiers of the Western Front, death had become almost an occupational hazard, something that many soldiers had accepted that, more than likely, would happen to them at some point. Their only hope was that their end would be quick and painless and that their bodies would receive a decent burial. The evidence in plain sight told them that a decent burial was by no means guaranteed.

Another issue facing the army with regards to recovering the dead was public opinion back at home. The war was being reported in detail not only in the newspapers on a daily basis but also by soldiers returning home on leave who felt able to tell their closest confidants the truth of the Western Front. The British Army from 1916 onwards was no longer an army of professional soldiers and reservists who had made soldiering their trade. This was now the people's army, made up of postmen, bakers, butchers, husbands, brothers and sons. In short, the British public expected their fallen loved ones to be treated correctly, with respect and dignity, a point that the then General Douglas Haig was all too aware of when he stated in 1915, '… On the termination of hostilities, the nation will demand an account from the government as to the steps which have been taken to mark and classify the burial places of the dead'.[3]

On 29 June 1917, Fabian Ware wrote a letter to his representative in France, Captain Taylor. In the letter, Ware highlighted the current situation on the Somme battlefields in France and his fears of the effect on public opinion in the UK should the situation be reported. Large numbers of bodies still lay where they had fallen on the battlefields of the Somme several months after the battle officially concluded in November 1916:

> We are on the verge over here of serious trouble about the number of bodies lying out still unburied on the Somme Battlefields. The soldiers returning wounded or on leave to England are complaining bitterly about it and the War Office has already received letters on the matter. There is every reason to expect that the question may be raised in Parliament any day and I do not see what defence the Government could offer for the neglect of the Army in the field in this connection.[4]

These were strong words from Ware accusing the army of 'neglect' and the British government as being defenceless on the issue. Ware's fear was that the excellent work to date achieved by himself and his organisations with regards to locating and registering the graves of the fallen may get caught up in the potential scandal and harming the reputation of the DGR&E in the process:

---

3   Gibson and Ward, *Courage Remembered*, p.45.
4   Commonwealth War Graves Commission Archive (CWGCA) CWGC/1/1/1/34/1 (SDC 4).

> We of course have no responsibility in the matter but I feel most strongly that a lot of the good impression our work has created will be undone if a public scandal should arise in regards to this … this kind of scandal will be used … with great effect by the pacifists, and by others who are endeavouring to assist the enemy by obstructing the proper prosecution of the war.[5]

The main problem faced by the army in 1916 was the lack of organisation and procedure for dealing with losses on this scale. Quite simply, the manpower was not available to deal with the issue. The army had to act; it was their responsibility to provide burial parties from their ranks to deal with the issue of clearing the dead.

The creation of the corps and divisional burial officers in 1916 went some way on helping to solve the lack of organisation. Known colloquially as the 'Body Snatcher' or the 'Cold Meat Specialist', the corps and divisional burial officers would, in liaison with the DGR&E, select and organise army burial parties to clear the dead from predetermined areas of the battlefield while guided by the army publication *SS 456* 'Burial of Soldiers' of August 1916, which finally gave instruction to the burial parties involved in the recovery process. Ideally, though not always possible, personnel from the GRU would also be present when the body recoveries were taking place in order to register the location of the grave and place a grave marker on the site of the burial.

By January 1917, it was accepted that more provisions needed to be made for burying the dead, with the main discussion being whether if units were to bury their own dead or were separate units to be given the task? Interestingly, there were pros and cons for both arguments. The main concern was the impact on the morale of the men detailed to bury their own comrades or even family members and the impact on men who were due to be sent back to the front. What was overlooked, however, was the fortitude and sense of duty of the men given the task of body recoveries. For many, it was not only a necessary job but was also the right thing to do – no doubt in the hope that, if they met the same fate, their remains would be treated accordingly. This sense of duty was particularly strong when men were tasked with burying their comrades: 'Even when Cavalry and other branches were sent out to bury, the men of the units offered much opposition as the feeling was very strong on the question of burying their own dead, and it was thought that the effect of coloured men carrying out this work will be very bad on the soldiers'.[6]

The task of clearing the dead from the battlefield was not only unpopular but also deeply unpleasant and often distressing for the men of the units involved. The 47th Divisional Chaplain, Reverend D. Railton, noted in 1916:

---

5   CWGCA: CWGC/1/1/1/34/1 (SDC 4).
6   Peter E. Hodgkinson, 'Clearing the Dead', *WWI Resource Centre* (2007), <http://www.vlib.us/wwi/resources/clearingthedead.html>, accessed 19 Aug. 2020.

> Men who have stood it all, cannot stand this clearing of the battlefield … no words can tell you all I feel, nor can words tell you of the horrors of clearing a battlefield. This Battalion was left to do that, and several men went off with shell shock … caused not just by the explosion of a shell nearby, but by the sights and smell and horror of the battlefield in general. I felt dreadful and had to do my best to keep the men up to the task.[7]

Although the task of body recoveries was equally repugnant for the burial parties across the Western Front, depending on the year of the war, local conditions could either help or hinder the task. The ground conditions in some areas of the Somme were very different to the ground conditions in the Ypres Salient, the Somme being a chalky soil whilst the Ypres Salient being a wet, heavy clay with poor drainage characteristics. These local conditions influenced both the physical work involved in recovering a body and the rate at which a body would decompose. If the winter was particularly bad in a certain area and the ground frozen solid, it would be virtually impossible to dig for or rebury bodies, stopping all body recoveries until the ground conditions improved. Whatever the conditions and whatever the location, the burial parties had to deal with the job in hand no matter how repulsive it may have been. Private J. McCauley described his work when attached to a burial detail in 1918:

> Often I have picked up the remains of a fine brave man on a shovel. Just a little heap of bones and maggots to be carried to the common burial place. Numerous bodies were found lying submerged in the water in shell holes and mine craters; bodies that seemed quite whole, but which became like huge masses of white, slimy chalk when we handled them. I shuddered as my hands, covered in soft flesh and slime, moved about in search of the disc, and I have had to pull bodies to pieces in order that they should not be buried unknown. It was very painful to have to bury the unknown.[8]

The role of the burial parties was not only to recover bodies but also to exhaust every avenue they could in terms of identification. As Private McCauley so graphically described, this was by no means an easy or pleasant task. Quite often, the force of an explosion or projectile would have driven the casualty's identification tag deep into his now rotten corpse, making it difficult to find or retrieve. Identification tags were not the only method of identification and were only successful in identifying approximately 45 percent of the bodies recovered. There were other methods of identification. In October 1917, Lieutenant H. Knee was in charge of a burial party on the site of a

---

7   Hodgkinson, 'Clearing the Dead', <http://www.vlib.us/wwi/resources/clearingthedead.html>, accessed 19 Aug. 2020.
8   Hodgkinson, 'Clearing the Dead', <http://www.vlib.us/wwi/resources/clearingthedead.html>, accessed 19 Aug. 2020.

recently conquered German defensive position on the outskirts of Ypres known to the troops as 'Tower Hamlets'. Before burying the body in a makeshift grave, it had to be searched for identification:

> Orders had been given that we were to take from their pockets pay books and personal effects, such as money, watches, rings, photos, letters and so on, one identification disc had also to be removed, the other being left on the body. Boots were supposed to be removed, if possible, as salvage was the order of the day. A small white bag was provided for each man's effects, the neck of which was to be securely tied and his identity disc attached thereto. It was a gruesome job! Corpses, corpses everywhere in various stages of mutilation.[9]

Once the personal effects were removed from the remains, they were buried in a hastily prepared grave close to where they fell, with the site of the grave being registered. Corporal Joe Hoyles of the Rifle Brigade described burying the dead on the Somme in July 1916: 'There was a terrific smell … A smell of rotten flesh … they were seven and eight deep and they had all gone black … Wicked it was! Colonel Pinney got hold of some stretchers and our job was to put the bodies and, with one man at each end, we threw them into the crater'.[10]

Depending upon circumstances, a short burial service would sometimes be performed. Lieutenant H. Knee described at Tower Hamlets on the outskirts of Ypres in October 1917:

> Before we heaped the cold dank earth over the bodies I was able to read part of the Burial Service over them. It was a strange scene. One of the blokes had a Book of Common Prayer and it seemed scarcely decent to cover these poor 'bleeding pieces of earth' with filthy mud without giving them some sort of Christian burial – my father had been a lay preacher in his youth and I, too, had been a regular church-goer … at least we, their comrades, could show some measure of love and respect … My helpers gathered round as I stood by the burial fosse and reverently played the parson.[11]

By the end of the Great War, in excess of 720,000 dead of the armies of the British Empire lay dead on the Western Front, with approximately 195,000 of those lying in Belgium and the majority of those being in the Ypres Salient. Many of the dead lay in rough shallow graves dug by their comrades, and many still lie in the battlefields

---

9   Hodgkinson, 'Clearing the Dead', <http://www.vlib.us/wwi/resources/clearingthedead.html>, accessed 19 Aug. 2020.
10 Lyn Macdonald, *Somme* (London: Penguin, 1993), p.116.
11 Peter E. Hodgkinson, *Human Remains on the Great War Battlefields*. Unpublished. Birmingham University, MA.

where they had fallen. Many more were unaccounted for, simply listed as missing. Some were destined to be recovered and identified, but many were not. In the Ypres Salient alone, over 100,000 would eventually be recorded as 'Known unto God'.

From the instigation of the GRC in 1915 and November 1918, units of the British Army had registered approximately 95,000 isolated graves on the Western Front, with an extra 57,000 burials registered with their location noted as being 'unverified'. The end of the war was to bring a whole new set of challenges for the recovery of remains on the Western Front and the Ypres Salient. In November 1918, Fabian Ware stated, 'There is a strip of land right down from the North of France to the end of the British line some 50 miles broad, which is thick with isolated graves. Take the Somme Battlefield, we have 50,000 isolated graves which we have marked there and all around Ypres and Passchendaele the number is tremendous'.[12]

The next phase of the process of body recovery was about to begin.

---

12 Commonwealth War Graves Commission Archive (CWGCA) CWGC/2/2/1/6: Commission Meeting Minutes.

10

Post-War Body Recoveries

By the time of the armistice in 1918, the IWGC had recorded that approximately 500,000 men's bodies were listed as missing on the Western Front, and it quickly became clear that the existing level of manpower currently engaged in burial work fell far short of the numbers required to locate, exhume and rebury as many of these men as possible. Of course, the stark reality was that, in many cases, recovery would not be possible, as there was nothing left to recover, with Fabian Ware stating in 1916, 'I regret to say that not only have a large number of bodies been destroyed beyond all recognition by the enemy's artillery fire before burial but that all traces of graves themselves have in a large number of cases been obliterated'.[1] The official post-war exhumation program involving the army, DGR&E and IWGC started on 12 January 1919. However, because of severe frost making it impossible to dig, the work was halted on 20 January and did not recommence until 17 February 1919.

The exhumation program had been divided between the three British armies on the Western Front: the 1st Army would cover the Arras–Lys area, the 3rd Army would cover the Somme battlefront, and the 5th Army would cover the Ypres Salient and surrounding areas. Of the three armies, it was the 5th in the Ypres area that gave the best returns in the early days of the exhumation program, having started as early as late November 1918. It was noted that, up to 22 February 1919, the 5th Army had carried out 1,076 exhumations, the 3rd Army 376 exhumations and the 1st Army exhuming precisely zero. By the end of February 1919, the 5th Army in the Ypres Salient had an exhumation rate of around 500 bodies per week. The slow start in the 1st and 3rd Armies' areas was attributed to several factors: the weather conditions, lack of transport and of course levels of available manpower.

As a result of the slow start, arrangements were made in early 1919 to attract men with military experience to work in the exhumation units in France and Belgium. It was a strongly held view amongst the High Command and the IWGC that the men employed in the task should be volunteers because of the sensitivities of the work

---

1   CWGCA: CWGC/1/1/1/34/1 (SDC 4).

involved. Back in the UK, there was a huge pool of resources of 33,000 labour men who were retainable within the ranks of the British Army and could easily have been ordered to France and Belgium, but, as a result of the Adjutant General's views, it was decided to call for volunteers with the offer of a financial incentive of additional 2/6d a day. The Adjutant General stated in an undated document marked 'Secret' that the job 'required a certain class of men who must be volunteers. It could hardly be expected that men would come away from their firesides to grope about exhuming the dead'.[2] Lieutenant Colonel Ackroyd of the DGR&E stated that the job could be achieved within three months if they had 15,000 men focused on the task of exhumation. The reality was that, at that point in early 1919, there were only around 1,750 men involved in the task of searching for the dead, with that number slowly diminishing due to demobilisation. Ironically, at precisely this time, the army had a 'clearing-up force' in France and Belgium of around 120,000 men involved in clearing the battlefields and salving anything of use and value, none of whom were detailed in looking for the dead. The army clearly had questionable priorities.

Representatives from the Dominions also played their part in recovering the fallen from the Western Front. The Canadian authorities volunteered to take responsibility for exhumations in the Albert–Courcelette area in France, where they had fought heavily, providing 600 men for the task. Likewise, the Australians offered 1,000 men to clear the areas in France where they had fought heavily – for example, Pozieres and Villers Bretonneux. Although not performing any actual exhumation work in the Ypres Salient, the AGS (Australian Graves Services) had representation based in the town of Poperinge, 13 kilometres east of Ypres. Under the command of Major Alfred Allen, its job it was to oversee the exhumation of Australian graves by British units in the Salient. The Canadians also had administrative representation in the Ypres Salient under the guise of the CWGD (Canadian War Graves Detachment). Created after the end of the war, the role of the CWGD was similar to that of the DGR&E. Concentrating only on Canadian cases, they supervised the exhumation of Canadian soldiers and verified all records, and, much like the original GRC, they also offered a photographic service, sending photographs of Canadian graves back home to Canada.

In May 1919, the DGR&E assumed responsibility for the exhumation units on the Western Front, therefore bringing the command of the individual burial units under one umbrella. By June 1919, they had 33 GRUs operating on the Western Front, with 10 of those operating in the 5th Army Area, including the Ypres Salient. By the beginning of 1920, there were around 9,000 men on exhumation duty on the old Western Front, with only around half of them being available for work on a daily basis, as the hideous nature of the task they performed converted into an average daily sick parade of around 500 men.[3]

---

2   Commonwealth War Graves Commission Archive (CWGCA) CWGC/1/1/7/B/42 (WG 1294/3 PT.1: Exhumation France and Belgium Part 1).
3   Hodgkinson, *Human Remains*.

The work of exhumation attracted all types of men with all types of characters. Although the Adjutant General had hoped that the work would attract men of 'a certain class', this did not always to turn out to be the case. Granted, the majority of men volunteered because it was the right thing to do, driven by the memory of comrades who had fallen on the Western Front and, in some cases, haunted by survivor's guilt. These men not only volunteered to look for the dead, but some also stayed on in the years afterwards to work for then IWGC, tending to the graves of their fallen comrades. In fact, in the Ypres Salient today and in France, there are gardeners working for the now CWGC who are direct descendants of the first 'cemetery men' of the IWGC. For those men, it really was a labour of love. Some men, however, had different motivations. With the world plunged into a post-war economic crisis, this was the only chance they had for work and so grasped this opportunity with both hands. Some men simply did not want to go home, having fallen in love with a Belgian or French girl, and others did not want to give up a lifestyle that would be impossible for them to pursue back at home. The estaminets and brothels were still trading, and the heady mix of booze, sex and good pay meant that, in some cases, the inevitable disciplinary issues would follow. Of course, one of the reasons why the men drank and wanted to blow off steam was as a result of the abhorrent tasks they were performing. The sights and smells of the body recovery process must have taken a mental toll on some of these men, who then turned to alcohol for solace. Some men were able to cope better than others, as author and veteran Stephen Graham recounted when he returned to Ypres in 1920 and came across an exhumation unit, one of whose number told him, 'It's jolly hard work. But it 'as its better side. Some fellers the other day came on a dug-out with three officers in it, and they picked up five thousand francs between 'em'. Graham himself noted, 'It is a ghoulish work, but they have become as matter of fact as can be'.[4]

During March 1922, an article was published in the British press, part of which concerned the behaviour of British exhumation units in France. Two sections of the article covered the subject of body recoveries, one entitled 'The Interlopers' and the other entitled 'The Impossible Brigade', both of which accused elements of British exhumation units of behaviour not appropriate for the task they had to perform. The article questioned in particular the type of men recruited for the purpose:

> Convicts, cut-throats, vagabonds, drunkards, degenerates were dressed in Khaki and dispatched to France and Belgium, attached, for some inexplicable reason, to British regiments that had won undying renown in this and past campaigns … These 'Impossibles' did not stay out for very long; it soon became necessary to weed out and recall them … But the 'Impossible Brigade,' so promptly

---

4   Stephen, Graham, *The Challenge of the Dead: A Vision of the War and the Life of the Common Soldier in France, Seen Two Years Afterwards between August and November, 1920* (London: Cassell and Company, 1921), p.26.

demobbed, had done its wicked work; its shameless members had degraded the uniform of our King, and shown the captious foreigner to what depths even Britishers may sink. 'It is poor comfort to us,' complained one Englishwoman, who, when visiting the grave of her husband, had encountered some of them, 'to reflect that our beloved ones are entrusted to creatures such as these'.[5]

How much credibility that can be attached to this article is questionable, as its claims are not backed up by any hard evidence. However, it was taken seriously enough at the time to be entered into the archive of the IWGC archive. In its defence, the article does then go on to level the balance by saying, 'The men who remained till the end to bury our dead were a credit to their regiments and to the proletariat of their native land'.[6]

It was just not the British units who had some elements of poor discipline, the Australian units in France suffered with the same problems also. Australian Private William. F. Macbeath was serving in France in a burial party when he wrote home in 1919, 'I think they have got the roughest lot of officers they could find in the AIF [Australian Imperial Force] with this unit, and by Jove they want them as it is the roughest mob I have ever seen, they would just as soon down tools as not'.[7] New Zealander Ettie Rout was much more forthcoming in her criticism towards Australian burial units, saying in 1919 that there were 'scarcely any soldiers here at all – just masses of more or less unorganised soldiery, bribed with half crowns to undertake duties which only the very best of our citizens are fit to be entrusted with'.[8] Captain A. Kingston reported, 'The men were constantly getting drunk … The majority of the men were a bad lot and very inefficient. They were neither dependable nor reliable'.[9] In reality, the cases of ill behaviour were relatively low and, when you consider the tasks that the burial parties had to perform, were understandable in many cases. The main problem was that public expectations of the men who carried out this almost 'sacred' role was high. It was difficult for the general public to understand the reality of the effect these tasks had on the men's mental health. It is interesting to note that, in a lot of cases (but not all), the quotes above occurred in 1919 – the early days of body recovery when speed was of the essence. This year also meant that the bodies themselves were not fully decomposed, adding extra mental stress to those men as they picked through

---

5   Commonwealth War Graves Commission Archive (CWGCA) CWGC/1/1/7/B45 (WG 1294/3 PT.4: Exhumation France and Belgium Part 4): E. Stewart Smith, 'A New Entente Cordiale and Anglo French Animosities: Their Cause, Effect and Remedy', p.155.
6   CWGCA: CWGC/1/1/7/B45 (WG 1294/3 PT.4: Exhumation France and Belgium Part 4): Smith, 'New Entente Cordiale', p.155.
7   Hodgkinson, 'Clearing the Dead', <http://www.vlib.us/wwi/resources/clearingthedead.html>, accessed 19 Aug. 2020.
8   Bart Ziino, *A Distant Grief: Australians, War Graves and the Great War* (Perth: UWA Publishing, 2007), p.96.
9   Ziino, *A Distant Grief*, p.96.

the remains of dead comrades looking for evidence of identification. Private Henry George Whiting of the AIF summed it all up in a letter written in 1919:

> You will note by the above that we have left Belgium & came back to France. The reason for evacuating Belgium was because 10 of us volunteered for the graves detachment battn which is composed of 1,100 men, a few from each of the battn. Stan, Merv & myself volunteered for to assist in the raising of the bodies of our dead comrades and place them in cemeteries which we have surveyed for the purpose. The one which we are filling now is called the Adelaide Cemetery. We are raising the bodies of Tommies, Yanks, Canadians N Zealanders & Australians. We started on Monday last, and I can assure you it is a very unpleasant undertaking. Nearly all the men we have raised up to date have been killed 12 months and they are far from being decayed properly, so you can guess the constitution one needs. I have felt sick dozens of times, but we carry on knowing that we are identifying Australian boys who have never been identified. They nearly all have some means of identification on them, and we make a careful research for some, as it is cruel, for their people's minds not to set at rest to know that their sons have been located. Many mothers picture their sons blown to pieces and we record, so now we can hope to be able to identify 90 percent of the missing. Hilda, it is heart breaking to see the way the poor fellows are buried, perhaps I should not tell you, then again it is no harm, but we find dozens of them just in one big lump with all their coats equipment and gas helmet and all on, and a heap of earth placed over them. Today I dug two up that were buried together one was a Tommie and one an Aussie. The Aussie's head was blown clean off and sticking in his steel helmet and stuck in the middle of the Tommie's back. We have found many cases of a similar kind. We will be a hard-hearted crowd when we get back, after the sights we see and the many thousands that we will have raised by that time. All bodies are placed separately in large bags and buried that way. For my part I would be pleased to see them remain where they were first placed to rest. It seems cruel to see them taken up in pieces and placed away. We have a few hard-hearted fellows on the work and they annoy me the way they talk over the remains of the heroes … We could have been home by August, had we not volunteered for this, but my reasons are already explained, so God strengthen those who are awaiting our return. We will feel that we have completed our duty when this most important job is finished.[10]

The majority of those engaged in work were decent men with moral standards, and the number of cases of misbehaviour recorded was small in comparison to the size of the task and the nature of the work. The sensitivities of recovering the fallen meant that

---

10 Australian War Memorial (AWM) PR05609: Henry Whiting Letter, 17 April 1919.

the work of the GRUs was in the spotlight back at home, and, with a sensationalist press looking for stories to create scandals, it was essential that the process of body recovery was completed from start to finish in a manner befitting of the countries' heroes and that the behaviour of the men involved in the task should be beyond reproach. The public expected nothing less.

To be fair to the organisations involved in 1919, this was very much a learning curve. No real exhumation and search procedure existed, and regulations for dealing with certain situations were created only after a mistake had been made. William Macbeath wrote to his mother in 1919:

> Last Wednesday an English lady came here looking for her sons grave, she found out we were reburying him at the Adelaid Cemetery, she went round after we'd knocked off and found him lying in a bag on the ground … she fainted when she saw him and is in hospital suffering from shock, so English people are forbidden to travel to the battle areas now.[11]

Members of the Royal Engineers examining a skull recovered from the battlefield. (Photographer unknown. Courtesy of the In Flanders Fields Museum.)

11 Hodgkinson, 'Clearing the Dead', <http://www.vlib.us/wwi/resources/clearingthedead.html>, accessed 19 Aug. 2020.

By the 1920s, the exhumation units were a well-trained and efficient body of men. Most of the troublesome officers and men had been weeded out, disciplined and, in some cases, sent home. Of course, some problems persisted, particularly those related to excessive alcohol use, but that was to be expected and also understandable given the nature of the task the units faced on a daily basis. Writer and veteran Stephen Graham came across an exhumation unit on the outskirts of Ypres and asked one of the men if, after six months of sleeping on the battlefield, he saw ghosts: 'The man smiled. He saw none. He felt the presence of none. Imagination did not pull at his heart strings. If it did, he would go mad'.[12]

A gruesome reminder of the task faced by the men of the GRUs. (Photo by Corporal Ivan Bawtree. Courtesy of Jeremy Gordon-Smith.)

12 Graham, *Challenge of the Dead*, p.26.

11

Captain Crawford and the 68th Labour Company: 'The Pioneer Company in Work of this Kind'

The reason the 5th Army seemed to hit the ground running compared to the 1st and 3rd Armies can be attributed to the work of the 68th Labour Company in the Ypres Salient. The unit had been present on the Western Front since 1917, had been the first to answer the call for volunteers for post-war burial duties and had commenced work in the Ypres area in January 1919. However, the unit had little to no experience in burial work nor did they have any set procedure to follow apart from some rough guidelines issued by GHQ (General Headquarters). Under the command of their senior officer, Captain G. F. Crawford, the company's four other officers and 560 men started the work of body recoveries, clearing the area around the Menin Road on the outskirts of Ypres and using two burial sites in which to concentrate the bodies recovered, those being Birr Cross and Hooge Crater. The lack of hard and fast procedure and the relative inexperience of the men created exhumation units whose main focus was on the rate that they could recover and rebury bodies, with the focus on identification of those bodies being secondary. The units therefore became convinced that success and unit reputation was based on the pace of their burial returns, a misconception that would call into question the accuracy of their work later in 1919.

The task of body recovery faced by the 68th Labour Company was not an easy one. Not only was the job deeply unpleasant, but it was also inherently dangerous. Although the fighting had stopped, the old battlefields were still dangerous places, with tens of thousands of unexploded artillery shells littering the battlefields. To strike a concealed shell with a spade whilst digging for a body could and did have fatal consequences. There were also logistical problems to contend with. There was both a shortage of manpower and a desperate shortage of serviceable motorised transport, these vehicles being needed to convey the men of the exhumation units to their search areas and then deliver the recovered bodies to the designated cemeteries for reburial. Stores were also often in short supply, with units lacking the basic tools needed to do the job. Captain W. E. Southgate of the 83rd Labour Company reported in late 1919:

> This unit … has only been able to exhume and rebury 190 bodies. This is due to a lack of canvas … There is no motor ambulance doing duty with this unit, although one was detailed to report over two months ago … We have only 30 picks and there is a shortage of shovels (we have about 200 for nearly 500 men).[1]

The men of the exhumation units also lacked shelter. Four years of warfare had laid the Ypres Salient to waste, and, with the exception of the odd remaining bunker, there was very little in terms of shelter on the old battlefields. As some units slept in the areas they were clearing, a lack of tents and winter clothing became an issue. Work continued in the face of these hardships, however, with the units of the 68th Labour Company learning as they went until, eventually, they had perfected a system of best practice that was to become the benchmark for the rest of the exhumation units that were to follow.

In July 1919, the commanding officer of the 68th Labour Company, Captain G. F. Crawford, wrote a standard procedure for the process of exhumation based upon the experiences and mistakes made by the unit. The detailed procedure covered all aspects of the body recovery process, from the search for remains to logistical requirements and ending with the procedure for reburial in the designated burial ground. The detailed instructions of *Guidance of Exhumation Companies in the Future* make for fascinating reading. Under Crawford's procedure, prior to any search taking place, the area in question was to be assessed first by the DGR&E survey officer, who would then mark out the ground to be searched by placing a flag at each corner of the ground and then dividing the search area into quarter squares of roughly 500 yards per square. Once the ground was prepared, the responsibility for the search was handed over to the army burial officer. It was his responsibility to oversee the exhumations, making sure that the body with its effects and original burial cross (if any were present) were transported together for reburial in the concentration cemetery. Upon arrival at the cemetery, he was responsible for the reburial of the body on the site determined by the survey officer, whose role was also to lay out the concentration cemeteries. The army burial officer was also responsible for completing all the administration with regards to the exhumation and reinterment of the body. The task of exhumation itself was carried out by exhumation units, which were broken down into working parties or 'squads':

> The men employed upon the work of actual exhumation should be organised in squads, each under the command of an officer, with a sergeant, and a proper compliment of junior N.C.O.s. [non-commissioned officers] These squads should be sub-divided into parties of four, each with one O.R. [other rank] as a sanitary man. The ideal squad consists of 32 O.R.s. Each squad should be given

---

1   Hodgkinson, 'Clearing the Dead', <http://www.vlib.us/wwi/resources/clearingthedead.html>, accessed 19 Aug. 2020.

an area consisting of a map square of 500 yards, which must be thoroughly searched and cleared.²

Crawford then went on to detail the equipment that each exhumation squad needed in order to perform its task:

1. Sufficient stakes to mark the position of as many bodies as will provide them with at least 2 or 3 day's work.
2. 2 G.S shovels for each party of four.
3. 2 pairs of rubber gloves for each party of four.
4. Canvas and rope in which to wrap the bodies.
5. Stretchers.
6. Cresol.³
7. Wire cutters and shears.

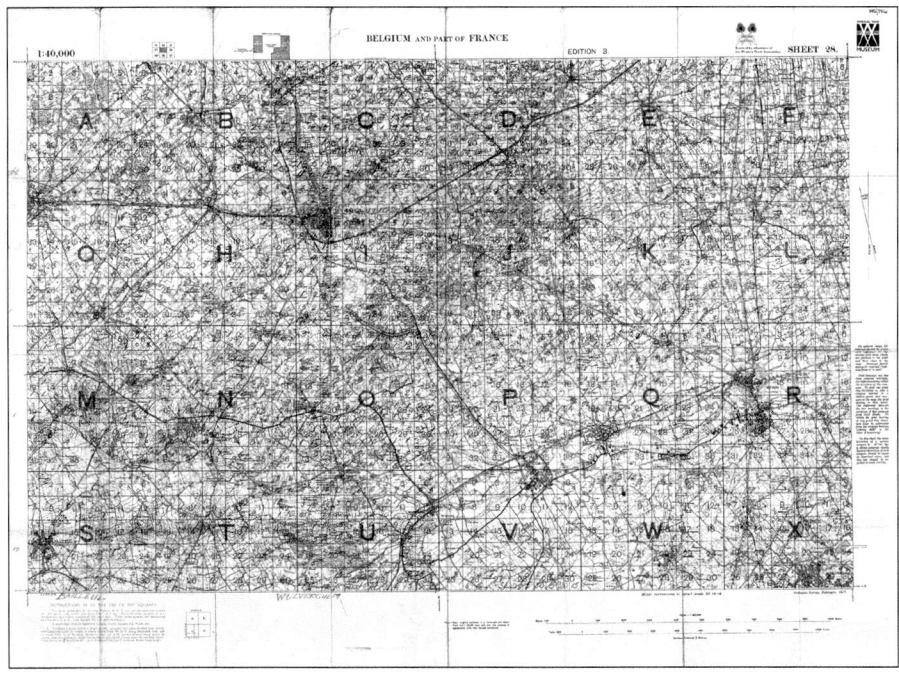

BDM (body density map). Marked out in 500-yard squares, with each square highlighting the known number of burials to be exhumed. (Courtesy of the Western Front Association/ Imperial War Museum)

2   Commonwealth War Graves Commission Archive (CWGCA) CWGC/1/1/7/B/48: Exhumations. Hooge Committee of Enquiry Report.
3   Cresol is a liquid disinfectant/antiseptic.

The officer of each squad was to be equipped with:

1. A map of the district, scale 1/20,000.
2. Labels to attach to the bodies.
3. Ration bags in which to preserve any effects found.
4. A notebook.
5. Stores such as stretchers, cresol, and canvas are to be sent up in the G.S wagons … but sufficient stakes, shovels, etc, should be taken by the men to ensure that work may be commenced even if the wagons are delayed.[4]

Captain Crawford was more than aware of the importance of thoroughness in the search process and of the value of the previous work completed by the GRC and then the DGR&E:

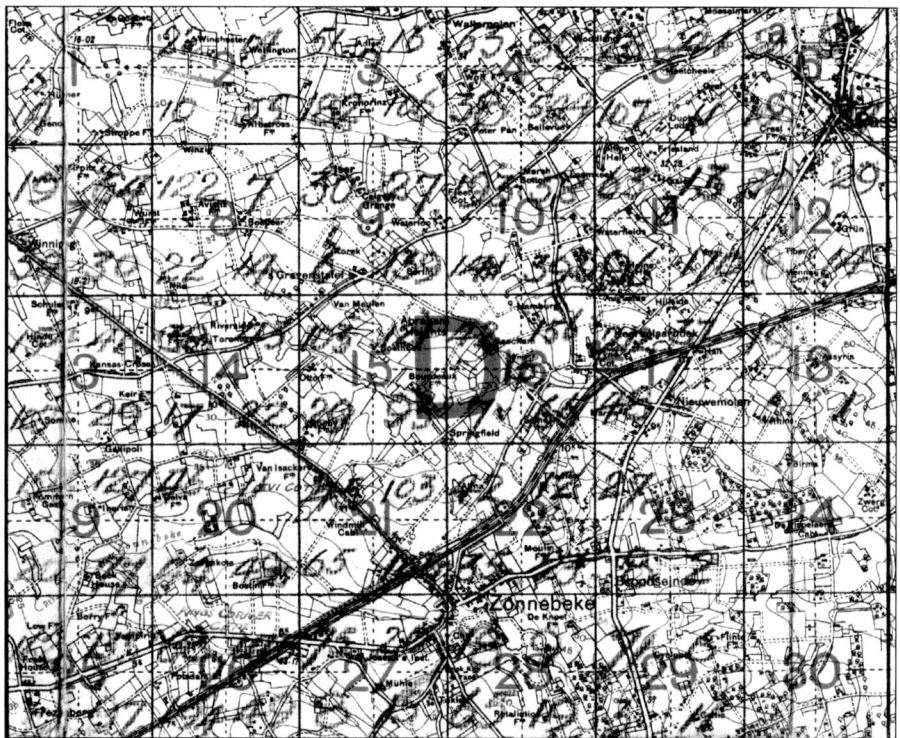

A close up of one map square showing the approach to Passchendaele, where heavy losses were incurred in October and November 1917. The numbers indicate the amount of visible graves known to exist for recovery. (Courtesy of the Western Front Association/Imperial War Museum)

4 CWGCA: CWGC/1/1/7/B/48: Exhumations. Hooge Committee of Enquiry Report.

At the company orderly room will be kept details showing the officer and men engaged, and the squares where they are working, together with a coloured map giving the areas cleared. There should further be kept at the Orderly Room a statement showing the number of bodies registered as buried in each square, and also any cemeteries which exist in each square, and each officer should be in possession of this knowledge regarding the square in which he is working. In most cases he will find many more bodies than are registered, and he should not be content to leave the square as soon as that number has been exhumed, but should satisfy himself that the area is cleared. The number registered as buried there will, however, give him some indication of the work to be done. G.R.Unit records must invariably be consulted before any square is put under concentration.[5]

In short, Captain Crawford realised that adequate planning and preparation was essential if the task was to be completed accurately and efficiently.

The reality of the ground to be searched and depicted on the BDM. (Photo by Corporal Ivan Bawtree. Courtesy of Jeremy Gordon-Smith.)

5   CWGCA: CWGC/1/1/7/B/48: Exhumations. Hooge Committee of Enquiry Report.

A GRU searching the battlefield, c. 1919. (Photo by Colonel Herbert Goodland. CWGCA, with permission.)

The art of 'spotting', c. 1920. (Photo by Corporal Ivan Bawtree. Courtesy of Jeremy Gordon-Smith.)

The next part of Crawford's new guidelines concerned the search procedure itself. Each 500-yard square, previously laid out by the survey officer, had to be searched thoroughly. Recommending that, in the heat of the summer, work should be carried out in the early morning, Crawford suggested searching small portions of ground at a time, working slowly and avoiding bunching. Wherever a body was found, a wooden stake was to be planted to mark the spot. With regards to old battlefield cemeteries, any cemetery located during the search containing more than 40 burials was to be marked with a blue flag, whilst smaller burial grounds of less than 40 graves were marked with a yellow flag and left untouched before further instruction was received from the DGR&E.

The art of searching for a body became known to those involved in the task as 'spotting'. Competency in the art of spotting could only be achieved with the hands-on experience of searching for bodies in the field, something that Captain Crawford had in abundance. There were, of course, obvious signs of a burial – for example, a rifle or cross marking a grave, small wooden stakes with markings burnt into the shaft left by the Germans as an indicator of where they had buried remains and, in some cases, bodies still lying exposed on the surface of the battlefield. However, the real skill of a spotter was to be able to spot unmarked burial sites from subtle signs that were not obvious to the untrained eye. Spotters would look for rat holes in the battlefield since the rats would often burrow down to get to the dead and would bring up small pieces of bone or pieces of equipment in the process. Other clues known to the spotters were depressions in the ground as it settled after a burial, discoloration of grass (as quite often it would turn a vivid blueish-green colour if a body had been buried beneath) and a change in colour of the earth and water, which turned to a greenish-black or grey if it concealed a body.

As their expertise grew, some spotters developed their own 'tools' over and above the official ones recommended by Captain Crawford. The machine gun rod was used by some men, particularly in the early days of body recovery when they were dealing with putrid remains. The long, thin metal rod was issued to the British Army primarily to clean the barrel of a Vickers machine gun, but, for the exhumation units, it provided an easy solution to identify the location of a concealed body. Having identified a suspicious site, the rod would be pushed into the ground as far as possible and then pulled out. The rod gave two chances of identifying a grave: first, it could detect a cavity below ground, as the rod could be more easily inserted; second, upon withdrawing the rod, one unlucky unit member would smell its end for evidence of a decomposing body. Many veterans described the smell as being similar to a decaying pork pie.[6]

Once the area had been thoroughly searched (sometimes as many as six times) and the body's location marked with a stake, then the work of exhumation could begin. Captain Crawford continued:

6   Interview with Paul Reed (10 June 2021).

Recovering the remains, c. 1920. (Photo by Corporal Ivan Bawtree. Courtesy of Jeremy Gordon-Smith.)

Each party of four should be sent to a spot staked, having with them shovels, rubber gloves, canvas and rope, cresol and stretchers. Of such a party the senior or best worker should be made responsible under his officer and N.C.O.s that the work of exhumation and identification is properly carried out … In the actual work of exhumation the men should be warned not to dig too closely to the bodies, but well outside them. Such a precaution renders the work easier, prevents disturbance of the bodies, and most important of all, reveals whether more than one man is buried at any particular spot … The body, having been exhumed, is placed upon the canvas, which has already been soaked in Cresol and a careful search is made for any effects which may lead to identification. The pockets should be searched, and a special examination made of the neck, wrists, and braces where identity discs may be found.[7]

Searching the remains for identification, c. 1920. (Photo by Corporal Ivan Bawtree. Courtesy of Jeremy Gordon-Smith.)

7 CWGCA: CWGC/1/1/7/B/48: Exhumations. Hooge Committee of Enquiry Report.

Once searched thoroughly, the body would then be wrapped and tied into the canvas, and any personal effects found with the body would be tied up in the ration bag. If the original grave had a grave marker (e.g., an old GRC wooden cross), this would be removed from the ground and kept with the body to be initially placed in the designated cemetery for reburial. The exhumation officer would then complete a label and attach it firmly to the wrapped body.

Personal effects recovered, in this case, those of an Australian soldier, c. 1920. (Photo by Corporal Ivan Bawtree. Courtesy of Jeremy Gordon-Smith.)

Crawford's procedure stated that:

> It is essential that the label be written by the officer, and <u>by no one else,</u> and it should bear the following particulars.
>
> A. Where identity has been established:
>   1. Sheet number of map used.
>   2. Map reference where body was found.
>   3. If a cross has been found, this should be stated.
>   4. No. and rank of deceased.
>   5. Name.
>   6. Unit.
>   7. List of effects found and sent with body, mentioning particularly where paybook is found, whether there is a will.
>   8. Whether a committal service is required. (This will depend upon whether in the opinion of the Officer present at the exhumation, the body has previously been properly committed or not.)
>   9. Religion, if possible.
>   10. Signature of the Officer responsible.
>
> B. In the case of unidentified remains:
>   1. Sheet number of map.
>   2. Map reference.
>   3. Unit if possible (e.g., from numerals).
>   4. List of effects, if any, from which identity may be established.
>   5. Whether a committal service is necessary.
>   6. Signature of Officer responsible.

> All kit, equipment, etc, which is useless for identification, is thrown back in the grave, cresol is poured on, and the grave is filled in.[8]

Once the excavation was completed, the body was then transported to the designated cemetery for burial, with Crawford stating:

> The work of transporting the bodies to the cemetery is usually carried out by G.S. wagons. No other transport can be used over the rough tracks which often have to be traversed. Motor ambulances are used when parties are working near the main road, or to take the bodies from the wagons as soon as they reach the

---

8   CWGCA: CWGC/1/1/7/B/48: Exhumations. Hooge Committee of Enquiry Report.

Refilling the grave, c. 1919. (Photo by Colonel Herbert Goodland. CWGCA, with permission.)

main road. A spare man from the Exhumation Company should be allotted to each G.S. wagon to see that the required stores are taken up to the working parties. He should walk behind the wagon when it is loaded with bodies to see that no accident happens on the way to the cemetery. A Union Jack should be provided to cover the bodies. Each G.S. wagon can take 5 loaded stretchers, 4 on the top and one in the bottom. A stretcher should be allotted to each body, except in the case of fragmentary remains.[9]

There is no doubt that Captain Crawford had a deep understanding of the exhumation task, insisting that, when more than one body was found in a grave, the remains should be kept together and labelled as such so that the cemetery officer would rebury them side by side, noting that 'This is essential because, among a group of bodies, some are already identified, while others are unknown. If the bodies are kept together,

9   CWGCA: CWGC/1/1/7/B/48: Exhumations. Hooge Committee of Enquiry Report.

A GS wagon loaded with bodies for transport, c. 1919. (Photo by Colonel Herbert Goodland. CWGCA, with permission.)

it is often possible from records to identify unknowns from the fact that they are known to have been buried with the identified men'.[10]

Crawford's perception was further highlighted when he advocated for the creation of special 'flying squads'. Realising that the Belgian landowners were returning to the Ypres Salient and that 'building and cultivation was proceeding at pace', he understood that there would be many bodies recovered in areas yet to be searched by the official exhumation units. The flying squads could quickly attend to these instances and recover the bodies using the correct procedure in order to not only give the best chance of identification but also prevent the bodies being covered over by an unscrupulous landowner.

The procedure created by Captain Crawford both concerned the act of exhumation and followed the process through to its conclusion of the reburial in the designated cemetery.

---

10 CWGCA: CWGC/1/1/7/B/48: Exhumations. Hooge Committee of Enquiry Report.

Once again, it was the job of the survey officer to lay out the agreed burial site using stakes and flags. Rows of graves to be dug were marked out in accordance with the instructions issued by the DGR&E, with the number of rows dependant on the estimated number of bodies to be recovered. Upon completion of this process, the survey officer would draw a plan of the cemetery and send it with a report to the DGR&E. The cemetery was divided into plots and rows separated by paths, with each row given an identification letter and each burial plot being numbered. An allowance of two feet of grave space was allotted to each individual grave. Having completed the marking out, he then handed over responsibility to the army burial officer and the cemetery parties. Crawford dictated that:

> A cemetery party consists of the Chaplain attached to the company, one officer, and a clerk, (who under supervision by the officer will see that all effects are taken from the bodies and checked with the particulars given upon the labels), a Sergeant or other N.C.O. or N.C.O.s in charge of the digging party, a sanitary man, and the digging party.[11]

The number of personnel required for the digging party depended upon the number of bodies forecasted to be recovered and reburied that day. Having received the forecast from the officer in charge of the exhumation unit, the officer of the cemetery party would make an estimate of the men needed based on the premise that it took 10–12 men per day to dig a four-foot-six-inch-deep burial trench large enough to accommodate 20 bodies. The use of POWs in the digging party was permitted provided they dug the graves only; they were not permitted to refill the graves and had to be outside the cemetery when the burial service was being read or the ground consecrated. Each cemetery party was issued with GS shovels, stakes, labels, hammer and stacks, ration bags, rubber gloves, a magnifying glass and a returns book.[12]

In a concerted effort to minimise the risk of misidentification, Captain Crawford put in place a system of checks and balances that was put into effect when the bodies arrived at the cemetery:

> The bodies being brought into the cemetery, all effects are examined carefully and compared with the labels attached. A magnifying glass should be used to read the discs. If any query arises as a result of the examination, the exhuming officer, whose signature will be on the label can be questioned when he reports to the cemetery, as he should each day … The ration bag containing the effects is detached from the body, and marked with the name of the cemetery, and particulars of the soldier to whom they belong. A return in duplicate … showing the graves allotted to each body is prepared and forwarded daily to

11   CWGCA: CWGC/1/1/7/B/48: Exhumations. Hooge Committee of Enquiry Report.
12   CWGCA: CWGC/1/1/7/B/48: Exhumations. Hooge Committee of Enquiry Report.

the D.A.D.G.R.E. [Deputy Assistant Director of Graves Registrations and Enquiries].[13]

Once the checks were completed, the body was placed into the grave in its respective position, and then the grave was filled. Depending upon the circumstances, a committal service may or may not have been performed. A stake bearing labels detailing the man's particulars was then placed at the head of the grave – the only exception being that, if the body arrived with a cross recovered from its original burial place, this cross was erected at the head of the grave instead of a stake. It was then the responsibility of the GRUs to erect permanent grave markers at the head of each grave. The final tasks to be performed fell to the sanitation man, whose job was to disinfect the stretchers, and to the cemetery officer to complete the remaining administration. The whole procedure from start to finish, when done correctly, was a time-consuming one. On average, six to nine men were required per body per day to exhume, transport and rebury.

Bodies being taken to place of burial, c. 1919. (Photo by Colonel Herbert Goodland. CWGCA, with permission.)

13 CWGCA: CWGC/1/1/7/B/48: Exhumations. Hooge Committee of Enquiry Report.

The bodies laid out, ready for burial, c. 1919. (Photo by Colonel Herbert Goodland. CWGCA, with permission.)

The cemetery party ready to perform the burials, c. 1919. (Photo by Colonel Herbert Goodland. CWGCA, with permission.)

The army chaplain reading the burial service, c. 1919. (Photo by Colonel Herbert Goodland. CWGCA, with permission.)

Captain Crawford's exhumation guide was not only a well-needed procedure but arguably was also way ahead of its time, with many of his recommendations still in use today in the field of forensic archaeology. Without these procedures, developed from the experiences of Crawford and the 68th Labour Company, many more soldiers of the British and Commonwealth forces killed in the Ypres Salient may have been lying in unidentified graves poignantly marked as 'Known unto God'.

However, the reputation of Crawford and the 68th Labour Company of 1919 was about to be severely tested when a potential scandal came to light in 1921.

12

Hooge Crater Cemetery Enquiry
Burial Discrepancies and Misidentification

In April 1920, the 68th Labour Company was officially disbanded. After serving three years on the Western Front, it was finally time for their compliment of five officers and 560 men to go home to their families and resume their civilian lives. For Captain Crawford, however, the demobilisation of the company was not the end of the story, as questions were being raised regarding their burial practices of early 1919 when the unit first volunteered for burial duty. As the first unit of their kind, engaged specifically in the task and with only very basic guidance in procedure from headquarters, which was later described as being nothing more than 'rough notes', the 68th Labour Company learnt as they went along, fine tuning working methods and learning from their mistakes with each exhumation. The exhumation units that were to follow in their footsteps would benefit from the experiences of the 68th Labour Company and, of course, the procedure put into place by Captain Crawford. The 126th Labour Company was one of those units. Commanded by Captain D. Coghlan, they quickly acquired a reputation for accurate and thorough work; however, the standard of excellence achieved by this company was arguably as a result of Captain Crawford's procedures and the experiences of the 68th Labour Company. Both companies were about to meet head on in a committee of enquiry starting on 13 January 1921 concerning the burials at Hooge Crater Cemetery on the outskirts of Ypres.

Started in October 1917 by the 7th Division burial officer and initially containing 76 burials, the cemetery quickly grew after it was designated as a concentration cemetery in 1919, with smaller cemeteries and isolated graves from the surrounding area being concentrated within its walls and eventually swelling its size to in excess of 5,900 graves. Hooge Crater Cemetery was one of six cemeteries used by the 68th Labour Company in the early days of their exhumation work, the other cemeteries being Birr Crossroads, Perth China Wall, Ypres Town Cemetery Extension, Duhallows Cemetery and Ypres Reservoir Cemetery. In 1920, Major Alfred Allen of the AGS (a man who would later accuse British burial units of chopping bodies in half in order to increase their burial returns, whilst facing a court of enquiry regarding his own dubious practices) reported a case of a duplicated burial concerning a soldier who had served with the AIF. A cross bearing the name of Private Williams of the 25th Battalion had been erected in both Underhill Farm Cemetery in Ploegsteert and in Hooge Crater Cemetery. Major Allen requested permission to exhume the grave at Hooge in order to try to solve the issue. Permission was granted, and the grave was exhumed by British exhumation units overseen by Major Allen on 2 October 1920. Upon opening the grave and examining the remains, it was found that the grave contained the body of a Private Hamilton of the 25th Battalion AIF and not the remains of Private Williams as indicated on the grave marker, Private Hamilton's remains being identified by a metal ID tag found in the grave. Worried by this turn of events, Major Allen then requested that the adjacent grave be exhumed and rechecked, the grave being marked as an 'Unknown Australian'. Once opened, this grave was also found to be incorrectly marked and contained a body identified by its identification disc as a 'T. Dodd', whose regimental number made it clear that he was definitely not an Australian. The body was, in fact, that of T. S. Dodd of the 18th Battalion, the King's (Liverpool Regiment), who died on 31 July 1917 at the age of 19.

The graves of Private Hamilton and Private Dodd today. (Photo by Patsy Mahieu.)

As a result of the exhumations, reports were sent to the DGR&E and to Australia House, with Major Allen requesting that further examinations of Australian graves in Hooge Cemetery be carried out. The request was agreed by the DGR&E, and these examinations were carried out between 25–27 October 1920 by the aforementioned 126th Labour Company under the command of Captain Coghlan. The findings were worrying, with the official report stating, 'The results of these test exhumations, which disclosed serious irregularities as distinct from purely technical mistakes'.[1] In other words, there was a suspicion of serious malpractice, and, as a result, an official Committee of Enquiry was opened in January 1921.

On the face of it, the suspicions of malpractice were confirmed when the detailed results of the further exhumations came to light. In all, 135 graves were exhumed and checked by the 126th Labour Company, with 117 of those being in plots one and two of the cemetery. These were the plots being used by the 68th Labour Company in the period up to July 1919, when Captain Crawford's procedures started to be used. Of the 135 graves exhumed and examined, six unidentified burials were able to be identified, 17 graves were found to contain no bodies, four graves contained sandbags and equipment but no human remains, seven soldiers buried as 'Unknown British Soldiers' were identified as coming from the Dominion countries, 12 soldiers' identifications were listed as 'doubtful', eight soldiers had partial identifications unrecorded on the grave marker, and two British soldiers were found to be incorrectly identified as coming from one of the Dominion countries.[2] Worse was to come when – on top of the empty graves reported and the misidentification issues – the 126th Labour Company found one body lying diagonally across three graves, at least one body being buried in a grave two feet deep instead of the required four feet and six inches, at least one body being buried head to foot in the grave and the body of a German soldier being buried in a grave marked as an 'Unknown British Soldier'. The report carried on in more detail:

> Plot 1, Row J, Graves 5–7. A bad reburial there were three crosses to unknown British soldiers on exhumation one body was found to be buried diagonally across the three graves.

> As regards to grave No. 9 … he could discover no trace of a body being there … the grave was 2 feet deep instead of four feet 6 inch.

> On opening up Grave No.10 a full body of a soldier was found with the Leicestershire numerals.

---

1   CWGCA: CWGC/1/1/7/B/48: Exhumations. Hooge Committee of Enquiry Report, p.35.
2   CWGCA: CWGC/1/1/7/B/48: Exhumations. Hooge Committee of Enquiry Report, p.11.

As regards Grave No.12 the following was on the cross 'Unknown British Soldier. No. 352 – 1st Division'. It is thought by the committee that if enquiry is made 'No.352 – 1st Division' might lead to some identification.

Grave No.15 had a cross showing Unknown British Soldier, body was discovered with disc and numeral on the arm. This points to carelessness – the body was also buried head to foot of grave.

Row G. Grave No.9. This grave was about 2 feet deep. Only the Unknown British Soldiers graves were opened in this case no body was found but it was possible that the body might have side slipped or be due to graves being badly spaced out.[3]

The committee then went on to describe in detail the issues found in the next row searched, that being Row H:

Row H. Grave No.3. To be amended to read Unknown Australian Soldier – to be considered later.

Grave No.4. The regiment viz., Lincoln Regiment omitted from the cross. There appears to be no reason for this as the numerals were found on the uniform. Appears to be carelessness.

Grave No.6. The cross was apparently the original one erected by the men of his unit as it is a white one … This procedure is irregular.

Graves Nos. 9 and 10. It appears that the bodies were buried under the wrong cross – 9 and 10 were transposed. This points to carelessness on the part of someone.

Grave No.14. Appeared to be empty.

Grave No.17. It would appear that the wrong body was put into the grave. The body was found to have a ring on it with the initials T.W.B. It is possible that the exhumation party accepted as correct the inscription on the cross and that the body was re-interred with the same cross without re-examination.[4]

---

3   CWGCA: CWGC/1/1/7/B/48: Exhumations. Hooge Committee of Enquiry Report, pp.6–7.
4   CWGCA: CWGC/1/1/7/B/48: Exhumations. Hooge Committee of Enquiry Report, pp.7–8.

Next came the findings for plot one, row one:

> Grave No.1. On opening up this grave a body was discovered with the disc No. 6622 Private Dunville, R.F.A. [Royal Field Artillery] and there is no doubt that this is the right identification and not that shewn on the cross.
>
> Grave No.5. Also points to bad work. Canvas, sandbag, paper, woodchips in tin. No human remains.
>
> Graves Nos.10 and 12. No remains were found. May possibly be a case of crosses being moved and no bodies found underneath them.[5]

Then on to plot two, row A:

> Grave No.4. Points to carelessness.
>
> Grave No.5. The Unknown Australian Soldier does not appear to have been carefully examined before re-interment. His identification could have been established.
>
> Grave No.6. Apparently, a German soldier was buried instead of a British soldier. This appears to be an indisputable case of carelessness.
>
> Grave No.14. The regiment was omitted from the cross – the Monmouthshire Regiment numerals were discovered.
>
> Grave No.16. Instead of an Unknown British Soldier should have been inscribed Unknown Australian Soldier. It is possible that the company who did the work had no instructions to differentiate between British and Colonial soldiers.[6]

Plot one, row F:

> Grave No.3. On the cross was Unknown British Soldier, The King's, and in the grave was an Australian soldier no. 5451 (?) Glenney, 25th Australian Infantry, Roman Catholic. Careless work.

---

5 CWGCA: CWGC/1/1/7/B/48: Exhumations. Hooge Committee of Enquiry Report, pp.7–8.
6 CWGCA: CWGC/1/1/7/B/48: Exhumations. Hooge Committee of Enquiry Report, pp.8–9.

> Grave No.9. Instead of Unknown British Soldier identity was established by two discs as a Corporal R. Morgan.[7]

Plot one, row G:

> Grave No.1. Under the cross of Unknown British Soldier was found the full body of an Australian soldier which was identified by numerals and badges on collar.
>
> Grave No.5. Only a sandbag was found filled with earth.[8]

Plot one, row E:

> Graves Nos. 13 and 14. The Unknown British soldiers were found to be bodies of Australian Soldiers.[9]

The purpose of the Committee of Enquiry was not to attach blame to units and individuals but rather to learn from the mistakes made in order that they should not happen again, as the president of the enquiry, Colonel W.H.V. Darell explained during its convening on 13 January 1921, '[The enquiry] was not held with a view to fixing responsibility for mistakes that may have occurred, but to advise how such mistakes might be rectified, and to make a recommendation with regard to future policy'.[10] In order to understand how such mistakes could have occurred and in the interest of fairness, Captain Crawford was invited to attend a follow-up enquiry. The meeting took place on 19 January 1921 at Australia House in the presence of Colonel W.H.V. Darell (the enquiry president), Lieutenant Colonel G. J. Hogben and Major Phillips. Captain Crawford, now of the IWGC, was attended by Mr. H. Shaylor, a former lieutenant and burial officer at Hooge Crater Cemetery.

Captain Crawford started the meeting by explaining the role that the 68th Labour Company had with regards to exhumations and reburials in the Ypres Salient and defending the work of his colleagues by stating, 'The 68th Labour Company commenced exhumations in January 1919, under Lieutenant Colonel L.C. Arbuthnot, the Army Burial Officer, 5th Army, and I never have met a more capable officer at his work'.[11] The committee then proceeded to question Crawford and Shaylor on the

---

7   CWGCA: CWGC/1/1/7/B/48: Exhumations. Hooge Committee of Enquiry Report, pp.8–9.
8   CWGCA: CWGC/1/1/7/B/48: Exhumations. Hooge Committee of Enquiry Report, pp.8–9.
9   CWGCA: CWGC/1/1/7/B/48: Exhumations. Hooge Committee of Enquiry Report, p.8.
10 CWGCA: CWGC/1/1/7/B/48: Exhumations. Hooge Committee of Enquiry Report, p.1.
11 CWGCA: CWGC/1/1/7/B/48: Exhumations. Hooge Committee of Enquiry Report, p.15.

issues found at Hooge, and it quickly became apparent that blame could not be laid solely on the shoulders of the 68th Labour Company. When asked of the procedure for marking the graves in the cemetery and its accuracy, Captain Crawford replied, 'It would have been the duty of G.R.U. to erect a cross bearing the same particulars as on the post which my officers erected. This I noticed was not done in March 1920, although my work was completed in August 1919. It was, therefore, impossible for the tabs on the posts to have withstood climatic conditions all this time'.[12] It seemed that the fault of incorrect information being entered on the grave markers was due to the inability of the GRUs of the DGR&E to replace, in a timely manner, the temporary grave markers that had been placed by Crawford's team.

The original GRU cross of Gilbert Talbot, 7th Battalion Rifle Brigade, the inspiration for Talbot House. (Courtesy of Talbot House Museum.)

12 CWGCA: CWGC/1/1/7/B/48: Exhumations. Hooge Committee of Enquiry Report, p.25.

When questioned on the discovery of sandbags in graves, Crawford replied that, at Hooge, 'Which was on the edge of trenches thousands of such sandbags were thrown in to fill up the earth'.[13] Lieutenant Shaylor then made a statement bringing to light issues that had influenced the early work of the company. For example, they had been instructed by the burial officer that 'The particulars on a cross could be taken to be that of the soldier buried beneath', those instructions being cancelled in the following months.[14] The fact that this instruction was issued in the first place is strange, as many crosses placed on battlefield graves were knocked over by explosions and then replaced by a well-meaning Tommy but not necessarily in the right place. Therefore, checking that the details on the cross corresponded to the body buried below was an essential part of the identification process. Lieutenant Shaylor also called into question the testimony of Captain Coghlan of the 126th Labour Company, particularly focussing on Coghlan's claim that very few identification discs were found and the fact that he did not mention the correct way of labelling a body, a procedure followed religiously by Shaylor and his team. The subject of the misidentified German soldier was also explained by the former Lieutenant:

> I notice … that a body of a German was found in a grave marked U.B.S. [Unknown British Soldier]. I distinctly remember this incident. The body was discovered while a grave trench was being dug. At that time, there was no German cemetery available, the fact was mentioned to the Army Burial Officer (Colonel Arbuthnot) and in order to dispose of the matter it was decided to leave the remains and erect a cross as a U.B.S. There was no place where he could have been re-interred and we had no mortuary.[15]

Shaylor also went on to confirm that they did distinguish on the grave markers between British and Dominion soldiers when known. Turning to the subject of bodies not corresponding to crosses or not being in the correct place during the exhumation, Shaylor outlined the following relevant information: 'Our instruction was to dig a trench 4ft deep, usually 40ft long and leave a space of 2 ft between each body … I am of the opinion that if in the reconstruction of Hooge Cemetery has been carried out on a 2ft 6 inch basis that considerable confusion has resulted'.[16]

After examining the cemetery officer's burial books and considering the testimony of Captain Crawford and Lieutenant Shaylor, the committee felt that the situation

---

13   CWGCA: CWGC/1/1/7/B/48: Exhumations. Hooge Committee of Enquiry Report, p.18.
14   CWGCA: CWGC/1/1/7/B/48: Exhumations. Hooge Committee of Enquiry Report, p.19.
15   CWGCA: CWGC/1/1/7/B/48: Exhumations. Hooge Committee of Enquiry Report, p.19.
16   CWGCA: CWGC/1/1/7/B/48: Exhumations. Hooge Committee of Enquiry Report, p.19.

was so serious that all unknown soldiers buried in the cemetery should be exhumed and their remains re-examined for any signs of identification. Accordingly, orders were issued to Major Gardiner of the DADGR&E (Deputy Assistant Director of Graves Registrations and Enquiries) that Captain Coghlan and the 126th Labour Company were to commence work exhuming the approximate 3,000 unidentified graves in November 1920.

In the meantime, a report of the committee's findings of January 1921 was compiled and sent to the Army Council. Whilst finding the work of the 68th Labour Company to be below the standard required in the early days of exhumation, the committee concluded that this was partly due to extenuating circumstances, stating that the 68th Labour Company:

> … Commenced work in the second week of January 1919 … Some notes were issued by G.H.Q. for their guidance; they were expressed to be no more than rough notes and were in fact much less precise than the later instructions that the DGR&E found it necessary to issue. At that time the speedy clearing of the battlefields was probably of higher importance, from sanitary and other considerations, than the minute accuracy in establishing the identity of the bodies that were found. The lack of experience of the 68th Labour Company in this kind of work, the want of detailed instructions, difficulty of housing and administration, the quality of the personnel engaged, were further factors that contributed to a system under which mistakes were apt to occur.[17]

The report went on to give credit to Captain Crawford for realising the shortcomings of the limited instructions issued and for producing a more detailed procedure based on the problems encountered by the 68th Labour Company:

> In May 1919 the Directorate of G.R. & E. assumed responsibility for all the future work of concentration, and in July of that year adopted for general use the complete and able instructions 'For the guidance of exhumation companies in the future', drawn by the officer when commanding the 68th Labour Company, which are acknowledged to have led to an efficient service of identification and reburial. Mr G. Crawford was in command of that company …[18]

The Committee of Enquiry also acknowledged that the unit carrying out the exhumations on behalf of the enquiry, the 126th Labour Company, had distinct advantages over the 68th Labour Company:

---

17 CWGCA: CWGC/1/1/7/B/48: Exhumations. Hooge Committee of Enquiry Report, p.2.
18 CWGCA: CWGC/1/1/7/B/48: Exhumations. Hooge Committee of Enquiry Report, p.2.

It must be remembered that the 126th Labour Company who conducted the exhumations in October 1920 had by that time reached a very high standard of efficiency in establishing identifications and that they were reviewing the work of another company with a not unnatural eagerness to find fault … Moreover after the lapse of twenty months from the date of concentration and very nearly two years from the day that the last shot was fired, the further decomposition of the remains may not only have made a more careful examination less disagreeable but also have revealed clues to identity that were buried in the flesh by the wounds that caused death.[19]

Of the 135 graves examined, the men of the 126th Labour Company were able to establish the identity of three of the 80 unknown graves and disprove the identity of five of the 55 knowns, giving a success rate of 3.75 percent for new identifications. This rate and the fact that the committee believed that the burial errors only occurred up to the date of when Captain Crawford's procedures became policy led to the committee recommending the cessation of the exhumations in the rest of the cemetery:

There are in the cemetery some 5,000 graves in all, of which 3,000 are graves of unknowns. It would be quite impossible … to exhume the unknowns without also exhuming those whose identity has been recorded, for the reason that each row of graves is a continuous trench.

Therefore, apart from the sentimental objections that might be raised by the relatives of those whose identity is recorded, the committee is of the opinion that further exhumation would yield no higher percentage than 3.75 of total new identifications and probably less in inverse proportion as the 68th Labour Company gained experience.[20]

The conclusion of the Committee of Enquiry, the scale of the task, the spectre of finding more errors and the potential bad publicity that would follow no doubt influenced the War Office telegram received by the DADGR&E in Poperinghe in early January 1921 suspending the exhumation work in Hooge Crater Cemetery. By March 1921, the suspension had been confirmed as permanent, with the War Office stating, 'That no good purpose would be served by the carrying out of any more exhumations in this cemetery'.[21]

It seems, however, that mistakes were not just limited to the work of the 68th Labour Company in the Ypres Salient. In March 1921, exhumations took place in Lancashire Cottage Cemetery, and 11 graves were found to contain no bodies; in April 1921, a duplicated grave was opened in Potijze Burial ground and was found to

19   CWGCA: CWGC/1/1/7/B/48: Exhumations. Hooge Committee of Enquiry Report, p.4.
20   CWGCA: CWGC/1/1/7/B/48: Exhumations. Hooge Committee of Enquiry Report, p.5.
21   CWGCA: CWGC/1/1/7/B/48: Exhumations. Hooge Committee of Enquiry Report, p.2.

be empty.[22] In reality, the problem extended right across the Western Front and across all nationalities, with the Australians reporting their own problems in the early 1920s. In fact, in the six months that ended on 28 February 1921, the IWGC reported that 1,200 graves had been examined for the purpose of identification, with around 400 being either completely or partially identified.[23]

The policy of exhumation for identification would soon be scaled back, as plans were put into place in December 1920 for the disbandment of the DGR&E the following year, with the IWGC taking over the majority of its roles.

I will leave the last words on this subject to a 'Canadian bereaved parent' who wrote a letter to the editor of *The Times* whilst searching for her son's grave on the outskirts of Ypres in July 1919:

> Sir, I came from Canada to Belgium a month ago on a very sad errand, to locate the bones of my son killed in battle in Sanctuary Wood, near Ypres in June 1916 … I came 4,000 miles to find the body and give it a decent burial.
>
> What was the surprise and joy of his mother and myself to find his grave and the cross, five minutes after our arrival on the scene, in a cemetery by the roadside at Hooge, two miles east of Ypres, on the Menin Road. The 68th Labour Company had been working in this vicinity since January last, clearing the battlefield of our heroic dead, and gathering them into orderly cemeteries. My son's body was one of the first to be found and removed.
>
> I deem it only fair to these officers and men who are so persistently and faithfully doing this by no means attractive work, that I should acknowledge the debt thousands of parents owe to them, and that I should bespeak for them a little greater recognition and consideration from the public at large. In a dogged and unostentatious way, they are labouring day after day to reclaim the mortal remains of many a beloved son … These trained men go out, search the ground, discover, and, with tender hands, re-bury thousands of graves no-one ever expected to find.[24]

---

22 Commonwealth War Graves Commission Archive (CWGCA) CWGC/1/1/5/26 (WG 1294 PT.1: Exhumation by IWGC).
23 Commonwealth War Graves Commission Archive (CWGCA) CWGC/1/1/3/8 (ADD 1/3/4: Taking Over of DGR&E by IWGC).
24 Commonwealth War Graves Commission Archive (CWGCA) CWGC/8/1/4/1/1/58: *The Times*, 'The Graves Labour Companies, A Visitors Testimony (1919)'.

The grave of Private Hagarty, the son of the aforementioned 'Canadian bereaved parent'. (Photo by Patsy Mahieu.)

13

The Lost Army
Abandoning the Search

Between November 1918 and September 1921, British and Dominion exhumation units had, in the most arduous conditions, recovered, attempted identification and then reburied in excess of 200,000 bodies on the Western Front. In the space of three short years, and largely as a result of Captain Crawford's procedures, the exhumation units had evolved into an efficient and highly specialised body of men skilled in the task of spotting areas where bodies may be concealed, those areas being often invisible to the untrained eye. With most of the old battlefield having been searched between a minimum of six to 20 times and with official recovery rates starting to decline, the question now was how much longer would the British Army continue to look for the missing? The problem facing the War Office was that an estimated balance of nearly 300,000 bodies still needed to be located, recovered and reburied. In short, the search potentially could continue for years, and, at this point, it was far from being completed. In fact, the reality was that, even with the reduced level of personnel engaged in the search, bodies were still being found at a rate of 200 per week.

From as early as December 1920, meetings were being held with the IWGC exploring the aim of disbanding the DGR&E and handing over their roles to the Commission in an effort to devolve the army from its role and responsibility of recovering the missing. In March 1921, it was officially announced by the War Office that the DGR&E was to close down, with the IWGC taking over all of their responsibilities with the exception of the task of body recovery. That task would remain the responsibility of the army exhumation units until their demobilisation and as long as manpower allowed. The IWGC officially took over the remaining duties from the DGR&E during April 1921, with the army setting a target date of September 1921 to have the battlefields of the Western Front completely searched and all visible isolated graves exhumed and reburied in a designated IWGC cemetery. It then planned to cease the search. On 6 August 1921, Lieutenant Colonel James Dick-Cunyngham of the DGR&E stated that, with some exceptions, 'The whole of the battlefield areas of France and Belgium have been finally researched for isolated graves, both British and German. It cannot be guaranteed that no graves either with or without surface indication remained in the area'.[1]

The decision of the army to disband the DGR&E and cease the search for the missing was greeted with surprise and a certain degree of shock by the organisations involved in the recovery of the dead. In order to justify its position, the War Office had cited two main reasons for ceasing the search: the cost to the British taxpayer and the decline in the numbers of bodies being recovered. To those on the ground, however, the decision not only was premature but also, when made known to the British public, had the risk of creating a scandal of huge proportions. For the public, the cost would be immaterial. Their missing fathers, sons and brothers had answered their country's call and had made the ultimate sacrifice, and, as such, the government had a sacred pact with them – everything possible should be done to locate and identify the missing so that their loved ones could receive the burial they deserve. Costs should not be an option. Furthermore, the claim by the War Office that recovery figures were reducing was not strictly true. On paper, they were reducing, but crucially, at the same time, so was the manpower employed in looking for them. The number of men looking for bodies on the Western Front had been in a steady decline since the end of the war. Demobilisation had meant that the original paper strength of around 9,000 men engaged in exhumation work in 1920 had been reduced to eight officers and 1,086 individuals of other ranks by January 1921, with a commitment to reduce it further to 24 officers and 557 other ranks by 1 April 1921 on the dissolution of the DGR&E. To put it quite simply, the fewer people you have looking for bodies, the fewer you will find. The reduction in men was to have a dramatic effect on the level of body recoveries, dropping from between 600–800 per week to an average of 200 per week by September 1921.

The race was now on to complete the search task before the date of demobilisation of the remaining exhumation parties by the end of September 1921. To maximise the number of bodies recovered, the search teams were relieved of certain duties. They no longer exhumed remains already interred in cemeteries for identification purposes or removed cemeteries or groups of graves within cemeteries, focussing purely on locating and exhuming isolated graves. Special exhumations for identification were only to take place if overwhelming evidence could be produced of the likelihood of a positive outcome.

In terms of the Ypres Salient, a large search area still needed to be covered and was designated as still open for searching. The search area contained Steenstraat, Poelcapplle, St. Julian, Boesinghe, Zonnebeke, Becelaere, Gheluvelt, Zandvoorde, Messines, Wytschaete, Voormezeele and Zillebeke.[2] In fact, it was most of the British Army area of operation during the four years of war in the Ypres Salient. There was

1 Hodgkinson, 'Clearing the Dead', <http://www.vlib.us/wwi/resources/clearingthedead.html>, accessed 19 Aug. 2020.
2 CWGCA: CWGC/1/1/3/8 (ADD 1/3/4: Taking Over of DGR&E by IWGC).

little doubt in the eyes of the IWGC that 'a considerable number of bodies still remain in this area and the only limitation which could be placed on the time during which this kind of work would be productive of results is the length of time during which the ground will remain uncultivated'.[3] The reclamation and cultivation of the ground of the Ypres Salient by the returning population was about to have a dramatic impact on the body recovery figures in the coming months and years.

It quickly became obvious that, in the run up to the September deadline, bodies lay everywhere in the Ypres Salient, not only buried in isolated graves but, in many cases, also lying exposed or partly exposed on the surface. As the deadline approached, the list of unattended bodies and graves continued to grow, with minimal staff or agreed procedure in place to deal with them except for the two specially created flying squads who were working flat out from dawn to dusk in an effort to recover the isolated graves and exposed bodies as they were reported. On 16 August 1921, Australia House had already raised its concerns to the IWGC when it asked for confirmation of the arrangements that had been put in place for future exhumation work. A second letter followed, acknowledging the procedure put into place with the French but querying what the procedure was to be in Belgium. Major Allen of the AGS in Poperinge had already run into problems. Having discovered several sets of remains, he had proceeded to report them as usual to the local British Army labour company, the unit in question being the 126th Labour Company under the command of Captain Ryan. The letter stated:

> A telegram has been received this day from the Inspector, Australian Graves Services, Belgium stating that a large number of bodies have been discovered in isolated graves and are now awaiting reinterment. He also states that the Exhumation Companies in his area are unable to deal with this question as they are now in the process of disbandment.
>
> It will therefore be very much appreciated if you can advise this Office when you can anticipate that the Imperial War Graves Commission will be in a position to deal with this question.[4]

The letter was dated 8 September 1921, and it is interesting to note that, even at this late stage, there seems to have been no clear instruction on what to do with the bodies as the exhumation companies demobilised and that there was the misconception that the IWGC would be responsible for the exhumation and recovery of the bodies. This was not and was never intended to be the case. Major Allen's list of bodies highlighted the true picture of the state of body recoveries in the Ypres Salient, and it was a very different picture to the one painted by Lieutenant Colonel James Dick-Cunyngham in

---

3   CWGCA: CWGC/1/1/3/8 (ADD 1/3/4: Taking Over of DGR&E by IWGC).
4   Commonwealth War Graves Commission (CWGCA) CWGC/1/1/7/B/45 (WG 1294/3 PT.4: Exhumation France and Belgium Part 4).

the August of that year. In his report, Major Allen lists 20 instances of isolated graves and exposed bodies, some instances describing multiple bodies and burials and nearly all in the Ypres Salient. For example:

3. Remains of British Soldier behind ruined house used as shelter and pillbox … these remains were exposed to view …
4. Remains of two Brit. Soldiers on the right of the Zonnebeke-Langemarck Road.
5. Body of an English Soldier wrapped in canvas and situated approx. 100 yards beyond St Julien Cemetery …
6. Several bodies close to Picketts factory.
7. Twelve or more bodies (British) … behind Cheddar Villa Cemetery.
10. Body of a Scotch Officer … Part of this body was exposed to view but has been covered with soil.
11. Body of a British Soldier about 50 yards from Irish Cemetery … partially uncovered and at foot of tree.
14. Remains of two bodies close by Railway Line, Poelcapelle.
15. Eight bodies at different locations in Sanctuary Wood …
17. Trench … containing three or four bodies exposed to view. Reports have been received that this trench is full of bodies.
20. Two British Soldiers off road from Langemarck to Zonnebeke.[5]

On 12 September 1921, all exhumation personnel of No.1 District (incorporating the Ypres Salient) proceeded for dispersal to finally be sent home to their friends and family. Having achieved what they did in terms of body recoveries and the level of professionalism that they had attained meant that a bad taste must have been left in the mouths of some of these men, knowing that the task was far from completion and that it was about to be left in the hands of those who could not give it the same love, care and attention.

In the short term, something needed to be organised to bridge the gap between the departure of the exhumation units and the start of the new procedures in the Ypres Salient. Bodies were being reported on a daily basis, and there was little to no organisation in place to deal with them. In a document dated 19 September 1921 and sent to Fabian Ware, the situation in Belgium was inferred to as being at crisis levels. Major H. F. Chettle of the IWGC started the report that was entitled 'Exhumation in Belgium' by stating, 'I have to report as follows on the question of exhumation in Belgium, I am submitting a separate report as regards France, where the crisis is less

---

5   CWGCA: CWGC/1/1/7/B/45 (WG 1294/3 PT.4: Exhumation France and Belgium Part 4).

acute'.⁶ The situation in the Ypres Salient was indeed dire, but, as in all situations, people pull together in an effort to relieve the pressure. A Belgian gang master whose men were engaged in battlefield clearance volunteered to erect crosses on the sites where remains were discovered, and 'Colonel Roy and Major Williams, helped by Major Allen and using British gardeners (who are glad to help), are removing the remains in box cars, identifying them, and lightly burying them in Hooge Crater Cemetery pending the receipt of instructions for final reburial'.⁷

The discussions on how to replace the work of the exhumation units had started at an early stage. The two consistent themes of the discussion were the War Office's insistence that there should be no permanent presence of army exhumation units on the Western Front and the IWGC's insistence that they could and would not be responsible for the search for and exhumation of bodies, with Major H. F. Chettle of the IWGC stating:

> It is not considered practicable for the Commission to set up or maintain a special exhumation staff on the lines recently maintained by the army, but that the limit to which the Commission can go in this matter is that of seeing that bodies brought to light and notified to them have proper burial and are seen before internment by an officer competent to identify.⁸

After much discussion, and with various solutions being put forward (including the use of IWGC gardeners for exhumations), it was agreed that the IWGC would be responsible for 'founds' only, that is to say, a body reported by a third party such as a farmer. Upon the receipt of such a report, a representative of the IWGC would attend the scene. The actual work of exhuming and removing the body would be performed by local workers employed as and when needed, with the work being overseen by the IWGC officer. There was to be no active search program. One of the motivations of the IWGC in pursuing this policy was to detach themselves from any potential bad press that may have arisen because of the potential lack of experience and professionalism of Belgian workers employed in the task. Lieutenant Colonel H. Ellissen of the IWGC recorded his thoughts on the subject in a memo dated 1921. Commenting on a discussion regarding the future procedure of exhumations in France and Belgium and, in particular, the proposed (but ultimately denied) use of IWGC gardeners, he stated:

---

6   CWGCA: CWGC/1/1/7/B/45 (WG 1294/3 PT.4: Exhumation France and Belgium Part 4).
7   CWGCA: CWGC/1/1/7/B/45 (WG 1294/3 PT.4: Exhumation France and Belgium Part 4).
8   CWGCA: CWGC/1/1/5/26 (WG 1294 PT.1: Exhumation by IWGC).

I thought the reason for this procedure was in order to avoid the possibility of scandal attaching to the Commission in the event of any irreverence in the manner of carrying out the duty of reinterment. No.1 of Col. Gell's minute seems to contemplate the very thing which it was desired to avoid i.e., the possibility of a visitor to a cemetery seeing a Commission gardener carrying remains on his bicycle about the country.[9]

By December 1921, the new procedure was in place in the Ypres Salient, and No. 1 Area's establishment was at full strength. An Australian representative was also attached to the unit, and the civilian labour required had been obtained on an as-and-when-needed basis. The use of unskilled and 'foreign' labour in the task of exhumation was to prove to be a controversial one. The professionalism and success in the art of body spotting of the exhumation units of the army had not gone unnoticed nor had their success rates in identifying the remains recovered. In fact, the IWGC had raised fears of the accuracy of the work of third-party work units engaged in exhumation when they stated:

Unless previously experienced personnel are employed, I am of the opinion 80 percent of the bodies which still remain to be picked up, would never be found. Unexperienced men on search parties would never be able to trace were remains were buried under the present conditions. The principal factor i.e., that the remains which are still to be found, and those, which previous search parties have passed over unnoticed, must not be lost sight of, and this only further emphasises the importance of the employment of men who have previous experience and local knowledge, this latter being as equally important as the former.[10]

As previously agreed, the DGR&E, upon the cessation of their duties, presented the IWGC with a certificate of work completed, with special reference being made to work completed since 31 March 1921. The certificate was carefully worded and somewhat ambiguous with regards to the areas searched and the areas left to be searched. Clearly designed to absolve the DGR&E from any future criticism and possible scandal, it also served (and rightly so) to provide the IWGC with a degree of protection should future questions be asked on the subject of the withdrawal of the army in the search for bodies. The certificate stated, 'The areas allotted and known as the British Zone have been cleared of all visible isolated graves, as a result of careful search by Exhumation Parties. This should not be taken to mean that all isolated British remains have been picked up, and that the areas are definitely and finally

9   CWGCA: CWGC/1/1/5/26 (WG 1294 PT.1: Exhumation by IWGC).
10 CWGCA: CWGC/1/1/5/26 (WG 1294 PT.1: Exhumation by IWGC).

cleared'.[11] In essence, the certificate stated that the exhumation work was far from being completed in all areas, with the recognition that many bodies may still lie in the areas previously declared as searched and closed by the army. The phrase 'visible isolated graves' was a carefully chosen one, as the IWGC clearly noted, 'This term is certainly ambiguous. To the average person walking over the Battlefields, very few signs of graves would be discovered, but to an experienced Search-Exhumation party many would still be found'.[12]

And that exactly was the point. Not only had the army ceased the search for the missing, knowing it was far from completed, but it had also disbanded and dispersed the only men who had experience in searching for them, leaving the IWGC to deal with the problem with a limited budget and men of little experience. If the army had delayed the withdrawal for another 12 months, the scenario could have been very different, with the IWGC reporting that:

> It will be noticed that Major Williams is strongly against the abandonment of the research work; and he believes it could be completed, with this staff, in nine months (so far as Belgium is concerned). He assures me that he and Captain Ryan could maintain the high standard of conduct of the men of 126 Exhumation Company if they had twenty men of that Company under them as civilian exhumers.[13]

But this was not to be, and, within a few days, on 12 September 1921, Captain Ryan and his experienced team of exhumers were on their way home for demobilisation. It was now down to the IWGC to attempt to recover the fallen in the Ypres Salient.

Just as Captain Ryan and his team were arriving back in England and going through the process of demobilisation, the story broke in the national press that the army's role in the search for the missing on the Western Front was about cease. On 12 September 1921, the *Daily Mail*, under the heading 'SOLDIER'S GRAVES. BITTER AUSTRALIAN PROTEST. ARMY CEASING WORK OF RECOVERY', ran a story based on a cablegram received from Mr. Edward Hempenstall, J.P., a leading businessman of Queensland Australia. The details of the story had been substantiated by a *Daily Mail* reporter before publication, and the article did not make for good reading for the authorities. Mr. Hempenstall alleged that:

> Bodies are being recovered in the Ypres, Passchendaele, Zonnebeke, and Pozières districts and average over 300 weekly. In the past three months April to July, 10,000 were recorded, with a big percentage fully identified.

---

11   CWGCA: CWGC/1/1/5/26 (WG 1294 PT.1: Exhumation by IWGC).
12   CWGCA: CWGC/1/1/5/26 (WG 1294 PT.1: Exhumation by IWGC).
13   CWGCA: CWGC/1/1/7/B/45 (WG 1294/3 PT.4: Exhumation France and Belgium Part 4).

> I have today (September 9) seen a written notification of nearly 100 British and Australian bodies found. Sixteen were found this day in one hour and I undertake to point out 1000 covered. Yet the officials here are powerless to take any further steps, and these bodies, now easily recoverable by the expert, highly experienced military working staffs, must soon be ploughed into the earth by farmers or covered over by builders.[14]

The article continued with Mr. Hempenstall outlining the percentage of Australian bodies found and then criticising the use of civilian labour versus expert military personnel, closing with the statement, 'I consider the London handling of this national matter an utter disgrace'.[15]

The *Daily Mail* asked the War Office for comment, who, plainly stalling for time, replied that 'The matter did not come under their department', with the IWGC stating that 'The matter was now under consideration and would be dealt with later'.[16]

More allegations were to follow when Mr. Hempenstall sent a second cablegram to the editor of the *Daily Mail*, the details of which they duly printed the following day. The article alleged the discovery of more unrecovered bodies, including 'One area at Passchendaele was declared to be clean by London last September, but between that month and February of this year 8,000 further bodies were recovered from this area'.[17] The editors of the *Daily Mail* expressed a degree of disbelief that the search for the fallen was being abandoned. Anxious to give the War Office the benefit of the doubt, the newspaper commented, 'We can only assume that a misunderstanding has occurred in connection with the transference of the Director of War Graves sad duties to the War Graves Commission, and we hope that the fears expressed by Hempenstall may prove unfounded'. They followed up by declaring, 'A clear and satisfactory official statement should be made at once'.[18] By this point, several other newspapers had picked up on the story and were asking the War Office for clarification and an official statement, with London's *Evening Standard* printing on 14 September 1921, 'Officialdom today declined to discuss the subject – I cannot understand why. A full and frank statement is certainly very essential. And it must be prompt'.[19]

---

14 CWGCA: CWGC/1/1/7/B/45 (WG 1294/3 PT.4: Exhumation France and Belgium Part 4).
15 CWGCA: CWGC/1/1/7/B/45 (WG 1294/3 PT.4: Exhumation France and Belgium Part 4).
16 CWGCA: CWGC/1/1/7/B/45 (WG 1294/3 PT.4: Exhumation France and Belgium Part 4).
17 CWGCA: CWGC/1/1/7/B/45 (WG 1294/3 PT.4: Exhumation France and Belgium Part 4).
18 CWGCA: CWGC/1/1/7/B/45 (WG 1294/3 PT.4: Exhumation France and Belgium Part 4).
19 CWGCA: CWGC/1/1/7/B/45 (WG 1294/3 PT.4: Exhumation France and Belgium Part 4).

The decision to cease the search had the whiff of scandal about it, something that the committee of the IWGC had already recognised and wanted to disassociate themselves from in an effort to protect their own credibility. During the thirty-seventh meeting of the IWGC on 18 October 1921 – attended by (amongst others) Secretary of State for War Sir Laming Worthington-Evans, High Commissioner for Australia M. L. Shepherd, Rudyard Kipling, Sir Robert Hudson and H. Maddocks – the committee recorded their fears and objections:

> Mr. Kipling desired that it should be made quite clear that it was the War Office who had stopped the exhumation and search.
>
> Mr. Maddocks thought it should also be made clear that the whole ground had been covered by the war office search parties. They must consider public sentiments in this matter.
>
> Sir Robert Hudson said that if it was known to the public that bodies were being found at the rate of 200 a week at the time the search parties were disbanded, the public would want an explanation.[20]

The War Office knew, of course, that the story would break sooner or later and that an official statement would have to be released in order to address 'public anxiety'. After questions were raised in the Houses of Parliament, Secretary of State for War Sir Laming Worthington-Evans, having attended the meeting of the IWGC in October, released a statement that was subsequently printed in *The Times* on 10 November 1921. He had clearly done his homework:

> Since the Armistice the whole battlefield area in France and Flanders has been systematically searched at least six times. Some areas in which the fighting had been particularly heavy, were searched as many as 20 times. In the spring of 1920, the work was easy and rapid owing to the number of surface indications, but since then in the cases of, approximately, 90 percent of the bodies found, there was no surface indication. These invisible graves were found by various local indications recognised by the experience of the exhumation parties. It is probable that a number of these invisible graves have not yet been found, and are likely to be brought to light during the work of reconstruction and in the opening up of areas at present inaccessible owing to the thickness of undergrowth, the marshiness of land etc. The searching, however, was most thorough, as the whole of the battlefield area was divided into map squares, to which a platoon under a subaltern was allotted. The actual search party usually

---

20 Commonwealth War Graves Commission Archive (CWGCA) CWGC/2/2/1/6: 'IWGC 18 October 1921', Commission Meeting Minutes.

consisted of about 12 men under a senior non-commissioned officer. These parties systematically searched the whole of the surface of the areas.[21]

The statement did little to allay the fears of the public. After all, the facts were there for all to see: 300,000 sets of remains were still missing on the Western Front, and only a percentage of those would have been completely destroyed by wartime action.

---

21 Hodgkinson, 'Clearing the Dead', <http://www.vlib.us/wwi/resources/clearingthedead.html>, accessed 19 Aug. 2020.

14

The Recovery Restarts
The IWGC Takes Up the Torch

Meanwhile, back in the Ypres Salient, the situation had started to improve. No. 1 Area's compliment of staff was up to full strength, reporting one officer, seven field assistants, one part-time clerk and 14 local labourers, of which 10 were British and four were Belgian. The staff were being kept busy, as bodies were starting to appear in previously searched areas. In some numbers, remains that were invisible in the winter became visible in the summer as the sun dried the water in the shell holes, revealing the horrors that had been concealed in its murky depths, whilst 'Remains that are invisible in summer are occasionally visible in winter'.[1]

The main reason for the continuing recovery of bodies in the Ypres Salient was the reconstruction work that was taking place. Since the early 1920s, the local population had started to return to the so-called 'devastated regions', anxious to rebuild their properties, clear their land and resume farming. In order to clear and level the old battlefields, gangs of workmen were employed by the Belgian government to clear the land of war materials, fill in shell holes and level the land. Each gang consisted of one foreman and 250 men; the gangs worked in pairs, with one gang roughly levelling the land and the second gang then digging it over. Each gang covered roughly two-and-a-half hectares per day and was paid by piecework; in other words, the more work they completed, the more they were paid.[2] The fact that they were paid in this way was initially to prove problematic with regards to them reporting any British bodies they may recover. The gangs were under strict instruction to report all body finds by the Belgian authorities, but, in practice, many did not because they lost time and therefore pay by doing so, thus either leaving the remains exposed or simply ploughing them over. A further disincentive for them to report British bodies was the fact that

---

1 CWGCA: CWGC/1/1/7/B/45 (WG 1294/3 PT.4: Exhumation France and Belgium Part 4).
2 CWGCA: CWGC/1/1/7/B/45 (WG 1294/3 PT.4: Exhumation France and Belgium Part 4).

the Belgian and French governments paid them two francs for every Belgian, French and German body reported. The British, however, paid them nothing, and, since the withdrawal of the DGR&E, there was no personnel to supervise their work as had been the case previously. At that point in 1921, the IWGC estimated between 30–40 gangs working in the devasted areas of Belgium and that approximately 25 sets of remains would be reported per week if they did not pay the two francs and around 70 sets of remains reported if they did. The lack of a two-franc incentive for the recovery of British bodies resulted in a macabre fraud amongst some of the more unscrupulous individuals of the agricultural community and the men of the Belgian clearance teams, with British equipment being removed from a British body and replaced with an item of German, French or Belgian equipment in order for the man who found the body to be able to collect his 'reward'.

Not all of the gangs were so mercenary in their actions, as many of them adhered to the law not only out of necessity but also because of their own moral values and the sense of what was the right thing to do. One such foreman was Monsieur Oscar-Joseph de Groote of Ste. Croix, Bruges. It was Monsieur de Groote who had previously volunteered to mark graves with wooden crosses and name labels when there were no British personnel available to do perform the task. Monsieur de Groote was in charge of a working party of 500 men and had discovered and reported several hundred British bodies. The IWGC reported that 'Monsieur de Groote, who takes a personal interest in our dead and sacks his men if he finds them failing to report, is an unexpected exception to the general attitude of the "reconstruction" personnel'.[3] As a result of these findings, and in an effort to increase body finds and cut out the macabre practice of swapping equipment on bodies, a bounty of two francs was made available for each British body reported to the IWGC by local civilians and workers.

Work continued at pace in the Salient, with new body recoveries being reported every day and large areas of the Salient still needing to be researched. In December 1921, Lieutenant Colonel Gell of the IWGC reported on his recent tour of the Western Front that, in contradiction to Sir Laming Worthington-Evans' statement to the House of Commons the previous October, in terms of search, 'Patches of country are left untouched'.[4] On 19 December 1921, Gell arrived in the Ypres Salient and started a three-day inspection of the area. His report provides fascinating insight into the conditions of the Ypres Salient at the time:

> To Railway Wood, where a body was reported by an intelligent gang foreman … His regiment was the Cheshire … probably an N.C.O.

---

3 CWGCA: CWGC/1/1/7/B/45 (WG 1294/3 PT.4: Exhumation France and Belgium Part 4).
4 Commonwealth War Graves Commission Archive (CWGCA) CWGC/1/1/5/26 (WG 1294 PT.1: Journal of Lieutenant Colonel Gell).

I walked across to Railway Wood Cemetery … Just outside the cemetery I found two graves, but it was impossible to identify them even as British when they were disinterred. They will be reburied as 'Unknown Soldiers'.

To Tower Hamlets (Gheluveldt). Body reported by one of a gang. This not identified even partially, though careful search was made, the boots scraped, and the coloured silk handkerchief examined. This was probably a 1914 soldier as the date of his boots was 1914. It is therefore remarkable that the silk handkerchief should have been so well preserved, but I am assured that there is nothing other than metals which resists decay better than silk. In this case every bit of cloth was completely decayed, but after washing the silk handkerchief would be as bright and good as on the day it was buried. We walked towards Shrewsbury Forest along the Houthem Road. A man stood beckoning to us from among some mounds of debris. He told me that he had uncovered two skulls, and that two bodies lay in this and that direction. One proved to be British, of the Hampshire Regiment (pay book also recovered); the other was a German. It looked from their position that they had killed one the other, and that a shell had come along and buried them where they lay. The Germans bayonet was of the saw variety.

To St Eloi, where we found a lorry waiting to receive the seven bodies picked up yesterday by Assistant Hubbard and a small party … Thence to Messines. The foreman of the gang working here was interviewed. One point I noticed here which is common to nearly all the areas in which the gangs are clearing. The whole area is seldom completely cleared before the gang is moved to another. Patches of country are left untouched. The reason may be that a private owner has asked to be allowed to level his own property, or that the money estimate for this particular plot of land has been exceeded. It will readily be understood that this complicates the task of our re-interment personnel, as it is necessary for them to watch the movements of these private owners in addition to those of the gang foreman. Comparatively few British bodies have been found on the Messines Ridge, and very few, if any, since the Commission took up the duty of re-internment.

To Dam Strasse. This is a road about one and a half miles long … It is evident that the position must have cost many British lives … I felt certain that many more British bodies would be uncovered if any sort of reconstruction was attempted. Clearing was taking place in the vicinity and the gangs were invited to report any bodies found.

To Tyne Cot. Picked up a blanched skull just behind the battalion H.Q. dug-out in the embankment of the Broodseinde Cutting. This will be reburied tonight in La Brique, but will not be registered. An entombed R.F.A. observing officer was found close by this spot today, in an old O.P. [observation post] that had been knocked in by a shell. The telephone and receiver were beside him.

To Polygone Butt. Nearby I watched the lifting of a New Zealander and an Australian. Both were in shell holes. The latter was identified by his tunic which was of Australian pattern …

Out past St Jean on the road to Langemarck, where a body was reported. Having received a 'phone' message that the work of removing two British plots from Hazebrouck C.C. [Civilian Cemetery] had commenced, I went there to see that all was in order and the proceedings being properly watched … The Fossayeur [grave digger] asserts confidently that some of the graves marked with one cross and one name, contain three or four bodies. He says the burials of this kind took place at the time of the first gas attack and resulted from it.[5]

By the end of April 1922, there were still large areas to be cleared in the Ypres Salient between Grafenstafel and Zonnebeke, Blackwatch Corner and isolated patches of ground that had been left uncleared due to ground conditions or because of a difficult owner. All the woods and wooded land still needed to be cleared, as did, to a large extent, any areas of waterlogged ground. There were still several land-clearing gangs in operation in the area, with a reported nine large gangs of around 30 men each and 20 gangs of around 10 men each occupied in different parts of the Salient. Lieutenant Colonel Gell reported that, by that time, 'Half of the remains being found at the moment are found by cultivators ploughing deep or cutting drains after the clearing and levelling has been finished. The farmers now report well, telephone messages often being received'.[6]

Eventually, the work of the Belgian clearance gangs would cease, as each piece of land was cleared and its usage given back to its rightful owners. In September 1921, Major Williams of the IWGC predicted that 'Reconstruction will be complete in less than nine months from now', whilst the Belgian foreman Monsieur de Groote suggested a time frame of six months, with Sanctuary Wood being levelled and Observatory Ridge being blown up by Christmas.[7]

As time passed, the amount of labour engaged in clearing the Salient dwindled. However, the rate of body recoveries was to remain fairly consistent for at least the next 10 years, with around 52 percent of the total being reported by metal searchers, 30 percent by farmers or others and 18 percent by official government search parties. The actual body recover figures themselves are truly astounding and reveal the army's decision to cease the search for the missing in 1921 as being, at best, premature and, at worst, reckless. Even as late as 1927, newspapers were reporting that 4,000 bodies were still being recovered in France and Belgium each year. Between the years of 1921

---

5   CWGCA: CWGC/1/1/5/26 (WG 1294 PT.1: Journal of Lieutenant Colonel Gell).
6   CWGCA: CWGC/1/1/5/26 (WG 1294 PT.1: Journal of Lieutenant Colonel Gell).
7   CWGCA: CWGC/1/1/7/B/45 (WG 1294/3 PT.4: Exhumation France and Belgium Part 4).

and 1937, approximately 38,000 bodies were recovered by the IWGC and civilian clearance teams.

The interesting question is how many extra bodies would have been found if specialist search teams had remained in use on the Western Front? We will never know for sure, but if you work on the IWGC assumption that 80 percent of bodies would be missed by inexperienced workers, it raises the possibility of a total of 152,000 bodies could have been recovered in France and Belgium as opposed to the actual 38,000 recovered during the period of 1921–1937, which is a large proportion of the War Office's official figures of 175,000 missing sets of remains as estimated in 1927. A simplistic calculation I know, and the reality is that a large proportion would not have been found. However, logic dictates it could well have been of huge benefit had the search teams stayed on. Whatever the figures, that window of opportunity was closed when the DGR&E disbanded in 1921, leaving many families without a grave to visit and the process of closure a much more difficult task to achieve.

15

Bringing the Boys Home?
The Question of Repatriation

> *The country took him and the country should bring him back ...*
> Ruth Jervis, bereaved mother.[1]

There is no doubt that Sir Fabian Ware was a man of principle and strong will, attributes that would come to influence his decision-making process, in particular, concerning a policy that was to turn out to be one of the most controversial with regards to the management of war graves, that policy being the ideal of equality in death. Right from the start of his association with the GRC and perhaps reflecting the changing politics of the time, Ware was of the belief that in death – irrespective of background, rank and colour – all members of the British armed forces should be treated equally, each man or woman having fought and died for the same cause, each one of them giving the most precious, irreplaceable commodity that they owned: in short, their future, their life. It was because of this belief that Ware decided there should be no official policy of repatriation of war dead of the British Empire's armies. This decision was to prove to be even more contentious than the topic of the recovery of the dead and be a topic that persistently hounded the DGR&E and the IWGC, a topic that caused questions to be raised in Parliament and at higher levels.

There had been repatriations of British war dead from the Western Front in the early days of the war. Between August 1914 and October 1915, there were 53 repatriations of the bodies of British army personnel from the Western Front. Of the 53 repatriations, only two came from the ranks. A staggering 51 of the repatriations were officers, with many coming from wealthy and influential families, the highest rank being Field Marshall Sir Frederick Sleigh Roberts killed on 14 November 1914. The case that spurred Fabian Ware into action was that of Lieutenant William Glynne

---

1   Richard Van Emden, *Missing: The Need for Closure after the Great War* (Barnsley: Pen and Sword, 2019), p.146.

Charles Gladstone of the 1st Battalion Royal Welsh Fusiliers, a lord lieutenant and the grandson of late Prime Minister W. E. Gladstone. KIA in France on 13 April 1915, Lieutenant Gladstone's body was disinterred under fire and had arrived back at the family seat of Hawarden Wales, where it was reburied on 23 April 1915 with 'an almost state-like funeral'.[2] It had been the wish of William's mother that his body should be brought home, and so his uncle Henry Neville Baron Gladstone contacted Herbert Henry Asquith, the British prime minister of the time, who in turn communicated with the King. It was with the King's approval that the War Office issued the necessary orders for the retrieval of the body of the 29-year-old King's Lieutenant. Henry Gladstone then proceeded to France, where he was given every assistance by the military authorities in order to affect the recovery of his nephew's body.

In terms of the Gladstone family, the retrieval of William's body was commendable and understandable, giving comfort and closure to his grieving mother and family. However, there was one factor that the majority of grieving mothers in Great Britain at the time did not, as the Gladstone family did, possess – that factor being privilege. As a long-standing family of the British upper class, the Gladstones could make use of their social connections in order to get the desired result, an option that the proverbial Mrs. Smith, a mother of a 19-year-old factory worker, would definitely not have had. Fabian Ware was acutely aware of this. Determined that this imbalance in British society should not be used to discriminate against the poorer classes – whose loss of their loved ones was felt just as keenly, and was no less important than, the loss of a member of the aristocracy – Ware approached the Adjutant General of the army and persuaded him to issue an order to stop the practice of exhumation and repatriation for the duration of the war. The Adjutant General agreed and issued the order 'On the account of the difficulties of treating impartially the claims advanced by persons of a different social standing'.[3] Ware had, in the short term, bought himself some breathing space. If the policy of non-repatriation was to be followed through, then careful thought needed to be applied to the subject, as it was sure to become an emotive issue and a political hot potato.

During the first meeting of the IWGC on 20 November 1917, it was announced that an agreement had been reached on 9 August 1917 with the Belgian government for land to be gifted in perpetuity to accommodate the graves of British and Dominion soldiers who fell on Belgian soil. After being recorded in the meeting as 'a noble and generous act', Rudyard Kipling went a step further when he said:

---

2   'Gladstone, William Glynne Charles', *Flintshire War Memorials*, <https://www.flintshirewarmemorials.com/memorials/hawarden-memorial/hawarden-sodliers-2/william-glynne-charles-gladstone>, accessed 25 June 2021.
3   Philip Longworth, *The Unending Vigil: A History of the Commonwealth War Graves Commission, 1917-1967* (Barnsley: Pen and Sword, 2020), p.14.

> There was no portion of the Empire and hardly any race within the Empire that was not represented among the vast cloud of witnesses to freedom that lie on the Flanders front; and there was no portion of our Empire that would not be moved with gratitude to Belgium the great-hearted country that had taken our dead to her breast for ever.[4]

The decision of the Belgians, and of the French a few months before them, in gifting the land for the cemeteries for the armies of the British Empire was one that was to be used by the IWGC in the coming years to justify and reinforce their strict policy of non-repatriation.

The immediate problem faced by the IWGC was that the official ban on repatriation only lasted for the duration of the war, and, upon its conclusion, the IWGC almost immediately started to receive correspondence requesting the repatriation of soldiers' remains. The IWGC made their stance on the subject very clear when, in response to the growing list of requests, they published the following statement in a report dated December 1918:

> With regards to the removal of bodies to their native countries, the Commission were aware of a strong desire in a small number of cases that such exhumation should be permitted; but the reasons to the contrary appeared to them overwhelming. To allow removal by a few individuals (of necessity only those who could afford the cost) would be contrary to the principle of equality of treatment, to empty some 400,000 identified graves would be a colossal work and would be opposed to the spirit in which the Empire had gratefully accepted the offers made by the Governments of France, Belgium, Italy and Greece to provide land in perpetuity for our cemeteries, and to 'adopt' our dead. The Commission felt that a higher ideal than that of private burial at home is embodied in these war cemeteries in foreign lands, where those who fought and fell together, officers and men, lie together in their last resting place, facing the line they gave their lives to maintain. They felt sure (and the evidence available to them confirmed the feeling) that the dead themselves, in whom the sense of comradeship was so strong, would have preferred to lie with their comrades. These British cemeteries in foreign lands would be the symbol of future generations of the common purpose, the common devotion, the common sacrifice of all ranks in a united Empire. This view has already been expressed in some of the Overseas Dominions, and the Commission were strongly of opinion

---

4   Commonwealth War Graves Commission Archive (CWGCA) CWGC/2/2/1/6: 'IWGC 20 November 1917', Commission Meeting Minutes.

that it would commend itself to the large majority of the British people, as the higher and nobler course.⁵

The Commission had set out their stall and was determined to defend their principles no matter what and whom they came up against, firmly believing that not only was it the right thing to do but they also had the support of the majority of the public. This was, however, only the start of what was to turn out to be a long and protracted bone of contention amongst some elements of British society. The Commission, of course, had foreseen the potential for unfavourable reactions and so, in an effort to remove themselves from the direct firing line, had negotiated with both the French and Belgian governments to ban exhumations of soldiers on their soil no matter what their nationality unless it was for concentrating isolated graves into a pre-agreed burial ground, with the Belgian government citing hygiene reasons and the possible delay on the reconstruction of its lands caused by a mass removal of human remains. Both the French and Belgian governments had willingly agreed to this, with it being written in the Anglo–French agreement of 26 November 1918 and finally being passed into Belgian law by December 1919.⁶ This was, in effect, the Commission's 'get out of jail card' with regards to repatriations in 1919 and the early 1920s, with many written requests for repatriation receiving a reply that, in part, passed on the responsibility for the decision onto the Belgians and the French.

During the course of 1919, there was a steady stream of letters, at a rate of around 90 per week, arriving at the door of the IWGC requesting information on how to repatriate remains. In October 1919, the Commission received a request from a Mr. Thompson of Sydenham to organise the repatriation of his son. The request was refused, with Mr. Thompson receiving what was to become a fairly standard reply: 'I deeply regret to inform you that permission cannot be obtained from the French authorities for this exhumation to take place. The exhumation and transportation of the bodies of Officers and men who fell and are buried in France is forbidden under a decree made by the French Government'.⁷ On 12 December 1919, the IWGC received a request for repatriation from Australia House in London. The request in question referred to the body of Major General William Holmes of the AIF buried in Steenwerck Cemetery near Armentieres, France. Major General Holmes was killed by a German artillery shell close to Messines and died of his wounds on 2 July 1917. Holmes was the most senior Australian officer to be killed on the Western Front, and

---

5   Commonwealth War Graves Commission Archive (CWGCA) CWGC/1/1/7/B/43 (WG 1294/3 PT.2: Exhumation France and Belgium Part 2).
6   CWGCA: CWGC/1/1/7/B/43 (WG 1294/3 PT.2: Exhumation France and Belgium Part 2).
7   CWGCA: CWGC/1/1/7/B/43 (WG 1294/3 PT.2: Exhumation France and Belgium Part 2).

the people of New South Wales thought it would be a 'splendid tribute' to bring his body home.[8] The request was again refused.

The argument continued to rage with questions being asked in the Houses of Parliament. Letters were received quoting the wording of the Treaty of Versailles in an attempt to circumvent the regulations, and questions were asked on the legalities of the decision and who actually owned the bodies in question, the state or the families? The IWGC stood firm in the face of this pressure and continued to refuse all requests for repatriation. The pressure grew when, in 1920, the BWGA (British War Graves Association) was formed by a Mrs. Sarah Smith and, within a few months of its creation, reported a membership of 2,000 members, all of whom did not agree with the Commission's policy, many of them being mothers and wives of the fallen in Belgium and France. The BWGA continued to apply pressure by organising petitions, mass meetings and questions to be raised in the House of Commons. The BWGA quickly found they had friends in high places – in particular, Lady Shelbourne, who showed a surprising lack of acknowledgement of the political situation in Europe when she published an article entitled 'National Socialism in War Cemeteries' and accused the IWGC of 'collectivism and socialism in which individuals' rights were swept away by the stroke of the pen'.[9] Lady Shelbourne seems to have missed the point. It was the individuals' rights that the IWGC were trying to protect, the rights of everybody for fair and equal treatment, not just those who had a life of privilege and influence. Again, to their credit, the IWGC stood firm. It was not all voices of denunciation, however, with the IWGC receiving support for their policy from people of influence to the man in the street. In December 1918, Henry Cook from Guildford wrote to the IWGC:

> I hope you will pardon my writing to express my thanks to you on your decision in bringing into the cemeteries the bodies buried in isolated graves. I am a father of two dear boys buried in isolated graves, much as myself and many dear parents would like to have them buried in their own parish cemetery, yet where the brave lads who fought and fell together is a very fitting place for them to rest in peace.[10]

The IWGC were to lose the protection afforded by the French and Belgian decrees banning the exhumation and movement of bodies in late 1920s. As a result of the French bowing to American pressure to allow the repatriation of their war dead, public pressure mounted in France and Belgium for the repatriation of their own

---

8   CWGCA: CWGC/1/1/7/B/43 (WG 1294/3 PT.2: Exhumation France and Belgium Part 2).
9   CWGCA: CWGC/1/1/7/B/43 (WG 1294/3 PT.2: Exhumation France and Belgium Part 2).
10 CWGCA: CWGC/1/1/7/B/42 (WG 1294/3 PT.1: Exhumation France and Belgium Part 1).

soldiers. Accordingly, both decrees were no longer extended, denying their use as a reason for non-repatriation to the IWGC. The decision galvanised organisations such as the BWGA and individuals to further press for the repatriations of their loved ones. A steady stream of complaints and demands followed, and questions were again raised in the House of Commons, all leading to an official announcement in early 1922 that a final decision was made and that there was to be no repatriation. On 3–4 March 1922, Britain's press ran with the following headlines: 'Our War Dead, No Bodies to be Brought to English Graves', 'Bodies not to be Brought Home for Reburial' and 'Equality of Treatment: No removal of Remains'.[11]

The formidable Sarah Smith and the BWGA would continue their campaign right into 1924, when it seems that they had admitted that they had lost their fight. By 1922, safe in the knowledge that they had the support of the government and the majority of the British public, the IWGC had adopted a policy of indifference towards the BWGA, ignoring much of their correspondence and getting on with the job at hand – that of providing a fitting resting place for the fallen. It is quite plain, however, that, although the Commission felt safe in the knowledge of their support, they would take nothing for granted.

There can be no doubting the sincerity of Mrs. Sarah Smith and the members of the BWGA. Many of them had lost loved ones on the Western Front and were desperate to bring their bodies home. As time passed and the cemeteries were completed, it became harder for them to argue their case, as visitors returned from the Western Front and described the fitting settings the IWGC had created in which their heroes lie. During October 1922, the British Legion had sent a repatriation enquiry to the IWGC on behalf of one of their members, which was refused. On receipt of the reply, the Legion acknowledged the reasons given and offered the IWGC their full support, asking for permission to publish the reply in their journal so that all members would understand the reasons for why the policy was in place. In their reply, the IWGC respectfully requested that the reply not be printed, stating that 'There is a minority of a few influential people with money who are ready at all times to re-open this question' and adding that the letter or extracts 'might stimulate anew the demands of the few … and for their part the Commission would prefer that no publication was made'.[12] It seems that the IWGC were trying to diffuse the situation with a policy of 'letting sleeping dogs lie'.

There were, however, many organisations that were looking forward to the prospect of repatriation and the potential for the large earnings that it would generate. From as early as January 1919, the Commission were receiving communications from the British Undertakers Association asking for a meeting to discuss the exhumation of

---

11   CWGCA: CWGC/1/1/7/B/45 (WG 1294/3 PT.4: Exhumation France and Belgium Part 4).
12   CWGCA: CWGC/1/1/7/B/45 (WG 1294/3 PT.4: Exhumation France and Belgium Part 4).

soldiers in France, 'For the purpose of re-internment in Family Vaults, etc'.[13] Even earlier, on 15 November 1918, just four days after the armistice, the IWGC received a letter from the press bureau of the *Daily Telegraph*. They had received a request for the following advertisement to be printed:

> CREMATION IN FRANCE; Relatives who desire that the Remains of Officers should be exhumed and cremated in France and the ashes sent home for internment please write John R. Wildman, Cremation Specialist, 158, Fleet Street, London.[14]

On being asked if this advertisement could be published, Fabian Ware replied the following day in no uncertain terms, 'Certainly not. At present all exhumation forbidden by French (and British) order and it would raise hopes in some relative's minds that can probably never be fulfilled'.[15] A similar advertisement was placed in the Toronto press in Canada. On 31 January 1920, Monsieur E. Teysseyre (an undertaker from Paris, France) announced that 'Through his Canadian representative Mr. Robert U. Stone, that he will accept commissions from relatives who so desire, to exhume, prepare and transport to Canada, the Sacred Remains of their soldier dead, now in France and Flanders'.[16] At the same time, the aforementioned Robert U. Stone announced that 'He proposes personally to visit the British Isles at an early date and will accept commissions for removal to Canada of the Remains of Soldiers buried in England, Ireland or Scotland'.[17] Such adverts served no purpose, as the IWGC had made up their mind on the repatriation issue and there was to be no exceptions to the rule. The adverts did, however, create false hope for the families of the fallen and extra administration for an already overworked IWGC to cope with. The IWGC countered the adverts by asking for a contradictory notice to be placed in the Toronto press and for the details of the French undertaker so that they could press him on the matter.

Some individuals and organisations would employ different tactics in the hope of securing the permission needed for the repatriation of an individual. Using the technique of acceptance by assumption, they would often write as permission was assumed and just needed the finer details in order to carry the exhumation. In January 1922, Funeral Directors John Bye and Company of Manchester tried exactly that

---

13 CWGCA: CWGC/1/1/7/B/42 (WG 1294/3 PT.1: Exhumation France and Belgium Part 1).
14 CWGCA: CWGC/1/1/7/B/42 (WG 1294/3 PT.1: Exhumation France and Belgium Part 1).
15 CWGCA: CWGC/1/1/7/B/42 (WG 1294/3 PT.1: Exhumation France and Belgium Part 1).
16 CWGCA: CWGC/1/1/7/B/43 (WG 1294/3 PT.2: Exhumation France and Belgium Part 2).
17 CWGCA: CWGC/1/1/7/B/43 (WG 1294/3 PT.2: Exhumation France and Belgium Part 2).

when they wrote to the Home Secretary, asking about what the regulations were for importing corpses in Great Britain. The Home Secretary duly forwarded the letter to the Commissioners of Customs and Excise, who replied on 22 March 1922 that 'imported packages containing corpses should be accompanied by the certificate of the Civil Registrar of the place where the death occurred stating that the body is being removed for internment and also by a certificate of verification by the British Consul'.[18] The receipt of such details inferred to John Bye and Company that the exhumation may well be possible. After all, why would such details be given if it was not possible? Circumventing the IWGC, John Bye and Company then replied on 30 March to Customs House in London:

> Dear Sir,
> Since writing you yesterday, yours of the 29th March which has come to hand for which I thank you. The body which is desired to be exhumed is that of an Officer of the RAF who was killed on 13 June 1917 and was interred in the Military Cemetery near the church of Hoogstaadt, Belgium on 15 June, will you kindly say if permission will be granted to exhume, and what procedure is necessary.[19]

It is interesting to note that this letter had been written only three weeks after the IWGC had made the official announcement of non-repatriation that was widely circulated in the British press, that the mention of repatriation of a set of military remains did not come up until the second letter and that no letter had been addressed to the IWGC. Although not a clear deception, the letters were designed to try to muddy the waters just enough in the hope of gaining permission by assumption. However, between sending the second letter and receiving a final reply dated 18 April 1922, the request had found its way to the offices of the IWGC via the secretary of Customs House, to which the IWGC directed them to reply in their usual forthright and business-like manner, 'I am to say that they regret that they are unable to give permission for exhumation from any of the Military Cemeteries abroad ... the decision is universal and does not admit exception'.[20] Another attempt to circumvent the system had been thwarted.

The policy of repatriation was always going to be a difficult one for the IWGC to deal with. After all, it was first and foremost an emotive subject, involving the families of the fallen, whose loved ones had been so cruelly taken from them. Hand in hand with the emotions involved, the IWGC had to balance the logistical realities

---

18 CWGCA: CWGC/1/1/7/B/45 (WG 1294/3 PT.4: Exhumation France and Belgium Part 4).
19 CWGCA: CWGC/1/1/7/B/45 (WG 1294/3 PT.4: Exhumation France and Belgium Part 4).
20 CWGCA: CWGC/1/1/7/B/45 (WG 1294/3 PT.4: Exhumation France and Belgium Part 4).

of bringing back the dead. It would be a huge undertaking with a cost that the British government was unwilling to cover, meaning that families would have to pay the costs themselves, which in turn would mean that families who could not afford to pay would be left broken hearted as they would have to leave their loved ones abroad. This scenario also raised the spectre of cut-price funerals, soldiers' bodies being transported home in less than ideal circumstances and a raft of pauper's funerals taking place in the UK. In the eyes of the IWGC and most of the population, such a scenario was unthinkable. All of the fallen deserved to be treated equally, buried together in the same ground with uniform headstones, generals lying next to privates, identified and unidentified soldiers side by side, each man in his own grave in beautiful surroundings, in land guaranteed for perpetuity and tended with love and care by the gardeners of the IWGC. This vision of Fabian Ware was as revolutionary as it was utopian, as the fallen would really be treated as heroes, receiving burials in settings far superior to what they would have had in civilian life. The publication of a 16-page booklet written by Sir Rudyard Kipling in 1919 and entitled '*The Graves of the Fallen*' by the IWGC was a masterstroke. For the first time, the British public could see the results of the IWGC's vision, and, as a result, even the most diehard critics of the IWGC started to fall silent.

The Graves of the Fallen by Rudyard Kipling. (CWGCA, with permission, CWGC/1/1/5/7/1, SDC 19.)

I am lucky enough to live in the Ypres Salient surrounded by the cemeteries tended superbly by the men of the now CWGC, each one immaculate with hardly a blade of grass out of place. As a battlefield guide here since 2010, I can recount many stories of people being moved to tears in cemeteries, not only because of the incredibly sad stories of the men and women who lie within their boundaries but also by the sheer beauty of the cemeteries. It is a hard man who can walk into Tyne Cot Cemetery and not be moved by the banks of roses and fields of white headstones. For me, the policy of non-repatriation was the correct one. Without it, the soldiers of the Great War would be denied the fitting burials they have today, with their graves scattered across England and easily overlooked and forgotten. The policy of equality in death and uniformity was indeed a triumph.

16

The Business of Death
Body Snatching and Illegal Exhumations in the Ypres Salient

The strict enforcement of the policy of non-repatriation was to have a direct impact on the Ypres Salient. Many of the letters requesting repatriation received by the IWGC concerned burials of soldiers in and around the Ypres area, some of the correspondence coming from wealthy families and some coming from families of a lesser social standing, all of which received the same response, that repatriation was not possible. For a few families, however, the response of the IWGC was not acceptable, and their continual denial of their requests would lead them to consider and, in a few instances, actually take more drastic measures.

After the announcement in 1921 that the search for bodies was to cease on the Western Front, an incensed Sarah Smith of the BWGA threatened that her members would be 'taking the law into their own hands in bringing the dead home'.[1] Although the BWGA and the majority of their members never made good on their threats, it does go to show the depth of feeling amongst those who believed that they should be able to bring the bodies of their loved ones home. Those feelings of frustration, anger and despair proved to be a dangerous cocktail for some, leading them to take action that would make most people recoil in horror, that action being the clandestine removal of their loved one's remains – in short – digging the body up. A clandestine exhumation was not an easy task to organise and would require collusion and assistance from people and organisations with local knowledge. As in all things in life, there is always someone willing to perform a task, no matter how ghastly, if the price is right.

The first recorded instance of an attempted illegal repatriation of a member of the British armed forces in the Ypres Salient and its surrounding area took place in February 1920 and was an attempt to remove a body by exploiting a perceived loophole in the law. Captain Christopher Guy of the 29th Squadron of the Royal Flying Corps

---

1 Commonwealth War Graves Commission Archive (CWGCA) CWGC (WG 783 PT.1: War Graves Association).

was killed on 29 August 1917 at the age of 23, and his body was buried in Wynendaele German Cemetery. The fact that Captain Guy was buried in a German cemetery led his father, the Reverend Frederick Guy, to believe that he had the right to exhume and repatriate his body. Article 225 of the Treaty of Versailles concerned the treatment of war graves and had stated that 'Furthermore they agree to afford, so far as the provisions of their laws and the requirements of public health allow, every facility for giving effect to requests that the bodies of their soldiers and sailors may be transferred to their own country'. This article had not gone unnoticed and had been used as justification for repatriation requests by previous correspondents to the IWGC. The Commission, however, had always stated that this article applied only to soldiers buried in foreign territory (e.g., Germany) and not France or Belgium, and indeed there are at least three repatriations from Germany being recorded as having taken place.[2] As a precedent had been set regarding the recovery of bodies from Germany, Reverend Guy attempted to apply the procedure to his son's body, which was buried in a German cemetery that was, technically, in Reverend Guy's opinion, enemy territory.

In early February 1920, Reverend Guy circumvented the normal channels for repatriation and entered a request to the DGR&E at St. Pol, rather than contacting the IWGC, and was given permission to exhume the body and remove it from the German cemetery. Later that month, Major Ingpen of the IWGC received a letter from the Belgium authorities and, as a result, sent an urgent telegram to the DGR&E, which read:

> INFORMED BY BELGIAN MINISTRY OF WAR THAT IT IS PROPOSED EXHUME AND TRANSFER ENGLAND BODY CAPTAIN GUY BURIED GERMAN CEMETERY WYNENDAELE   STOP   THIS CONTRARY TO AGREEMENT BETWEEN GOVERNMENTS   STOP   PLEASE TAKE NECESSARY STEPS PREVENT ANY ACTION   STOP.[3]

It seems that Reverend Guy had been somewhat economical with the truth when he had spoken with Colonel Chapman of the DGR&E, the officer who had issued him with the relevant permits, as he was also in the process of communicating with the local Belgian authorities to remove his son's remains to England, no doubt claiming that he had the relevant permit from the DGR&E to do so. This was, of course, contrary to all agreements between the Belgians and the IWGC with regards to the exhumation of graves, and so the Belgian authorities had refused permission and informed the IWGC accordingly. For Reverend Guy, the game was up, and his attempt to arrange the repatriation of his son's body by subterfuge had failed. As a

---

2   Andrew Featherstone (2021), 'Recovery of Remains'. E-mail (20 April 2021).
3   CWGCA: CWGC/1/1/7/B/43 (WG 1294/3 PT.2: Exhumation France and Belgium Part 2).

The grave of Captain Guy. (Photo by Patsy Mahieu.)

result, he finally agreed to have his son's body reburied in Poperinge New Military Cemetery, where he still lies today in plot II, row L, grave 9.

Whilst the case of Captain Guy seems to have been the first involving the remains of a member of the British armed forces in the Ypres area, it was by no means the first attempt of an illegal exhumation from an IWGC cemetery in the area. From as early as 1919, reports were being received by the IWGC of illegal exhumations of French soldiers whose bodies had been buried in British cemeteries. Although the Belgian and French governments had passed laws in 1919 prohibiting the exhumation of any soldier's body no matter what nationality on their soil, it seems that illegal clandestine exhumations of French and Belgian soldiers from their cemeteries by family members was becoming almost commonplace. The actual act of exhuming a body, often at night, with leaving minimal surface evidence of the removal, was no easy task and required specialist knowledge. A small shadowy industry involving local undertakers, grave diggers and bribed officials quickly sprang up in order to serve the needs of those wishing to bring the bodies of their loved ones home. In July 1919, the newspaper, *Le Journal*, covered the story, suggesting an increase in illegal exhumations and the involvement of shadowy commercial operations or, what the journalist called, 'mercantils de la mort' ('merchants of death').[4] Belgian Juul Filliaert described such actions that were taking place in the French military cemetery in the town of Nieuwpoort, close to where he lived:

> When the population returned after the war, it was their care to preserve this French cemetery as it was during the war. This became a competition in decorating the graves, flowering and maintenance. It looked like a blossoming flowerbed, simple but naively beautiful. Not one object, not even those recognised as theirs, was taken away. Then, the French cemetery was an important place of worship. Innumerable families came to visit and honour their dead. The French Government supported the visitors and paid their transport costs. It didn't last too long, before we saw families exhuming their beloved dead. With the passing of the months, these exhumations became a daily event.[5]

With significant numbers of French and Belgian soldiers interred in IWGC cemeteries in the Ypres Salient, the practice of illegal exhumation was bound to impact those IWGC cemeteries sooner or later, and impact it did, with reports of illegal exhumations in Lijssenthoek Cemetery amongst others being received. The situation was deemed serious enough for the IWGC to send circulars on three separate occasions to the Belgian authorities, who then distributed them to the provincial governors and the town mayors. The third circular contained a direction to the town mayors to post warning notices reminding the inhabitants that any infringements of the rules concerning the exhumation of military dead would be severely dealt with. The town mayors were also warned that they must report every case of reported exhumations to the relevant military authorities.[6] Although the Belgians had gifted the land for the British and French cemeteries for military burials, they had retained legal control over said land, meaning that the British and French authorities had no power of prosecution for those caught engaging in illegal acts in their cemeteries. It was up to the Belgian authorities to prosecute offenders.

In January 1920, the French Etat Civil Officer had a meeting with the IWGC in Brussels to discuss an alleged illegal exhumation of a French Soldier in Lijssenthoek Cemetery, a few miles from the city of Ypres. It is very clear in the British memo of

---

4   CWGCA: CWGC/1/1/7/B/42 (WG 1294/3 PT.1: Exhumation France and Belgium Part 1).
5   Dominiek Dendooven, 'Bringing the Dead Home: Repatriation, Illegal Repatriation and Expatriation of British Bodies during and after the First World War', in Paul Cornish and Nicholas J. Saunders (eds), *Bodies in Conflict: Corporeality, Materiality, and Transformation* (London: Routledge, 2013), p.69.
6   CWGCA: CWGC/1/1/7/B/42 (WG 1294/3 PT.1: Exhumation France and Belgium Part 1).

the meeting that the French believed an illegal local business operation was involved in the exhumation of the body:

> He informed me that his people down there thought they had every prospect of laying their hands on one of the persons, believed to be an undertaker, who is carrying out the exhumations in that area at what is believed to be an extortionate profit.
>
> As soon as he has any evidence, he will let me know, and we shall approach the Belgian authorities together, with a view, if possible, to a prosecution, and are agreed that we should ask for a stiff punishment with a view to putting the fear of God into other persons tempted to do the same thing.
>
> We agreed that it is impossible to take, or to ask the Belgians to take, any legal steps against the parents of the soldiers so exhumed.[7]

The protection of the parents in these matters was always a concern of the IWGC. Not only was it a recognition that the drastic actions of the parents were driven by grief, but it also protected the IWGC from any bad publicity that could arise from their actions. As we have already seen, there were plenty of organisations in Britain ready to utilise any opportunity presented to them in order to attack the IWGC on their policy of non-repatriation.

Meanwhile, the Belgian government had their own worries with regards to illegal exhumations. Like every European country at the time, its ruling classes were threatened by the rise of socialism and so were desperate to avoid the same situation that the Russian aristocracy had found themselves in. Historically split between French and Flemish speakers, with the educated classes speaking French and the working classes speaking Flemish, the situation had already become a bone of contention during the war, with the Belgian Army narrowly avoiding a full-scale mutiny when it was believed by the rank-and-files that only French speakers were being promoted within its ranks. The end of the war and the new freedoms gained by the working classes meant that the Belgium government wanted to avoid at all costs any accusation of favouring the rich, as revealed in a discussion between the Director of the Office for Military Burials in Belgium and the IWGC in Brussels in September 1919. It was stated in the records of the meeting that, on the question of the Belgian policy as to exhumation:

> The Belgian Policy is – THAT EXHUMATION SHALL NOT TAKE PLACE EXCEPT FOR THE PURPOSES OF CONCENTRATION INTO MILITARY CEMETERIES – and they are doing their utmost to see that this policy is carried into effect.

---

7 CWGCA: CWGC/1/1/7/B/43 (WG 1294/3 PT.2: Exhumation France and Belgium Part 2).

> A very great difficulty is that CLANDESTINE EXHUMATION is almost impossible to prevent, and that in almost every case, the clandestine exhumation is of an officer's body.
>
> The Belgian authorities fear that as a result of this, people will say, on entering a Belgian Military Cemetery and seeing no officers' graves … the conclusion is obvious!
>
> The Belgian authorities are very anxious to avoid any such inference being drawn, and are now seriously tackling the problem, and propose to proceed with utmost rigour against any Local authority who reburies a clandestinely exhumed military body.[8]

The following year, in June 1920, the Belgians published a story in the newspaper, *L'Étoile Belge*, concerning the illegal exhumation of a French sergeant from a cemetery in the town of La Neuvillette, in the Reims area of France. The story concerned the mother and father of the soldier, who had paid two workmen to secretly exhume the body of their son and transport it back to their hometown, the city of Brest. Upon being discovered, the city authorities in La Neuvillette fined the couple 200 francs for the violation of the grave. Although taking place in France, this story was printed in the Belgian press to serve as a warning to those considering a similar course of events in Belgium, with the fine imposed representing the best part of two-weeks' work in France at the time. By the end of that year, in the face of public pressure, both the French and Belgian authorities scrapped their policy banning exhumations and opened the gateway for the bodies of their soldiers to be brought home.

Meanwhile, in the Ypres Salient, further attempts had been made by relatives of British soldiers to illegally exhume and repatriate the bodies of their loved ones. In mid-June 1920, Herbert Baron had travelled from Hull in order to bring home the body of his brother Frank Foster Baron of the RFA. Frank had been killed on 16 September 1918, and his body had been buried in Westoutre British Cemetery, approximately 11 kilometres southwest of Ypres. Upon arrival in Belgium, Herbert seems to have had a definite plan in place, which raises the possibly that he had already made arrangements with a firm of 'body snatchers' prior to his arrival. Herbert visited the British Consul in Antwerp, where he claimed that he had permission to exhume his brother's body and needed information on how to proceed with regards to shipping his remains back to Hull. On 14 June at 4:00 p.m., Herbert, assisted by two local men and a hired hearse, had already exhumed the remains of his brother and placed them into a coffin when two Belgian gendarmes attended the scene and arrested everybody involved, thus preventing the transportation of Frank's remains to Antwerp in order to be shipped to Hull.

---

8 CWGCA: CWGC/1/1/7/B/42 (WG 1294/3 PT.1: Exhumation France and Belgium Part 1).

The grave of Frank Foster Baron. (Photo by Patsy Mahieu.)

Having finally caught somebody in the act of body snatching, the IWGC and the authorities decided to take a strong stance on the issue. Not only was this an opportunity to publicly punish those involved, but it could also be the break they needed in the identification of the bodysnatching firm they believed to be operating from the Poperinge area, the same firm that was believed to have been involved in the illegal exhumation of the French soldier from Lijssenthoek Cemetery in January the same year. The determination of the IWGC to pursue this lead is highlighted in a document dated 8 July 1920, written by the IWGC in Brussels and addressed to Colonel Sutton in Poperinge: 'Above all get me those names and addresses if you can, as they may be the particular firm of body-snatchers I and the French Officer here are after. If we can only get enough evidence, they will be severely hotted by special request of the IWGC and the French Etat-Civil'.[9]

The investigations had a positive outcome for the IWGC, with Herbert Baron being ordered by a Belgian court to pay a fine of 26 francs and pay all legal costs whilst the fate of the two Belgian accomplices remain unknown. Herbert Baron had

9   CWGCA: CWGC/1/1/7/B/43 (WG 1294/3 PT.2: Exhumation France and Belgium Part 2).

failed in his attempt to bring his brother home, having achieved no more than being able to exhume his remains, which had then, upon the discovery of the exhumation, been reburied in the same grave. There was one further known attempt of an illegal exhumation and repatriation documented in the Ypres Salient, which was a lot closer to being successful, that being the case of Private G. C. Hopkins of the PPCLI (Princess Patricia's Canadian Light Infantry).

Private Grenville Carson Hopkins, a university student from Saskatchewan, Canada, was 21 years of age when he volunteered for overseas service with the CEF (Canadian Expeditionary Force) in April 1917. The only son of Mr. William Hopkins, a successful businessman and ex-mayor of Saskatoon, Grenville had volunteered to join the 196 Battalion, a battalion composed mainly of university students from Western Canada. Having received a few weeks of basic training in Canada, he embarked from the port of Halifax on the SS *Olympic* on 2 June 1917 and arrived in Liverpool a week later on 9 June 1917. After receiving further training in the UK, he then left for the Western Front, joining his unit in the Ypres Salient on 2 November 1917 during the Second Battle of Passchendaele. Two days after arriving in the field, on 4 November 1917, Grenville was transferred to the PPCLI, which was severely understrength due to the heavy losses they had incurred during the fighting in late October 1917 on the Passchendaele Ridge. After spending 10 days at rest behind the lines at Scotts Camp, the PPCLI received orders to return to the front, and so, on 14 November 1917, Grenville and his comrades found themselves defending a line of muddy-water-filled shell holes on the Goudberg spur near Passchendaele. The battalion war diary for the period of 14–17 November reads, 'During the period 14/15/16 the weather was fair but cloudy with frequent ground mists and the whole of the support area – hit particularly 1 and 2 Coys was subjected to heavy artillery fire. This lasted practically continuously – and also throughout the 17th … The front and rear areas were shelled with gas during the nights 15/16 and 16/17'.[10]

It was during this period that Grenville was to lose his life. Officially listed as KIA on 15 November 1917, Grenville was buried in the mud of the battlefield next to one of his comrades, Private L. J. MacEwen, by the members of their unit. Private Grenville's record of service was as short as it was violent – having joined up in April 1917 and, within the space of seven months, the brown-haired and blue-eyed body of Private G. C. Hopkins lay rotting in a makeshift grave in the cold, wet clay of the Ypres Salient.

The news of Grenville's death hit the family hard, particularly his mother and sister, with the emotional blow being amplified by the news that Grenville was listed as missing since his makeshift grave had been destroyed in subsequent fighting. So, in 1919, his father resolved to travel to the Western Front to locate his son's grave. Grenville's father, William, was a man of some influence, being the ex-mayor of

---

10 Princess Patricia's Canadian Light Infantry Museum & Archives (PPCLIMA) War Diary January 1917-March 1918.

Saskatoon and a prominent financial supporter of the Canadian government. On 27 January 1919, the British authorities in Belgium received a letter informing them of his forthcoming visit. Mr. Hopkins had contacted the Canadian High Commissioners Office, informing them that he had information supplied to him by his late son's comrades on the location of his burial site. Having been warned of the bad condition of the ground around Passchendaele, Mr. Hopkins was given permission to make his own arrangements to locate his son's grave. Unfortunately, the search was to prove unsuccessful, and so Mr. Hopkins returned home in 1919 without recovering the remains of his son. Undeterred and driven by the grief suffered by his wife, upon arrival back in Canada, Hopkins recontacted his late son's comrades, who provided him with further information on the location of Grenville's grave, and so he determined to return to the Ypres Salient with his wife to continue the search.

No more was heard about Mr. Hopkins until 16 November 1920 when Fabian Ware completed an DGR&E enquiry form on his behalf, stating that he would be visiting the area in order to search for his son's grave but on arrival would first of all call at the

William Hopkins. (Portrait of William Hopkins, Saskatoon Public Library, Local History Room, Photograph Collection, LH-9163.)

Private Grenville Carson Hopkins. (*University of Saskatchewan, University Archives and Special Collections, The Sheaf, February 1918, p.90, 'Grenville Hopkins'.*)

DGR&E Enquiry Bureau in Ypres. On 24 November 1920, the DGR&E received, in advance, copies of letters of introduction given to Mr. Hopkins by the War Office, stating that Mr. Hopkins had been sent by Sir George Perley (the Canadian High Commissioner in London) and was to be given every assistance possible in the search of his son, including, placing at his full disposal, the use of an exhumation party should it be required.[11] It seems that Mr. Hopkins was using his political influence to its full extent. Two days later, on 26 November 1920, and armed with his letters of introduction, Mr. Hopkins reported to Headquarters, No. 5 District, where a hastily arranged search team from Austral Dump, on the outskirts of Ypres, was immediately detailed for his use. With the new grave location information given by his late son's comrades, Hopkins and the search party proceeded to the Goudberg Spur area, close to the Passchendaele Ridge.

It seems that the updated information given to Mr. Hopkins by his late son's comrades and the expertise of the exhumation unit paid dividends, as, during the course of the next few days, they located and recovered two sets of remains of soldiers of the PPCLI in the area where Privates Hopkins and MacEwen were reported to be buried. It was Mr. Hopkins who actually identified both sets of remains:

Re 219335 Pte. [Private] G.C. HOPKINS. P.P.C.L.I. – 15.11.1917 …

The remains of two P.P.C.L.I. soldiers were found at sheet 20.v.30.d.07.30, and identified by Mr. Hopkins as follows: -

a. First body was identified by Mr. Hopkins as that of the above-mentioned soldier by –
   1. Cranium wound.
   2. Inner pocket in tunic for fountain pen.
b. Second body was identified by Mr. Hopkins as that of 2193334 Pte. McKeown, L., [sic] P.P.C.L.I., as his remains were known to have been buried beside his son.

The remains of these soldiers have been interred in Tyne Cot British Cemetery as follows: -
Pte. HOPKINS … Plot 56, Row A, Gr.1.
Pte. McKEOWN [sic] … Plot 56, Row A, Gr.2.[12]

Not only had Mr. Hopkins located and recovered the bodies of his son and Private MacEwen, but he was also brave enough to examine and identify those remains, a ghastly and harrowing experience. In travelling over 6,000 miles in order to find his son's body, Mr. Hopkins had shown that he was both a determined individual and an

---

11 Commonwealth War Graves Commission Archive (CWGCA) CWGC/8/1/4/1/2/54 (CCM 16470: Pte G. C. Hopkins PPCLI).
12 CWGCA: CWGC/8/1/4/1/2/54 (CCM 16470: Pte G. C. Hopkins PPCLI).

incredibly devoted father. Having accommodation in Nice, France, both Mr. and Mrs. Hopkins attended the burial of their son in Tyne Cot Cemetery on 30 November 1920 and, once concluded, returned seemingly satisfied to their apartment in Nice. Things, however, were about to take a decided, and somewhat macabre, turn for the worse.

The following year, on 5 January 1921, from his apartment in Nice, Mr. Hopkins wrote a letter to Sir George Perley, the Canadian High Commissioner in London, that was to set in motion a set of events culminating into the most extreme act imaginable:

> Dear Sir,
> We have been successful in locating the body of our boy and have decided to take the remains back to Canada with us, and anything you can do to help us in this sad task will be greatly appreciated. We would like to hear from you as to the proper course to take. The body is in very good condition considering the long time it has been lying in No Man's Land. We were able to identify it without a shadow of a doubt.
> Yours sincerely
> (Sgd) [Signed] H. Hopkins.[13]

On 17 January, Sir George Perley wrote to Major General Fabian Ware of the IWGC, enclosing a copy of Mr. Hopkins' letter and explaining that Mr. Hopkins was a prominent citizen and ex-mayor of Saskatoon Canada. Detailing the course of events, Sir George Perley confirmed that that his office had explained to Mr. Hopkins the policy of non-repatriation and asked if the IWGC could send a kind and sympathetic answer to Mr. Hopkins request. Therefore, on 14 February 1921, the IWGC sent a carefully worded letter of refusal to Mr. Hopkins. The circumstances of the case were not lost on Fabian Ware, as he was quick to realise that Mr. Hopkins had friends in high places and was a man of some financial means, both factors that he had used in the process of locating his son's remains and factors that no doubt he assumed would secure him the right to repatriate those remains back to Canada. Whether this change of direction from Mr. Hopkins was pre-planned or decided upon after the funeral of their son as the two parents sat in their apartment in Nice over the Christmas period of 1920 while contemplating their loss, we will never know, but, whatever the reason, Fabian Ware and the IWGC were to stand firm in their policy. The letter sent outlined the non-repatriation policy and the reasons for this policy, the letter concluding with:

> I need hardly say that the Commission regret deeply having to convey this decision to those to whom it necessarily causes pain, but in view of the common sacrifice of rich and poor alike, and of the equality and comradeship of officers and men where they now lie together, I feel sure you will appreciate the ideal of

---

13   CWGCA: CWGC/8/1/4/1/2/54 (CCM 16470: Pte G. C. Hopkins PPCLI).

treating all alike, an ideal which met with an almost universal response among the armies in the field and the relatives of the fallen.[14]

Upon sending the letter, Fabian Ware and the IWGC assumed that the matter was concluded and that Mr. Hopkins had been treated fairly and sympathetically. The problem was that, on receipt of the letter, Mr. Hopkins did not 'appreciate the ideal of treating all alike' nor did he agree with 'the universal response … of the relatives of the fallen'. The letter that had been intended to diffuse a delicate and potentially difficult political situation had, in fact, infuriated Mr. Hopkins. The blue touch paper had been well and truly lit.

The first inkling that the IWGC had of the trouble looming on the horizon was upon the receipt of a letter sent by Mr. Hopkins in reply to the aforementioned IWGC letter. Dated 18 February 1921, the letter had a very different tone to that sent by the IWGC 11 days earlier:

> Dear Sir,
> In reply to your letter of the 14th inst: re the taking home of our boy's body, we regret that the Imperial War Graves Commission have taken the stand that we cannot take the body home. This decision may be quite right so far as the Imperial War Graves Commission is concerned, but it is not at all satisfactory to us, we are the parties who have authority in this matter. The body is ours, it does not belong to the to the Imperial War Graves Commission, in fact, we have more authority in this matter than ever as Empire bodies have been brought back to Canada and none of the cases are more urgent than ours. The Americans who did so little in the war were permitted to take their bodies home. Surely no objection can be raised to us who fought so faithfully.
>
> Perhaps you are not aware of the fact that we made two voyages across the ocean all the way from the City of Saskatoon a distance of over six thousand miles and at no small expense, in my first voyage I was unsuccessful in discovering the body but on my second voyage I was more fortunate 'I found the body', 'The Government failed', how can any reasonable body of men say to us we cannot have it. We must ask the Imperial War Graves Commission to reconsider this decision and kindly farm us with a favourable reply.
> Yours
> Very Sincerely
> H. Hopkins.[15]

A few days later, the Commission received more correspondence from the Hopkins. Dated 21 February, it was Mrs. Hopkins who penned this curious letter, perhaps in

---

14 CWGCA: CWGC/8/1/4/1/2/54 (CCM 16470: Pte G. C. Hopkins PPCLI).
15 CWGCA: CWGC/8/1/4/1/2/54 (CCM 16470: Pte G. C. Hopkins PPCLI).

the realisation that her husband might have been too forthright with his comments. Citing the fact that her husband did 'not seem satisfied to go back home without the body', that he had 'become very nervous since the loss of our dear' and that he had barely slept over two hours since the decision, Mrs. Hopkins added that 'I have tried to reason with him but to no avail' and that 'It should not affect him in this way I know'. The letter concluded with Mrs. Hopkins asking the IWGC to reconsider their decision and that 'Mr. Hopkins does not know I have written this note, for I believe he should not wish me to tell you first how badly he is feeling'.[16]

Does Mrs. Hopkins' letter paint the picture of a man wracked by grief and under intense pressure or of a man used to getting his own way in life and who cannot accept in that, in this case, his requests have been denied? I cannot say, as I am no psychologist. Maybe the fact that Mrs. Hopkins does not want her husband to know that she has written the letter tells a story? Who knows? But what I can say is that more letters followed from Mr. Hopkins to the Canadian High Commissioner and that more polite letters of refusal were sent from the offices of the IWGC to Mr. and Mrs. Hopkins, with the last being dated 16 March 1921. In terms of communication, all went quiet until early May 1921, when Mr. and Mrs. Hopkins visited their son's grave in Tyne Cot Cemetery and mentioned that they were going to obtain permission to remove the body to Canada. Although the correspondence had ceased, the matter was clearly not dropped in the mind of Mr. Hopkins.

On the morning of 18 May 1921, the IWGC gardeners of Tyne Cot Cemetery reported for work as normal, ready for a day's work of maintaining the graves of the fallen. Upon approaching plot 56, row A, one of the gardeners realised that something was amiss and, upon approaching grave no. 1, was horrified to find that the grave had been desecrated – the coffin had been exhumed, broken open and the remains removed. It seems that, during the night of 17–18 May, a person or persons (up to that point it was unknown) had entered the cemetery with the sole aim of illegally exhuming a body and removing it from the cemetery. The body in question was that of Private Grenville Carson Hopkins.

The foreman gardener of Tyne Cot Cemetery immediately reported the situation to the Director General of Public Safety, who in turn informed the Belgian police. Urgent enquiries were made, and the investigation quickly led to Antwerp, where Private Hopkins' remains were located in a mortuary ready to be shipped abroad. The guilty parties were quickly apprehended and detained. It soon emerged that the instigator and financier of the clandestine illegal exhumation and attempted removal of Private Hopkins' remains was none other than his own father. It transpired that Mr. Hopkins, having had his requests for the repatriation of his son's remains refused, decided to take the law into his own hands. During his time in Belgium, he had contacted an ex-assistant director of the DGR&E, No. 5 Area, a certain Lieutenant Colonel Cawston, who had been relieved of his duties with the DGR&E in 1919

16 CWGCA: CWGC/8/1/4/1/2/54 (CCM 16470: Pte G. C. Hopkins PPCLI).

after being 'not considered suitable for this (specialists) work', a decision that Cawston appealed against as he felt he had been unjustly treated.[17] After being sent back to the UK in August 1919, Cawston ended up as a captain (temporary lieutenant colonel) in the Royal Berkshire Regiment and, in November of that year, applied to spend a leave of absence between 12 November and 22 December 1919 in Belgium since he was suffering from rheumatism. His request was granted, and so he proceeded to Antwerp, giving his address as 'Rue des Tannems, Antwerp, Belgium'. It seems that he had then set up business in the Ypres area, offering tours to pilgrims visiting the Ypres Salient, under the name of 'Battlefield Historic Sites Bureau' and based in the Chateau des Trois Tours, Brielen, Ypres. It was no coincidence that Cawston chose this address, as the IWGC at the time had offices in the same building, which in turn added an air of credibility to Cawston's enterprises. It seems that Mr. Hopkins had found a sympathetic ear in Cawston, who no doubt was attracted not only by a healthy financial reward but also by the opportunity to hit back at the DGR&E, whom he felt had treated him unjustly. So it was Lieutenant Colonel Cawston and a team of men whom he had selected for the task – under the direction and supervision of Mr. Hopkins – who had exhumed the coffin, broke it open and transported the remains in a valise to Antwerp. Upon arrival, the remains were then placed in a coffin and stored in a morgue ready for shipment to Canada with the Canadian Pacific Steamships Ocean Services Ltd.

The apprehending of Cawston and the recovery of Grenville Hopkins' remains were not the end of the story. Two things now had to be considered by the British authorities: the first, being quite straight forward, what to do with Private Hopkins' remains, and the second, a much more delicate topic, what to do with the perpetrators?

After taking legal advice, the IWGC in Brussels lodged a formal complaint against Cawston on 14 June 1921, with an interview taking place on 23 June 1921. Present at the interview was Lord Stopford of the IWGC, Mr. Riches (Cawston's legal representative) and of course Cawston himself. During the forthright discussion between the three parties, Cawston and his legal representative tried several different avenues of attack to explain and justify their actions. It was suggested that Mr. Hopkins had received permission from the IWGC to remove the body quietly. Lord Stopford then queried, if that was the case, why was it necessary to remove the body at midnight? Cawston then went on to allege that many other bodies had been removed to Canada from the Western Front, but, when challenged for more detail, he could not come forward with any examples. In a tetchy interview, Cawston argued that, as Mr. Hopkins had found the body, he had every right to it and then launched into a diatribe concerning the work of the DGR&E and their identification of burials, unfortunately incriminating himself in the process since he was responsible for the work of the exhumation units he was criticising at the time. The ex-Lieutenant Colonel clearly

---

17 Cawston's name is misspelt in several documents as 'Caustin' and 'Causton'. The National Archives (TNA) WO-339/120758: Captain E. P. Cawston.

The missing grave of Grenville Hopkins in Tyne Cot Cemetery. (Author's photo.)

still had a chip on his shoulder over his removal from office in 1919. Lord Stopford was not shy in his criticism of Cawston:

> I told him that personally I was surprised at Colonel Causton [sic] who had been with the DGR&E so long, stooping to such work … I pointed out that he had lent himself to a very serious deception which was not authorised by those in authority over him and I was surprised to hear that he as a Colonel and a Senior Officer of the Directorate had done this and that if there were many others who had acted I the same way, naturally our work would be unreliable.[18]

Lord Stopford then questioned the credibility of Cawston's word by adding, 'If it was to be given on the same sort of conditions as in this particular case, it might be open to grave suspicions'.[19] Cawston, however, was unrepentant, claiming that 'He was not ashamed of what he had done as he understood from Mr. Hopkins that the Commission had no objection', and Cawston even admitted that it was 'His own men

18 CWGCA: CWGC/8/1/4/1/2/54 (CCM 16470: Pte G. C. Hopkins PPCLI).
19 CWGCA: CWGC/8/1/4/1/2/54 (CCM 16470: Pte G. C. Hopkins PPCLI).

did the removal and he was prepared to pay a fine or go to jail, if necessary'.[20] The Commission had their men, but what was to be done with them?

The question of what to do with Private Hopkins' remains was also discussed at the meeting. The Commission were firm on the issue, with Lord Stopford stating, 'The Commission were not prepared to withdraw their objection to the removal of the body from Belgium and that the body if not already re-buried, will be re-buried in a cemetery in Belgium'.[21] Two more letters, on 23 and 27 June 1921, were sent to Mr. Riches (the legal representative of Hopkins and Cawston) confirming the denial of request for repatriation and the confirmation of the planned reburial of Private Hopkins, not back in his original grave in Tyne Cot Cemetery but in Schoonselhof Cemetery, close to Antwerp. The IWGC clearly wanted to get Private Hopkins reburied in a British cemetery as quickly as possible in the hope that it would end all requests for repatriation and put an end to the matter before it attracted too much media attention. Citing Belgian law as their main reason for refusal in their second letter, the IWGC concluded the matter by taking the moral high ground in no uncertain terms:

> The Belgian authorities at Antwerp will not allow the remains of Private Hopkins to be taken out of the country, and have sent for the Commission's representative in Brussels, and requested him to arrange for the re-burial. In giving their aid to this request, the Commission will ensure that the remains are re-buried with all proper reverence and so makes amends, as far as they can, for the irreverent way in which the clandestine exhumation was done.[22]

Private Hopkins was indeed reverently reburied in Schoonselhof Cemetery on 28 June 1921, and the IWGC considered the matter of his reburial as closed. The matter of what to do about Lieutenant Colonel Cawston in the eyes of the IWGC was far from concluded, however. The IWGC were becoming increasingly concerned by reports of attempted clandestine exhumations and wanted to end the practice before it became public knowledge. The last thing they needed was for the story to serve as encouragement for others. As we have already seen in previous cases, there was a genuine fear that organised firms were prepared to carry out illegal exhumations to order. The Commission now wanted to show these organisations what the consequences would be if they were caught participating in clandestine exhumations, and Lieutenant Colonel Cawston could provide them with that opportunity. Refusing to suppress the discovery of the offences as suggested by Lieutenant Colonel Cawston's legal advisor in July of that year, the IWGC continued their enquiries into Lieutenant Colonel Cawston in the belief that he may be carrying out similar work on behalf of

20 CWGCA: CWGC/8/1/4/1/2/54 (CCM 16470: Pte G. C. Hopkins PPCLI).
21 CWGCA: CWGC/8/1/4/1/2/54 (CCM 16470: Pte G. C. Hopkins PPCLI).
22 CWGCA: CWGC/8/1/4/1/2/54 (CCM 16470: Pte G. C. Hopkins PPCLI).

other third parties in France and Belgium, quoting that such a suppression 'Would have been clearly be a neglect of the Commission's duty, not only towards the Belgian government but also towards the British relatives to whom the Commission are responsible for the sanctity of the Cemeteries'.[23] Eventually, however, it seems that Cawston was to benefit from the Commission's policy of keeping such instances as low profile as possible, as there seems to be no record of him being prosecuted by the Belgian authorities. It is possible, though, that he faced some unofficial sanction from his peers in Ypres – having been announced as the Belgium representative of the Ypres League in April 1921, with his battlefield tour company, Battlefields Bureau Ltd., being featured in their newspaper entitled '*The Ypres Times*' as a preferred battlefield tour operator, to having no reference of him or his company recorded in any publication of the Ypres League by 1922. Lieutenant Colonel Cawston did resurface in the UK in the coming years, where he was recorded as being involved in other dubious practices. But that is another story.

Mr. Hopkins resolved to continue the fight, and fight he did right into 1924, using all his political influence to approach the Canadian Prime Minister in 1921 and 1922, alleging that he originally had permission from Fabian Ware for the illegal exhumation and that he had evidence of the IWGC repatriating bodies from Belgium to the UK. Mr. Hopkins' arguments were ultimately discredited on both counts, the first being when he contradicted himself in a letter to the Canadian government when he stated that 'He could not get consent to bring the body home' and his second argument being based on a lack of geographical knowledge.[24] It seems that he had read a report detailing that British bodies had been recovered in Sanctuary Wood, on the outskirts of Ypres, and reburied in Bedford House Cemetery. Believing Bedford House Cemetery to be located in Bedford, UK, Hopkins thought he had positive proof of repatriations. Unfortunately for him, Bedford House Cemetery is not in the UK but is located in Belgium, less than a mile south of Ypres. Questions were raised in the Canadian Parliament on his behest again in 1924, but, as in all his correspondences, his requests for repatriation were refused, with the Canadian government firmly backing the policy of the IWGC.

Although both the Commission and the Canadian government viewed the persistence and refusal of Mr. Hopkins to accept their policy on repatriation as a potentially 'dangerous situation' that could 'be specially embarrassing for the Canadian Government', there seems to have been a degree of sympathy for him and his situation, with Colonel Osbourne, secretary of the IWGC (Canada), stating in a letter dated 29 September 1922 that:

> The Hopkins case has been a most unfortunate one, and one cannot but be most sympathetic with the parents. As stated in one of the enclosed memoranda, it

---

23 CWGCA: CWGC/8/1/4/1/2/54 (CCM 16470: Pte G. C. Hopkins PPCLI).
24 CWGCA: CWGC/8/1/4/1/2/54 (CCM 16470: Pte G. C. Hopkins PPCLI).

may be regretted that the enterprise of removing this body in a clandestine manner did not succeed. The whole case is however involved now in official proceedings and would on that account alone be almost impossible to deal with.[25]

Mr. Hopkins never achieved the repatriation of his son and died in January 1935. Private Grenville Carson Hopkins still lies where he was reburied after his illegal exhumation, in plot II, row A, Grave 77, in Schoonselhof Cemetery. The epitaph on the headstone simply reads, 'Remembered with Honour'.

The recorded acts of clandestine exhumations in the Ypres Salient are few, as they are on the Western Front, with only a handful being successful. The highest profile was that of Captain William Durie of the 58th Battalion of the CEF, who was illegally exhumed by his mother and accomplices from Loos British Cemetery and successfully transported to and reburied in Canada in 1925.

There is no doubt, however, that the IWGC viewed the subject of clandestine exhumations as a serious one – so serious, in fact, that they felt the need to republish their instructions to cemetery guardians on how to deal with the matter regularly

The grave of Private Grenville Carson Hopkins. (Photo by Lennert Bonkowski.)

25   CWGCA: CWGC/8/1/4/1/2/54 (CCM 16470: Pte G. C. Hopkins PPCLI).

The grave of Captain William Durie, illegally repatriated from France and reburied in St. James Cemetery (Toronto, Canada) in 1925. (Photos by Sophie Steward and Holly Kilbourn.)

throughout the 1920s. Not only were the IWGC concerned about illegal exhumations from families that wanted to bring home the body of a loved one, but they were also afraid of a much more sinister reason for the clandestine exhuming of the dead, that of the involvement of organised crime exhuming bodies of the sons of wealthy families and holding the bodies to ransom.

In order to deter such groups and punish apprehended offenders, the IWGC found themselves in a dilemma. The problem facing the IWGC was how to prosecute those involved in the practice without seeming heavy handed and insensitive. Whilst the Commission genuinely wanted to 'put the fear of god' into those apprehended engaging in such activities and to those thinking of taking the same path, they were aware of the potential PR disaster that could follow. Prosecuting a grieving mother whose sole aim was to reclaim the remains of her only son was not a good policy to pursue, and, as a result, the IWGC seldom, if ever, took the prosecution of a family member to its full conclusion, preferring instead to 'let sleeping dogs lie'. They even erected IWGC headstones over the graves of the few known successful cases of illegal repatriations in the cemeteries of their new places of burial in their home countries, leaving the prosecution of Belgians engaged in illegal exhumations to be dealt with by the Belgian legal system. The problem facing Fabian Ware of the IWGC is highlighted in a letter dated 21 April 1926 to Colonel Osbourne of the IWGC (Canada) regarding the successful illegal repatriation of Captain Durie from Loos in 1925:

> I am on the horns of a dilemma. We cannot allow our cemeteries to be violated in this disgraceful way with impunity – goodness knows the dreadful things that might happen if once it became known that this could be done. Though one doesn't want to breath the suggestion, some thirty or forty years ago there were several cases of bodies being stolen from cemeteries and held up for ransom! We have the sons of a number of important people etc. etc. over there.[26]

Fabian Ware was right to be worried, for the First Battle of Ypres in October–November 1914 had claimed the lives of many sons of the cream of the British aristocracy, with the old and esteemed cavalry regiments of the BEF suffering heavy losses. The only member of the British royal family to be killed in the war, Queen Victoria's grandson, Prince Maurice of Battenberg, was buried in Ypres Town Cemetery, and there were so many sons of influential families buried in Zillebeke Churchyard that it would eventually become to be known as the 'cemetery of the aristocrats'.

Whilst Fabian Ware was clearly worried about the acts of attempted illegal repatriations, he was equally worried about the effect that prosecuting the families would have on the image of the IWGC. Upon learning that the French police were to ask the Canadian police authorities to interview Mrs. Durie and her sister-in-law

---

26 Commonwealth War Graves Commission Archive (CWGCA) CWGC/8/1/4/1/2/62 (CCM 19578).

as the main perpetrators of the illegal exhumation of Captain Durie in 1925, Ware wrote in the same letter:

> What the Police are frightened of is that Mrs. Durie must have made use of some organisation existing in France to make money in this way and they have evidence to that effect ... From the point of view of our general policy, in our own interests and those of all decent sentiment, we ought now to leave Mrs. Durie alone ... It seems to me that you might get in touch with your own Police Authorities ... and possibly prevent the matter developing beyond the obtaining of the necessary evidence from Mrs. Durie to enable the French Authorities to prosecute and break up any organisation of body-snatchers in France.[27]

An early picture of the grave of Prince Maurice of Battenberg. (CWGCA, with permission.)

27   CWGCA: CWGC/8/1/4/1/2/62 (CCM 19578).

His grave today. (Author's photo.)

Up to this point, very little had broken in the press concerning the subject of illegal exhumations. A small column in *The Star*, subtitled 'Secret Exhumations By Mourners', was published in 1923 and told the story of an exhumation thwarted at the last minute and of an exhumation of an unknown soldier's grave by a family that believed the body was that of their son. Inevitably, the story finally broke on 3 May 1931 when the *Sunday Express* printed a full-page article entitled 'BRITISH WAR DEAD SMUGGLED HOME' with the subtitles 'Bodies Exhumed from Graves In Flanders', 'Belgian Smugglers £10,000 From Relatives' and 'Night Landings on Essex Coast'.[28] The article alleged that, for a period of 10 years, a Belgian gang of smugglers had illegally exhumed 'scores' of British bodies and, with the help of British accomplices, shipped the bodies back to the UK in small boats (landing the bodies on the Essex coast in the dead of night) or packed them into a crate marked as 'fruit and vegetables', for example, and shipped it across the channel as freight.[29] Upon arrival in the UK, the remains were placed in a cheap travelling trunk and

28   Commonwealth War Graves Commission Archive (CWGCA) CWGC (ACON 167).
29   CWGCA: CWGC (ACON 167).

left in the luggage office of a pre-agreed railway station. The relatives would then be sent the ticket receipt by post and would then proceed to collect the remains to take home to rebury. The article went on to allege that a Belgian trafficker would watch cemeteries for wealthy grieving widows and then approach them to offer his services, selecting families who had private burial vaults in the UK so that the reburial would go unnoticed. Once a large sum of money had been paid, two specialist gardeners would secretly exhume the body and replace the ground, leaving no surface evidence of the illegal exhumation. The following week, on 10 May 1931, the *Sunday Express* printed a follow-up, stating that, although the IWGC initially denied any knowledge of the subject, after questions were raised in the House of Commons and the Secretary of State for War had opened an investigation, the mixed Franco–British Military Cemeteries Committee admitted knowledge of the disinterment of a body, with the body being held up at the port before being reburied in a British military cemetery (this possibly could have been the Baron or Hopkins case). The *Sunday Express* then went on to state that, since the publication of the original article, they had received 'A number of communications on the subject', including (amongst others) ex-employees of the IWGC and an ex-British officer who had been involved with the official exhumation units of the DGR&E.[30] According to an ex-IWGC employee, it was not unusual for gardeners to find 'sunken graves' when they reported to work in the morning, claiming that the illegal exhumations 'Were usually carried out in secret, and generally results in more earth being thrown in and fresh turf placed on top'.[31] The unnamed ex-British officer added, 'It was generally known that there were two Belgians in the district that were believed to be trafficking in the bodies of British Soldiers'.[32]

Bearing in mind that the *Sunday Express* article was printed in 1931, 10 years after the Hopkins case and six years after the Durie case, with at least another six successful illegal exhumations and repatriations taking place in that period, the claim of the IWGC to have no knowledge of any cases goes to highlight the sensitive nature of the subject of repatriation and the IWGC fear that bodysnatching could become a serious issue if it was thought that it was easily achievable by grieving families.

What drove a minority of families to take these extreme and ghastly measures? To dig up the rotting corpse of a loved one is hardly showing reverence and respect to the individual, especially when, in some cases, not all the remains were taken, with odd bones being left behind in the shattered coffins by the grave robbers as they worked hurriedly in the dead of night. For some families, it was a matter of asserting their social standing, refusing to accept the decision of the IWGC and that they did not have more privilege than the average man. For most, however, the reason was grief – pure, desperate and inconsolable grief – the type of which stays with a parent for a

---

30   CWGCA: CWGC (ACON 167).
31   CWGCA: CWGC (ACON 167).
32   CWGCA: CWGC (ACON 167).

lifetime and is not dulled by the passing of the years. The *Sunday Express* did not hold back with their opinions on the matter: 'When wealthy persons are approached to pay for the transport of their war dead home to their family graves they should think first whether they are not rather dishonouring than honouring the dead by removing them from the great family of heroes'.[33]

---

33 CWGCA: CWGC (ACON 167).

17

The Reaper Returns
The Second World War and Post-War Era

The consistent rate of body recoveries in the 1920s had led the Director of Records of the CWGC to question the previously projected number of bodies still to be recovered on the Western Front, including the Ypres Salient. He recorded his concerns in a letter dated 24 February 1927, in which he stated:

> For some time I have been considerably exercised over the large numbers of bodies recovered in the French and Belgian areas. You will remember that a few years ago there was an almost constant figure of 100 per week, which about a year ago seemed to drop to approximately 30 a week … Looking at the results covering the last few weeks the numbers have mounted again to something like the original average …[1]

Having previously suggested that a total of around 5,000 bodies would be expected to be recovered in the 'next few years', the Director of Records significantly increased his projection, blaming the 'Inability of the War Office … to produce a correct and complete number of deaths in France and Flanders unmixed with those soldiers of the Expeditionary Force dying in the United Kingdom'.[2] In the same document, the Director of Records stated that he was 'surprised' to find that 174,479 bodies still remained unaccounted for on the Western Front. Making allowances for the soldiers who had died in the UK and for statistical errors, he estimated at least 100,000 bodies of British and Commonwealth soldiers still lay unrecovered on the Western Front,

---

1   CWGCA: CWGC/1/1/7/B/45 (WG 1294/3 PT.4: Exhumation France and Belgium Part 4).
2   CWGCA: CWGC/1/1/7/B/45 (WG 1294/3 PT.4: Exhumation France and Belgium Part 4).

which would lead to 'a constant stream of discoveries for perhaps the next twenty years'.³

The fluctuation of the annual body recovery figures can be attributed to several factors. Local weather conditions could influence the rate of body finds, as a particular hard winter or wet summer could hamper agricultural work, leading to fewer bodies being discovered. The price of scrap metal was also a factor. When prices were high, the iron seekers would be scouring the fields for scrap metal and would often turn up bodies in the process; when the price of scrap was low and taxes on it were high, as it was in 1932, fewer iron seekers were to be seen on the fields, which meant of course fewer bodies would be recovered. Also, as time progressed, more and more areas of land had been officially cleared by the teams of Belgian front workers, resulting in many of them leaving the area to look for alternative work. The equation is simple: the less people there are working on the land in various capacities, the less bodies would be found. None of these factors, however, changed the stark reality that over 100,000 bodies of soldiers of the British armies still had to be recovered from the battlefields of France and Belgium.

Somebody's son. Human remains recovered on the old battlefields. (Photographer unknown. Courtesy of the In Flanders Fields Museum.)

3   CWGCA: CWGC/1/1/7/B/45 (WG 1294/3 PT.4: Exhumation France and Belgium Part 4).

Ultimately, the Director of Records was proven right to be concerned, as, between the years of 1921 and 1939, in excess of 10,000 bodies of British and Commonwealth soldiers were recovered from the battlefields of the old Western Front, with approximately 30 percent of those being recovered in Belgium. Between the years of 1932 and 1939, roughly half of all bodies recovered were as a result of the work of the aforementioned iron seekers or metal searchers.

In 1939, the dark clouds of war once again formed above Belgium and the Ypres Salient, and the next generation of the BEF once again found themselves digging trenches and defensive positions in the old battlegrounds of the Ypres Salient. For the soldiers of 1939, the task was not only arduous, but it also had its inherent dangers of its own. Digging defences and trenches below the depth of the local farmers plough would often result in the discovery of unexploded ammunition from the Great War and of the bodies of their fellow soldiers who had fought over the same ground a generation before them. The digging of defensive positions in the Ypres Salient resulted in an increase of body finds in 1938–1939, when the rate of First World War body recoveries reached a level not seen since before the 1930s, with 155 recoveries being recorded that year in Belgium. An ominous sign of what was to come.

The threat of the impending conflict had led to the IWGC putting evacuation plans into place for their British staff and their families. In May 1940, the then IWGC had a recorded 540 staff members in France and Belgium. The German Army invaded Belgium on 10 May 1940, and, within the space of 18 days, it had achieved what the German Army of the Great War had failed to do in the space of four years: the complete defeat of Belgium. The speed of the German advance and the ensuing chaos meant that the evacuation plans of the IWGC were not as successful as hoped, with 206 of their staff members left behind in France and Belgium, of which 157 were captured by the Germans and interned in camps for the rest of the war and a further 11 listed as dead or missing.[4]

As the war neared Ypres itself, the plans for the evacuation of IWGC staff and families were put into action. In the early hours of Saturday, 18 May 1940, over 200 men, women and children assembled as planned in the school yard of the British school in Ypres to await transport for their evacuation back to the UK. All did not go to plan, however, when some of the prearranged transport failed to arrive, leaving some of the hopeful evacuees to find their own way to the coast as best they could. As a result, not all gained safety back to the UK. Some were captured and interned for the rest of the war in German camps, some went into hiding, a few joined the resistance, and unfortunately some were killed. By mid-May 1940, the IWGC no longer had a presence in the Ypres Salient and, therefore, no one to maintain the cemeteries and memorials of both the First World War and of those killed in this new conflict that yet again was consuming Europe.

---

4   Commonwealth War Graves Commission Archive (CWGCA) CWGC/2/1: 'Twenty Fourth Annual Report of the IWGC', Commission Annual Reports, p.10.

War physically returned to the Ypres Salient in late May 1940, when units of the BEF once again engaged with units of the German Army on the old battlefields of the Ypres Salient in a desperate attempt to slow the German advance in order to give the evacuation from Dunkirk a few more precious days. Hill 60, the Bluff, the Caterpillar Crater and St. Eloi were just a few of the notorious battle sites of the First World War that were again to witness the bloodshed of British and German soldiers. The fighting was as short as it was brutal. In three days of close and sometimes hand-to-hand combat, from 26–28 May 1940, the BEF were to lose approximately 600 men killed, with the Germans suffering a higher rate of over 800 men KIA.[5]

First World War bunker on Hill 60, scarred by battle damage from the Second World War in 1940. The bunker had taken several hits from a PAK 38 (t). (Author's photo.)

The dead lay where they had fallen: in fields, by roadsides, next to railway lines, in ditches and in people's gardens. Whilst the German graves units looked after the burial of their own dead, it seems to have been left to the local population to

---

5   Jerry Murland, *The Battle of the Ypres-Comines Canal 1940: France and Flanders Campaign* (Barnsley: Pen and Sword, 2019), p.113.

initially bury the dead of the BEF. As a result, multiple and single graves of British and German soldiers could once again be seen scattered across the Ypres Salient, buried in the spots where they had lost their lives. Local resident Ernest Blankaert found himself in the unenviable position of having the grave of a young German *leutnant*, Erdmann Hildebrand, in his garden. Hildebrand of the 12./I.R.30 had been fighting around Zillebeke on 27 May and had been buried where he had fallen, right in the middle of Blankaert's garden.[6] Eighty-one years after the event, Blankaert's granddaughter, Diana, told the story:

> My Grandmother and Grandfather had a house on the outskirts of Zillebeke close to the railway line at the road crossing. A German soldier had been killed in the fighting there in May 1940 and had been buried in the garden. I remember the grave had a cross bearing the soldiers name and was neatly kept. It had to be, as from time to time a German officer would visit the grave to lay flowers and to make sure that my grandfather kept the grave in a good condition. Sometimes flowers, forget me nots I think, would be sent from the soldier's family in Germany to be placed on the grave. Again, this was always checked by the Germans, if you didn't do as they said then you would be in serious trouble.[7]

By the end of May 1940, Belgium was in German hands and much of the fighting was over. The Belgian authorities, under the watchful eye of the German occupiers, now assumed responsibility both for the care of the British cemeteries and memorials of the Great War and for the burial of the British dead from this new conflict. By 1941, the Belgian Interior Ministry had handed this responsibility to two existing Belgian war graves associations, those being *Nos Tombes* and *Le Souvenir Belge*. These organisations not only maintained British cemeteries to a high level in difficult circumstances but also reverently buried the dead from the First World War as well as the Second World War, as, in spite of the German occupation, bodies of soldiers killed in the Great War were still being recovered in the Salient.

During those four years of occupation, the citizens of the Ypres Salient tried to get on with their lives as best as they could. Agricultural work and construction work continued, and so First World War bodies would have been discovered. It is, however, a matter of conjecture as to how many bodies of Great War soldiers discovered in the Ypres Salient during the Second World War were reported to the authorities and then reburied by the two Belgian organisations, as little record exists. Before the start of the Second World War, between the years of 1933 and 1938, bodies were being recovered from the battlefields of Belgium at an average rate of around 86 bodies per year. This was, however, with the 'finder's reward' still in place, which had been increased from

---

6 Henri Braem and Roger Verbeke, *De Slag om de Spoorweg en Vaart* (Zillebeke: Heemkunidge Kring Selebeke, 1990), p.111.
7 Interview with Diana Comeyne (15 August 2021).

two francs to 10 francs per body pre-Second World War. With no official IWGC presence in Belgium to record and recover such finds and with no finder's reward in place, one can only surmise that, in some cases, body finds were not reported, with the sites of the remains either marked for future collection or, more likely, ploughed through or built over by farmers and construction workers who wanted to have as little contact with their German occupiers as possible. Between March 1940 and February 1946, a total of 56 sets of remains of British Empire soldiers were recorded as having been recovered and reburied in the Ypres Salient, an average of only nine bodies per year, a figure well down on the pre-Second World War totals.[8]

In 1941, the German graves service removed the graves of their fallen from the fighting of 1940 to the German concentration cemetery in Lommel, close to the Dutch border. At the same time, the Belgian graves organisations exhumed the British bodies from the areas surrounding Ypres and then reburied them in several First World War British cemeteries in the area – for example, Bedford House Cemetery, which holds the remains of 69 British soldiers who were killed in the Second World War. The exhumation records of the British soldiers killed in 1940 tells a grim tale of brutal and violent death, with many having suffered bayonet wounds and many others with gunshot wounds to the back of the head or neck, indicating either mercy shots or cold-blooded executions.[9]

Belgium, like the rest of Europe, was to suffer as an occupied country until its liberation on 4 February 1945. The city of Ypres, and its surrounding areas, was liberated on 6 September 1944 by the 1st Polish Armoured Division, who lost several men in the process of freeing the city, those men then being buried at the Polish cemetery in Lommel.

The end of the Second World War saw the return of the IWGC to Belgium. Upon their return, the inspectors of the IWGC were pleasantly surprised to find that the First World War cemeteries and memorials had been largely left alone by the German occupiers. Although some were overgrown and some had suffered collateral battle damage, with the odd exception, there was no policy of systematic destruction of British cemeteries or memorials by the Germans on the Western Front. The return of the staff of the IWGC also signalled the restarting of the recording of First World War body recoveries in the Ypres Salient, with over 50 sets of remains recorded as having been recovered and reburied between the years of 1952 and 1957. Unfortunately, in the 1950s and 1960s, these figures would have been supplemented by the recovery of Second World War remains, particularly those of aircrew whose bodies lay deep in the ground with the mangled wreckage of their aircraft.

---

8   Commonwealth War Graves Commission Archive (CWGCA) CWGC/8: IWGC Burial Return C.R.3240/40/R. 31 March 1940, IWGC Burial Return C.R.3240/41/R. 31 March 1940, IWGC Reburial Return C/480/69/R 18 March 1957, and IWGC Reburial Return C/480/70/R 18 March 1957.

9   Braem and Verbeke, *De Slag om de Spoorweg en Vaart*, p.31.

After the Second World War, the Belgian Army (under the instruction of the Belgian government) now assumed the role for physically recovering the sets of First World War remains from the old battlefields as and when they had been reported, relieving the IWGC of the responsibility. Upon receiving a report of a chance find of human remains, a representative of the Belgian Army would attend the scene of the discovery, remove the remains and any surrounding artifacts and, once documented, would then notify the relevant authorities for collection, with the IWGC then collecting and taking responsibility for the remains of soldiers of the British armies of the time. In over 90 percent of cases, a body could at least be identified by nationality, normally by equipment found with the body. The remaining unidentifiable 10 percent would be reburied as unknown soldiers in the Belgian Army cemetery in Houthulst, a few miles from Ypres. The ethos of the Belgian authorities at the time was one of speed, being fully aware that, if a farmer or builder was to lose valuable time because of a site closure as a result of a body discovery, he would be less likely to report the find of a body in the future. In some instances, especially during harvest time, bodies were reburied on the spot where they had been found and the site marked in order for the farmer to work around the site and continue with his work unhindered, the body being removed in the coming weeks when the work had finished, thus giving the Belgian Army representative more time to search the area around the body and increase the chance that the body may be identified. This policy led to a greater level of cooperation between all the parties involved and certainly increased the rate of reported body discoveries. However, the system was somewhat primitive in today's terms and no doubt would have entailed a certain amount of educated guesswork in some cases of identification. This, of course, was all about to change with the passing of time and the development of technology.

18

Another Time, A Different Philosophy

From the 1960s to the 1990s, the level of body recoveries in the Ypres Salient continued at a steady rate, with the Belgian authorities handing over to the now CWGC an average of around 20 to 30 sets of remains each year. The recovery rate could fluctuate dramatically with the building of industrial estates, theme parks and housing in the Ypres Salient. These major works would often yield sets of remains from different nationalities and could often run into the hundreds, a good example being the discovery of Yorkshire Trench and dugouts in Boesinge on the outskirts of Ypres, when, in the 1990s, an amateur archaeology group named 'The Diggers' recovered in excess of 200 sets of remains on a site being cleared for the building of a new industrial estate. The lack of forensic technology available at the time meant that only one of the recovered sets of remains could be identified as an individual. Francois Metzinger was a French soldier serving in the 3e Zouaves and is believed to have been killed during the Second Battle of Ypres between 28 April and 24 May 1915.[1] Unlike the soldiers of the British Empire of the time, who were issued with ID tags that were later found to deteriorate in wet ground, the French Army issued their soldiers with metal ID tags that were more likely to withstand the test of time. It was one of these tags found with the remains of Francois Metzinger that allowed him to be identified as an individual and reburied in a named grave, no. 2562a, in St. Charles De Potyze French cemetery on the outskirts of Ypres in 1998.

The reason that major construction works would often turn up bodies in large numbers is not because of the size of the area they were developing but rather the depth they were digging at. In an effort to increase crop production, the Belgian government started to allow the farmers in the former devastated regions to deep plough again in the 1970s. This brought them into contact with ground at depths that had been left untouched since the end of the First World War, resulting in an increase in ammunition and body recoveries. By the time of the 1980s, the rate of

---

1   Francois Metzinger's headstone records his date of death as 21 May 1915; however, there is some discussion on the accuracy of this date.

The chemical makeup of the Flanders soil often preserves artefacts, in particular leather and wood as seen here, with the boots and rifle remarkably preserved. (Photo by Pol Lefevre, with permission.)

Human remains recovered by archaeologists in the Ypres Salient. (Photo by Pol Lefevre, with permission.)

body recoveries had levelled out and was dwindling, as the ground being turned over at this new depth had yielded the majority of what lay at that depth. That is not to say, however, that most of the bodies had been recovered. In fact, far from it, they simply lay buried deeper than the maximum depth of a farmer's plough. The ground at the maximum depth of a farmer's plough is called the 'plough pan', and everything that lies beneath that depth lies relatively undisturbed. With deep ploughing going down to a depth of around 50cm and bodies in the First World War often being buried in trenches or shell holes, often metres deep, it stands to reason that many thousands of bodies still lie unrecovered, out of reach of the farmer's plough. The only time these bodies are likely to be recovered is during construction works or by archaeologists on official digs.

As the First World War faded into history and its last veterans passed away, the ethos of body recovery in the Ypres Salient switched not only to one of recovering and identifying the body but also to one of the who, what and why of the body's location. The battlefields of the First World War had turned into sites of historical significance, with many becoming protected sites and the bodies of the missing becoming part of

The remains of a British soldier of the Royal Welsh Fusiliers. Found where he fell, still wearing his helmet, ammunition pouches and carrying his entrenching tool. (Photo by Pol Lefevre, with permission.)

A discovery of mixed remains, possibly as a result of artillery fire. (Photo by Pol Lefevre, with permission.)

This soldier was found where he had fallen, and the rifle grenades he was carrying are clearly visible. (Photo by Pol Lefevre, with permission.)

the jigsaw. By the late 1990s, teams of official archaeologists were playing a larger role in body recoveries, and, by the 2000s, archaeologists in Belgium were exclusively responsible for the physical recovery of remains from the old battlefields, whether they were on predetermined archaeological digs or they were responding to a chance find by a farmer. Between the years of 1998 to 2020, a total of 695 body finds were reported to the Flemish authorities.

Today, the remains of the fallen of the First World War in Flanders are governed by two separate legal entities: on the one hand, the Geneva Convention requires that the remains of soldiers come under the remit of the military authorities, whilst the authorities in Flanders class them as being 'archaeological heritage' and, as such, become subject to Flemish legislation regarding this. Both entities work in harmony, the end goal being the efficient recovery of the fallen with the highest possible level of identification whilst retaining the dignity of the fallen soldier. The court of Ypres confirmed in 2006 that the military fallen of both world wars in Flanders must be excavated and examined by archaeologists and forensic experts using the most up-to-date scientific methods and techniques, including anthropology and DNA (deoxyribonucleic acid) extraction.

The official system of body recovery differs in Flanders from that of the rest of Belgium and of France, with the procedure in Flanders being born out of years of experience of First World War body recoveries and of necessity. Whenever human remains are found, the first step is to call the police, who will attend the scene with a local heritage intercommunal group named 'CO7' and try to ascertain if the remains are the result of a suspicious death. If the remains are deemed to be those of a fallen soldier, the police will report this to the Belgian war graves service, the BWHI (Belgian War Heritage Institute), and to the FHA (Flanders Heritage Agency). It is the FHA who then assign a local archaeology company to the task of the recovery of the remains, who are given a maximum total of 30 days to recover the remains and artefacts, fully document them and then return them to the authorities. Time scale is an important factor in the process, as individuals and contractors are less likely to act in due diligence and report finds if it means their building works are going to be shut down for weeks on end. As a result, the allotted archaeological companies have to attend the scene within 48 hours of notification and try their best to remove a set of remains within two days if possible. This high level of efficiency has resulted in an increase in the reporting of chance body finds by local contractors since they are no longer subject to long periods of disruption and added costs.

The recovery of the remains is conducted as thoroughly as possible by the archaeologists, with the area surrounding the body being meticulously searched for any small artefacts that may aid in the process of identification. Each find is recorded, and its position in relation to the body is noted, as even the slightest detail may mean the difference between identification or not. Once the archaeologists are satisfied that the site has been searched thoroughly and all artefacts are recorded, the remains are carefully removed.

Personal effects found with a body can often help in its identification. (Photo by Frans Hoijtink, with permission.)

Once the remains and artefacts have been recovered from the site, they are taken to a location in Bruges operated by the archaeologists, where the artefacts are studied and catalogued whilst the human remains are cleaned and examined by anthropologists, who look not only for evidence of cause of death but also any other factors that might aid in identification. Once completed, a temporary report is made containing such information as body location and map, list of artefacts recovered and photographs of the remains and artefacts. This report is handed over to the police when the body is returned to their care. Upon receipt, the police will hand over jurisdiction of the body to the Belgian war graves service, who in turn will notify the relevant national authorities to arrange the collection of the remains. In the British and Commonwealth's cases, the CWGC are informed. In the meantime, the archaeology company compiles a final report, copies of which are sent to the Flemish authorities and to the owner of the land where the body was discovered.

Once notified by the BWHI, the CWGC representatives will make arrangements to collect the body from the Belgian authorities and take them back to their main depot in Beaurains, France. Upon arrival, the remains and artefacts are rechecked, and a new anthropology report is compiled. The CWGC then compiles their own 'Discovery of Human Remains' report, which replicates everything from the Belgian archaeologists' report previously completed and sent digitally to the CWGC. The file is then sent to the commemorations team at the CWGC head office in Maidenhead in the UK, whose job it is to research the location where the body was found, re-examine previous recoveries from that area and look for the names of men registered as missing in that area – all with the aim of compiling a list of names for potential identification. Once completed, the relevant potential national authorities are informed, who in turn consult their own records and conduct their own research in an effort to identify the individual.

Although each Commonwealth country's procedures are slightly different (e.g., Canada's regulations and way of working may differ slightly to those of Australia), the process across all Commonwealth countries is broadly the same. With this in mind, I will focus on the work of the UK authorities, the JCCC (Joint Casualty and Compassionate Centre).

Based in Gloucestershire, the JCCC (also known as the 'MOD (Ministry of Defence) War Detectives') are responsible for further research and the organisation of the reburials of casualties from the British Army. Upon receipt of the reports from the Belgian archaeologists and the CWGC, the JCCC will set to work in trying to identify the casualty. Using the information gained from the aforementioned reports, battalion war diaries, the medal roll index, pension records, regimental museums, historians and genealogy sites, the JCCC will attempt to identify the body to whatever level is possible. If the JCCC believe there is a chance of identifying the body as an individual, then a third-party forensic company is employed, who will visit the CWGC depot in Beaurains, France, in order to extract DNA for analysis and compile a further anthropological report. The forensic scientists are also able to separate mixed remains into individual bodies when required, thus ensuring a separate grave for each set of remains where possible. In order to extract the DNA from the remains, the scientists remove an unfilled tooth or part of the femur from the body and take it back to the UK for further analysis. Upon arrival in the UK laboratory, the remains are cleaned in a bleach solution to remove the possibility of third-party cross contamination and then dipped into liquid nitrogen and ground into a powder. The powder is then mixed with chemicals that release the DNA into a solution. The sample is then compared to DNA-test-kit results already sent out to the families of possible relatives to the body identified by the research of the JCCC. Once the tests are completed, the results are sent to the JCCC. If there is any doubt whatsoever on a personal identification by name, the soldier will be reburied as an unknown but to a certain level of identification – for example, an 'Unknown British Soldier' or an 'Unknown Sergeant'. Once the JCCC are satisfied that they have exhausted all possibilities in identifying the set of remains, a report is sent to the CWGC, and the process of organising the burial can begin.

In order to organise the burial, the JCCC are responsible for several tasks, including liaising with British Army regiments, organising a local undertaker and sending out invites to dignitaries and family members. There are two types of regimental burial parties to organise: one for the burials of unknown soldiers and one for the burial of identified soldiers. The burial party for the reinterment of an unknown soldier consists of 10 officials – a padre, six bearers to carry the coffin, one officer, one sergeant major and a bugler. The burial party for an identified soldier consists of 17 officials – a padre, six bearers to carry the coffin, one officer, one sergeant major, a bugler and a firing party of seven consisting of six riflemen and an NCO. It is also the job of the JCCC to organise a full rehearsal of the ceremony the day before it is due to take place and to dress the coffin in preparation for the reburial.

The role of the CWGC in the reburial process mainly relates to what goes on within the boundary of the chosen cemetery. The CWGC select the cemetery where the reburial is to take place, normally selecting a cemetery that has space for reburials close to the site where the body was recovered. The CWGC will transport the body from Beaurains to the allotted undertaker and are also responsible for organising the production and delivery of the headstone, digging the grave and refilling it afterwards. The management of the crowd within the cemetery during the service is another the responsibility of the CWGC. Large numbers of people attending the service means that areas need to be roped off so that the general public know where they can and cannot stand. This part of their responsibility is very important, as they announce each burial on their website in advance, inviting the general public to attend. As a result, it is not unusual to see crowds of several hundred attending burials in the Ypres Salient, a truly fantastic thing. Since the start of the millennium, all British and Commonwealth burials have come under the control of the British military, hence the use of military units in the burial services. Before this, the services were managed by the CWGC, with the British military attaché attending the services on behalf of the

Burials in short coffins. (Photo by Frans Hoijtink, with permission.)

armed forces. The switch in responsibility resulted in a marked improvement in the types of coffins used in the ceremonies. Previous to the switch, short coffins, roughly half the size of a normal coffin, were being used mainly for practical reasons and for cost effectiveness. The change to the use of military bearer parties resulted in a change of policy, and now all the recovered remains are interred in full-size coffins, which are more practical for the bearer parties and more aesthetically pleasing to the onlookers at the ceremony.

As a battlefield historian and author, with over 12 years of battlefield guiding experience in the Ypres Salient, hand on heart, I can tell you (the reader) that the remains of our war dead in Flanders are treated with the upmost respect from the minute the remains are found to their reburial. The identification process can take anything up to three years from recovery to reburial, and the organisations involved in the process will exhaust every avenue of investigation before they rebury a body as an unknown soldier.

We owe them at least that.

Multiple burials of unidentified soldiers in Hooge Crater Cemetery, an all-too-familiar sight in the Ypres Salient. (Author's photo.)

19

Finding Lance Corporal Cook

The year of 2020 saw the world once again plunged into a worldwide conflict. This time, however, the enemy was an invisible attacker that made no discrimination between age or race, an enemy that, although would eventually be supressed, would have a dramatic impact on the lives of everyone in the modern world.

The impact of COVID-19 was felt keenly in the Ypres Salient, where previously high levels of tourism related to the First World War fell almost instantly to zero. The iconic Last Post Ceremony, which has been performed almost continuously nightly underneath the Menin Gate since 1928, was severely curtailed, with no members of the general public allowed to attend and a restricted number of buglers being permitted to perform the ceremony. To the credit of the city of Ieper and the Last Post Association, the ceremony continued unbroken throughout the pandemic, an action that was not only born out of respect for the war dead of the British Empire armies of the Great War but also one of defiance to this new enemy, one that would help show the people of Ypres that life would go on and that normality would eventually return.

The strict COVID-19 restrictions put into place in March 2020 by the Belgian authorities would not be eased until October 2021. During this time, the population was subject to lockdowns and severe travel restrictions, which not only hit the local population but also stopped First World War tourism in Ypres dead in its tracks. The year of 2018 and the end of the Centenary commemorations saw huge amounts of British and Commonwealth First World War pilgrims visiting the battlefields of the Ypres Salient. In 2020, that figure was reduced to virtually zero. Accommodation, bars, restaurants and tour guide companies were all hit hard by the loss of visitors to the area caused by the pandemic. The situation was so serious that even the work of DOVO, the Belgian Army bomb-disposal service, was put on hold until the situation improved. In fact, at the time of writing this book, the collection teams were still only collecting from the Ypres Salient two days a week, as opposed to the daily collections they normally performed.

The international travel restrictions that were put into place during March 2020, in an effort to curtail the spread of the virus, resulted in the temporary cancellation of all British and Commonwealth military burials in the Ypres Salient, with around 27 burials being put on hold until the restrictions were lifted.[1] In early October 2021, burials resumed, with the reburial of 15812 Lance Corporal Robert Cook of the 2nd Battalion Essex Regiment (KIA on 2 May 1915) taking place on the twenty-seventh of that month. Rosie Barron of the JCCC takes up the story:

> Lance Corporal Robert Cook was born in Bishop Wilton, Yorkshire, on 6 June 1876. He was one of seven children born to James Cook and Rebecca Leak. In 1878 his mother Rebecca died. James then emigrated to South Africa with five of his children.
>
> Having travelled to South Africa as a young boy, Robert served with various British Colonial units. On 29 December 1895 he took part in the Jameson Raid as a Trooper with A Troop of The Mashonaland Mounted Police. In 1896 he qualified for the British South Africa Company Medal with 'Rhodesia 1896' reverse, whilst serving with the Matabeleland Relief Force. In 1899 he took part in the Second Boer War. He is listed as serving with Bethune's Mounted Infantry from 19 October 1899 to 19 November 1900, spending part of this time with The South African Light Horse. He took part in the relief of Ladysmith. On 23 April 1901 he was wounded at Boschmanskop whilst serving with French's Scouts. For this service he was awarded the Queen's South Africa Medal 1899–1902 and the King's South Africa Medal 1901–1902.
>
> In November 1914, Robert enlisted into The Essex Regiment in Cape Town. He arrived on the Western Front on 24 March 1915. The War Diaries of 2nd Battalion The Essex Regiment show that they moved into the front line near Ypres on 30 April 1915. At 5:00 p.m. on 2 May 1915 they were attacked with gas, they were shelled and then attacked by the enemy. Lance Corporal Cook was killed during the course of the fighting that day.
>
> Between 2014 and 2015, twenty-four sets of remains were found at what is believed to have been the site of Irish Farm Cemetery. In May 1915, Irish Farm was in use as a Regimental Aid Post and it was common for battlefield cemeteries to be established next to aid posts. It had been thought that all of the casualties buried in Irish Farm Cemetery had been concentrated into New Irish Farm Cemetery a short distance away after the Great War. Nineteen of the casualties found between 2014 and 2015 were buried in New Irish Farm Cemetery on 19 September 2017. None of these men were identifiable, although some were of known regiments including: four men who served with The Essex Regiment, one soldier belonging to The Monmouthshire Regiment, one soldier belonging to The Argyll and Sutherland Highlanders, one soldier of The Northumberland Regiment and a soldier of The Royal Irish Regiment.

1   Figures from the JCCC.

Five of the casualties found were not buried alongside these men in 2017 as it was thought they might be identifiable. After further research and unsuccessful DNA testing two of these men were buried as unknown soldiers of The Royal Fusiliers on 9 October 2019. Two more of these men, including another unknown soldier of The Essex Regiment, were buried on 5 November 2019.

This left one remaining soldier known as 'Casualty 19'. He was found with multiple artefacts including shoulder titles and a cap badge of The Essex Regiment and a medal ribbon bar. The shoulder titles and cap badge found with the remains were strong indications that this soldier was a member of The Essex Regiment. The location of where the remains were found indicated that this individual most likely belonged to 2nd Battalion and would have been killed between 30 April and 8 July 1915, when the battalion was located in the area moving in and out of the frontline.

CWGC records show that there is a total of a hundred and thirty-eight other ranks of 2nd Battalion The Essex Regiment still missing from during this period. These men are all commemorated on the Menin Gate, the majority having been killed in May 1915. Based on this information alone, it would not have been possible to narrow down the pool of candidates in order to identify 'Casualty 19'. JCCC therefore referred the case to Major Ret'd Peter Williamson MBE at the Essex Regiment Museum for further investigation.[2]

Having received the details of the then 'Casualty 19', Major Ret'd Peter Williamson MBE and his team set about the task in earnest in order to give this (so far) unidentified soldier the best opportunity of identification and affording him the dignity of being buried as a named soldier. Major Ret'd Williamson carries on:

> When JCCC first approached the Essex Regiment Museum for help in identifying these remains, all we had was a very blurry photograph of the medal ribbon bar and it wasn't even clear whether there were two medal ribbons on it or three. We knew that the soldier had been found at the site of the original Irish Farm Cemetery, and given the dates that Cemetery was in use we were able to say with some certainty that he had been serving with 2nd Essex in 1915. Our records showed that there were a hundred and forty-four members of that Battalion who had been killed during that period and had no known grave. A few weeks later we received a better photograph of the medal ribbon bar and were able to identify the medals concerned as the British South Africa Company Medal 1890–97, the Queen's South Africa Medal 1899–1902, and the King's

---

2   Rosie Barron, JCCC, *Summary of JCCC Case Research* (Unpublished, reproduced with permission).

South Africa Medal 1901–02, taking a comparison photograph of a mocked-up medal bar with the original.

Knowing the qualifying dates for the British South Africa Company Medal, we worked out that the soldier concerned must have been born no later than 1883 to have received it. This enabled us to eliminate from the 'no known grave' list all those who were born after that date.

Commonwealth War Graves Commission records gave us quite a lot of information, but we had to supplement that by researching the birth dates of many others using family history websites. We could also eliminate the two officers, because of the presence of shoulder titles. That left us with a short list of forty-seven.

We then consulted a book 'The British South Africa Co. Medal Roll 1890-1897' by Colin R. Owen, which lists all those entitled to the medal. That enabled us to eliminate many of the 1915 casualties simply because there was nobody of that surname on that roll.

That roll showed an R. Cook taking part in the Jameson Raid in December 1895 as a Trooper in the Mashonaland Mounted Police, then qualifying for the medal, with 'Rhodesia 1896' reverse, as a Trooper in the Matabeleland Relief Force. This information matched that on the CWGC record for Lance Corporal Robert Cook which includes the statement 'Served in Matabeleland (1896)'.

That gave us a stand-out candidate for this identification, but there remained question marks over ten others where 1915 casualty surnames also appeared on the British South Africa Co. medal roll. Detail was often sparse, but we studied each one in turn, gradually ruling them all out because we could see that they had not received the King's South Africa Medal, we could see from the 1901 Census that they could not possibly have received that medal, or on other grounds.

Finally, we came to the conclusion that these remains could only be those of 15812 Lance Corporal Robert Cook, killed on 2 May 1915 while serving with The Pompadours.[3]

The importance of the correct removal and cataloguing of artefacts during the body recovery process was highlighted in the case of Lance Corporal Cook. Upon closer examination of the remains, the shoulder titles and cap badge of the Essex Regiment were discovered. In addition to this, the remains of a medal ribbon bar were found on the remnants of the uniform, later identified as medals relating to the South African Wars prior to the First World War. The recovery of these artefacts by the archaeologists and later DNA testing pieced together a jigsaw that, upon completion, not only led to the identification of Lance Corporal Robert Cook as an individual

---

3   Major Ret'd Peter Williamson MBE, *Summary of Essex Regiment Museum Research* (Unpublished, reproduced with permission).

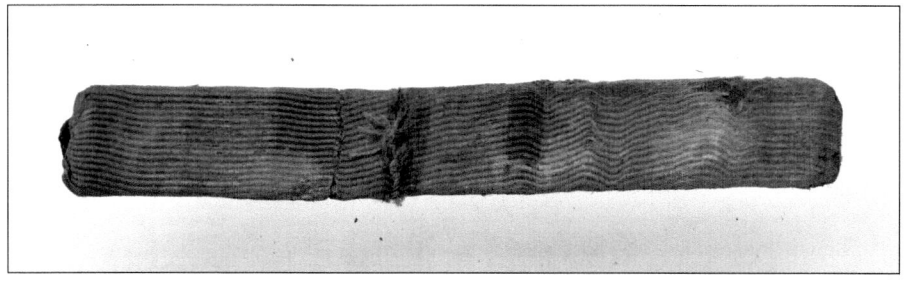

Personal effects found with the remains of Lance Corporal Robert Cook. (Photo by Agentschap Onroerend Erfgoed.)

but also enabled his modern-day family members to be traced so that they could both learn of the story of Robert Cook and attend his burial service, as he was finally laid to rest in the fields of Flanders.

After 106 years of being listed as missing in action, in the presence of members from his modern-day family, Lance Corporal Robert Cook was finally laid to rest amongst his comrades with full military honours on 27 October 2021 in New Irish Farm Cemetery, on the outskirts of Ypres, close to where he fell.

The burial of Lance Corporal Robert Cook, with members of his family in attendance. (Crown Copyright, JCCC, with permission.)

By the end of 2021, officials of the CWGC and JCCC had laid to rest 12 bodies of British and Commonwealth soldiers killed in the Great War in the Ypres Salient.[4] The sad reality is that even a global pandemic would not halt the relentless recovery of ammunition and bodies in the Ypres Salient from the Great War. The year of 2021 saw the usual amounts of ammunition recovered in the area; several accidents were reported as a result of ordnance recovered from the First World War, with one particularly nasty incident reported of a British hand grenade blowing up in the face of a local farmer's wife. Luckily for her, she did not suffer serious injuries. The discovery and recovery of bodies continued as always in the Salient, with local archaeologists recovering sets of remains across all nationalities during the year.

With millions of tons of ammunition still believed to be concealed beneath the surface of the fields of Flanders and tens of thousands of bodies of First World War soldiers still unaccounted for, the battlefields of the Ypres Salient of the Great War will still be releasing their secrets long into the future, long after you and I have faded into history.

A truly sobering thought.

---

4   Figures from the JCCC.

Bibliography

Archival Sources

Australian War Memorial (AWM)
2018.8.765: War Diary Australian War Graves Detachment
PR05609: Henry Whiting Letter

Commonwealth War Graves Commission Archive (CWGCA)
CWGC/1/1/7/B/48: Exhumations. Hooge Committee of Enquiry Report
CWGC/2/1: Commission Annual Reports
CWGC/2/2/1/6: Commission Meeting Minutes
CWGC/6/4/1/2/1572
CWGC/8
CWGC/8/1/4/1/1/58: *The Times*
CWGC ACON 167
CWGC ADD 1/3/4: Taking Over of DGR&E by IWGC
CWGC ADD 1/3/8 PT.1: Hooge Crater Enquiry Correspondence
CWGC CCM 12912: Lord Worsley
CWGC CCM 15034
CWGC CCM 16470: Pte G. C. Hopkins PPCLI
CWGC CCM 19578
CWGC DGRE 1: Narrative Letters and Reports
CWGC SDC 4
CWGC SDC 19
CWGC WG 783 PT.1: War Graves Association
CWGC WG 1294 PT.1: Exhumation by IWGC, Journal of Lieutenant Colonel Gell
CWGC WG 1294/3 PT.1: Exhumation France and Belgium Part 1
CWGC WG 1294/3 PT.2: Exhumation France and Belgium Part 2
CWGC WG 1294/3 PT.4: Exhumation France and Belgium Part 4

Princess Patricia's Canadian Light Infantry Museum & Archives (PPCLIMA)
War Diary January 1917-March 1918

The National Archives (TNA)
WO-95-40-48-09: War Diary of L of C Ypres Area Commandant April 1919–June 1919
WO-95-82-1: BEF France and Flanders GHQ Controller of Salvage July 1917 to Jan 1919
WO-95-82-2: BEF France and Flanders GHQ Controller of Salvage July 1917 to Jan 1919
WO-95-82-3: BEF France and Flanders GHQ Controller of Salvage July 1917 to Jan 1919
WO-95-82-4: BEF France and Flanders GHQ Controller of Salvage July 1917 to Jan 1919
WO-95-82-5: BEF France and Flanders GHQ Controller of Salvage July 1917 to Jan 1919
WO-95-82-5-017: War Diary of Controller of Salvage 3 Dec. 1918
WO-95-82-5-025: War Diary of Controller of Salvage 3 Dec. 1918
WO-95-82-5-033: War Diary of Controller of Salvage 3 Dec. 1918
WO-95-82-5-036: War Diary of Controller of Salvage 3 Dec. 1918
WO-95-83-6/1: War Diary Controller of Labour GHQ
WO-95-83-6/2: War Diary Controller of Labour GHQ
WO-95-83-7: War Diary Controller of Labour GHQ
WO-95-383-9: BEF Third Army Area Salvage Diary
WO-95-1016-1: 1st ANZAC Corps Salvage Coy
WO-95-1079-5: Canadian Corps Salvage Company
WO-95-2032-3: 18th Divisional Salvage Company
WO-95-2110: War Diary of 20th Divisional Troops, Division Salvage Company
WO-95-2110-4: 20th Divisional Salvage Company
WO-95-4048-9: Ypres Town Major War Diary
WO-339/120758: Captain E. P. Cawston

Newspapers and Periodicals

Commonwealth War Graves Commission (CWGC) – *A History of the Commonwealth War Graves Commission*
Commonwealth War Graves Commission (CWGC) – *Sir Fabian Ware. Founder of the Commonwealth War Graves Commission*
Daily Mail
Daily Telegraph Magazine
De Poperinghenaar
Evening Standard
Flanders Today
Kings Country Chronicle
Somme Times
Sunday Express

The New Annual Register, or, General Repository of History, Politics, Arts, Sciences, and Literature for the Year 1822
The Times
The Wipers Times
The Ypres Times

Published Primary Sources

Beaver, Patrick (ed.), *The Wipers Times* (London: Peter Davies, 1973)
Chaplin, Charles, *My Autobiography* (New York: Simon and Schuster, 1964)
Diary of 2nd Lieutenant John Glubb M.C. RE 7th Field Company (7 March 1916)
Edmonds, James E., *Military Operations: France and Belgium, 1917* (London: Battery Press, 1940), vol. II
Hague Convention of 1907
Siebert, Willi, *Journal* (Ypres: In Flanders Fields Museum, 1915)
Treaty of Versailles
War Office, *Statistics of the Military Effort of the British Empire during the Great War, 1914–1920* (London: HMSO, 1922)

Published Secondary Sources

Beckett, Ian F. W., *Ypres: The First Battle 1914* (London: Routledge, 2013)
Braem, Henri, and Verbeke, Roger, *De Slag om de Spoorweg en Vaart* (Zillebeke: Heemkunidge Kring Selebeke, 1990)

Connelly, Mark, and Goebel, Stefan, *Ypres: Great Battles* (Oxford: Oxford University Press, 2018)

Dendooven, Dominiek, 'Bringing the Dead Home: Repatriation, Illegal Repatriation and Expatriation of British Bodies during and after the First World War', in Paul Cornish and Nicholas J. Saunders (eds), *Bodies in Conflict: Corporeality, Materiality, and Transformation* (London: Routledge, 2013), p.69
Dendooven, Dominiek, and Dewilde, Jan, *The Reconstruction of Ypres: A Walk from Cloth Hall to Menin Gate* (London: Uniform, 2020)
Desreumaux, John, *Land van schroot en knoken: Slachtoffers van ontploffingen in de frontstreek 1918 - heden* (Leuven: Davidsfonds Uitgeverij, 2011)

Elliot, Sue, and Fox, James, *The Children Who Fought Hitler: A British Outpost in Europe* (London: John Murray, 2010)

Forbes, Arthur, *A History of the Army Ordnance Services* (London: Medici Society Ltd., 1929), vol. 3

Gardner, Brian (ed.), *Up the Line to Death: The War Poets 1914–1918* (London: Methuen, 1976)
Gibson, T. A. Edwin, and Ward, G. Kingsley, *Courage Remembered* (London: HMSO, 1989)
Graham, Stephen, *The Challenge of the Dead: A Vision of the War and the Life of the Common Soldier in France, Seen Two Years Afterwards between August and November, 1920* (London: Cassell and Company, 1921)

Haythornthwaite, Philip J., *The World War One Source Book* (London: Brockhampton Press, 2000)

Longworth, Philip, *The Unending Vigil: A History of the Commonwealth War Graves Commission, 1917-1967* (Barnsley: Pen and Sword, 2020)

Macdonald, Lyn, *1915: The Death of Innocence* (London: Penguin, 1997)
Macdonald, Lyn, *Somme* (London: Penguin, 1993)
Macdonald, Lyn, *They Called It Passchendaele: The Story of the Third Battle of Ypres and of the Men who Fought in It* (London: Penguin, 1993)
Murland, Jerry, *The Battle of the Ypres-Comines Canal 1940: France and Flanders Campaign* (Barnsley: Pen and Sword, 2019)

Passingham, Ian, *Pillars of Fire: The Battle of Messines Ridge, 1917* (Stroud: Spellmount, 2012)
Perry, Robert A., *To Play a Giant's Part: The Role of the British Army at Passchendaele* (Uckfield: Naval & Military Press, 2014)
Prentiss, Augustin M., *Chemicals in War: A Treatise on Chemical Warfare* (New York and London: McGraw Hill, 1937)

Starling, John, and Lee, Ivor, *No Labour, No Battle: Military Labour during the First World War* (Stroud: Spellmount, 2014)
Strachan, Hew, *The First World War* (Oxford: Oxford University Press, 2001), vol. 1: To Arms

Van Emden, Richard, *Missing: The Need for Closure after the Great War* (Barnsley: Pen and Sword, 2019)
Van Hollebeeke, Yannick; Derycke, Karen; Morisse, Annemie; Bostyn, Franky; and Reynaert, Steven, *1917: Total War in Flanders* (Brugge: Stefaan Gheysen, 2017)

Van Velzen, Marianne, *Missing in Action: Australia's World War I Grave Services, An Astonishing True Story of Misconduct, Fraud and Hoaxing* (Crows Nest: Allen and Unwin, 2018)

Zanders, Jean Pascal, 'The Destruction of Old Chemical Weapons in Belgium', in Thomas Stock and Karlheinz Lohs (eds), *The Challenge of Old Chemical Munitions and Toxic Armament Wastes* (Oxford: Oxford University Press, 1997), pp.199–230

Ziino, Bart, *A Distant Grief: Australians, War Graves and the Great War* (Perth: UWA Publishing, 2007)

Published Theses and Papers

Bowers, T., 'The Identification of British War Casualties: The Work of the Joint Casualty and Compassionate Centre', *Forensic Science International*, 318/110571 (2021), 1–5. https://doi.org/10.1016/j.forsciint.2020.110571

Dendooven, Dominiek, *Asia in Flanders Fields: A Transnational History of Indians and Chinese on the Western Front, 1914-1920*. 2018. University of Kent, PhD

Hubé, D., 'Industrial-Scale Destruction of Old Chemical Ammunition near Verdun: A Forgotten Chapter of the Great War', *First World War Studies*, 8/2–3 (2017), 205–34. DOI: 10.1080/19475020.2017.1393347

Martin, V., 'A First World War Example of Forensic Archaeology', *Forensic Science International*, 314/110394 (2020), 1–5. https://doi.org/10.1016/j.forsciint.2020.110394

Unpublished Thesis and Papers

Hodgkinson, Peter E., *Human Remains on the Great War Battlefields*. Unpublished. Birmingham University, MA

Index

A

Accidents, 33, 38, 48, 51–52, 54–56, 79, 82, 86–87, 90, 94, 103
   risk of, 56
Adjutant General, 122–23, 173
Ammunition, 24–25, 32–33, 35–37, 40, 42, 54–56, 61–62, 64, 69, 78, 80, 83, 88–89, 103, 229
   dangerous rusting, 48
   discovery of, 61
   live, 45, 49, 55, 64, 68, 103
   recovering, 39
   remaining in trench, 37
Ammunition collection, 37, 41, 53, 103
Ammunition deal, 40–41
Ammunition depots, 37
Ammunition dumps, ix, 36, 43, 50
   large German, 72
Ammunition empties, 27, 29
Ammunition packages, 98, 100
Ammunition recovery, 88
Ammunition workers, 42
Antwerp, 37, 187, 194–95, 197
Archaeologists, 214–15, 217–18, 225
Areas, work searching, 110
Armistice, 32, 47, 49, 121, 165, 178
Army burial officer, 129, 141, 150, 152
Army burial parties, 110, 117
Army exhumation units, 157, 161
Artefacts, 214, 217–18, 225
Article of commerce, 105–6
Artillery shells, 19–20, 23–25, 51, 55–56, 71, 73, 76, 94, 103
   buried, 55
   concealed, 47
   conventional, 43
   dud, 37
   large, 65
   rusting, 64
ASD (Army Salvage Department), 26, 28
Australian bodies, 164
Australian graves, 122, 147
Australian Graves Services, 122, 159
AWM (Australian War Memorial), 18, 27, 125

B

Baron, Herbert, 41, 187–88
Battenberg, Prince Maurice of, 201–2
Battlefields, ix–x, 23, 25–26, 29–33, 35–37, 45–48, 70, 104–5, 110, 113–14, 116–19, 126–28, 133–34, 207–8, 221–22
Battle of Messines Ridge (1917), 24–25
Bawtree, Corporal Ivan, 38, 132–33, 135–37
Beaufort, Duchess of, 111–12
Bedford House Cemetery, 198, 211
BEF (British Expeditionary Force), 13, 106–7, 110, 201, 208–10
BEF France and Flanders GHQ Controller of Salvage, 32, 37
Belgian archaeologists, 218–19
Belgian Army, 21, 49–50, 63, 70, 72–75, 77. 80, 84, 88, 94–95, 97, 102, 186, 212
   modern, 40
Belgian Army bomb-disposal service, 222
Belgian Army bomb-disposal site, 51
Belgian Army bomb-disposal units, 69
Belgian authorities, 39–40, 42–43, 84–85, 167, 183, 185–87, 197–98, 210, 212–13, 218, 222
Belgian War Heritage Institute, 217
Belgium, 13–14, 30–34, 37, 41, 62, 68, 72–76, 78–79, 109–10, 121–23, 159–61, 163–64, 167–68, 170–71, 174–79, 185–87, 194–95, 197–98, 206–8, 210–11
Bluff, The, 114, 209

235

Bodies, 52–53, 113, 115–16, 118–19, 124–25, 128–32, 134, 136–43, 146–50, 152–55, 157 65, 167–77, 182–87, 191–95, 203–4, 206–8, 210–13, 215, 217–21, 229
  decomposing, 115, 134
  exhumations of, 32, 161, 203
Body recoveries, 113, 117–18, 120, 123, 126, 128, 159–60, 206, 213, 215, 217
  early days of, 124, 134
  task of, 35, 117–18, 128, 157
Body Snatching and Illegal Exhumations, 182
Bomb-disposal units, 50, 62, 65, 68, 74, 80, 84
Bones, 105–6, 114, 118, 134, 155, 186, 204
Boveroux, Lieutenant Pierre, 73–74
Brass shell cases, 27, 42
British Army, 16–17, 24, 26–27, 33–34, 36–37, 41, 108, 110, 115–16, 120, 122, 219
British Army ammunition disposal sites, 41
British bodies, 167–69, 185, 198, 203, 211, 232
British cemeteries, 174, 184, 197, 211
British Empire, x, 17, 24, 29, 106, 172, 174, 211, 213, 222, 232
British exhumation units, 123, 146
British shells, 40, 46, 48, 59
  large, 68
  unexploded, 25
Brussels, 41, 79, 83, 185–86, 188, 195, 197
Building, 19, 45, 55, 65, 83, 87, 98, 100, 140, 195, 213
Burial officer, 150, 152
Burial parties, 117–18, 124, 219
Burials, 51, 54, 120–21, 128, 130, 134, 142–43, 145, 158, 160–61, 180, 182, 209–10, 219–20, 223
Burial service, 119, 141, 144, 220, 227
Burial sites, 108, 128, 190
BWGA (British War Graves Association) 176–77, 182

C

Canada, 122, 155, 178, 189–90, 192–95, 198–201
Canadian bereaved parent, 155–56
Canadian War Graves Detachment, 122
Cemeteries, 34–35, 58–59, 61, 112–13, 138–39, 141, 145, 153–55, 158, 174, 176–77, 181, 184–85, 194, 197–98, 200–201, 220
  civilian, 60, 170
  concentration, 129, 145
  designated, 128, 137–38, 140
Chambers, 86, 96, 98, 100
  inner, 98
  outer, 98
  second loading, 96
Chemical munitions, 42–43, 84–88, 96
Chemical shells, 61, 80, 83–87
  solid, 86–87
Chemical weapons, 23–24, 36–37, 41, 43, 50, 62, 75–76, 85–88, 90, 93
Children, 19, 46–47, 54–55, 57, 64, 78–79, 106, 208, 223, 232
  official Belgian poster warning, 56
Chinese Labour Company, 34, 37
Chinese Labour Corps, 33, 37
Clandestine exhumations, 182, 187, 197, 199
Clearing ammunition, 40, 50
Clearing the dead, 117–19, 124, 126, 129, 158, 166
Coffins, 51, 187, 194–95, 219–21
  short, 220–21
Controller of Salvage, 29–30
Cook, Lance Corporal Robert, 222-23, 225–28
Copper drive band, 46, 53
Cordite, 42, 45
Craters, 64, 118–19
  smoking shell, 53
Crawford, Captain G.F., 128–43, 145, 150–53
Crawford exhumation guide, 144
Crawford procedures, 145, 147, 154, 157
Cresol, 130–31, 136, 138
CWGC (Commonwealth War Graves Commission), 14, 17, 59, 61, 109, 111, 113, 181–82, 203–6, 213, 218–20, 229–31

D

Daily Mail, 163–64
Dangers, 48–49, 52, 55, 64, 68, 72–73, 76, 78, 84, 90, 109–10
Deactivations, 84, 87–88
Demobilisation, 31–32, 34, 122, 145, 157–58, 163
Deputy Assistant Director of Graves Registrations and Enquiries, 142, 153
Destruction of Munitions, 40, 97
Destruction process, 42, 96, 100

Destruction sites, 40, 43
Detonations, 47, 56, 73, 84–86, 89, 96, 98, 100, 102
Detonation chamber, 86, 96–97, 100
Devastated regions, 21, 39–40, 43, 45–46
DGR&E (Directorate of Grave Registrations and Enquiries), 113, 116–17, 121–22, 131, 134, 141, 147, 151, 153, 155, 157–59, 162, 171–72, 183, 194–96
Divisional burial officers, 117
Divisional Salvage Company, 26
DNA, 217, 219, 225
DOVO (Service for Clearance and Disposal of Explosive Ordnance) (Belgium), 50, 57, 62–63, 69, 71–77, 80, 82, 84–95, 97, 99, 101–3
  members of, 73, 76
Dud shells, 23, 25, 35–36, 48, 58
Durie, Captain William, 201–2

E

Effects, personal, 119, 137, 218, 226
Enquiry Report, 130–32, 136, 138–42, 147–54
Exhumation companies, 129, 139, 153, 159, 163
Exhumation parties, 148, 162, 165, 191
  remaining, 158
Exhumations, 121–23, 129–32, 134, 136, 138–42, 145, 147–55, 159–62, 165, 173–79, 183–86, 189, 203
  policy banning, 187
  task of, 122, 129, 139, 162
Exhumation units, 121–23, 127–29, 134, 141, 145, 157, 160–62, 191, 195
  official, 140, 204
Exhumation work, 122–23, 134, 136, 145, 154, 158–59, 163
Expatriation of British Bodies, 185, 232

F

Facilities, 43, 75, 82, 86–88, 103, 183
  ammunition destruction, 41
Families, 48, 51, 54–55, 106, 110, 171–73, 176, 178–80, 182, 185, 201, 203–5, 208, 227–28
Farmers, 55–58, 62, 68–69, 76, 78, 82, 88, 105, 161, 164, 170, 211–13, 217
Fatalities, 49–52, 54, 56, 80, 83, 103
Fils, 40–43, 84

First World War, 23–24, 55–56, 59, 62, 68–69, 71, 75, 78–79, 208–13, 215, 222, 225, 229, 232–33
Flanders Fields Museum, ix, 15, 18–20, 22, 28, 33–34, 56, 61, 104, 111, 115
Flanders GHQ Controller, 32, 37
France, 24–25, 29–32, 37, 40–42, 68–69, 107–10, 116, 120–25, 160–61, 170–71, 173–76, 178, 187, 202, 206–9, 217–19
Fuses, 46, 52–53, 56, 62, 65, 70, 76, 85–86, 89

G

Gardeners, 59, 61, 123, 180, 194, 204
Gas, 14–16, 21, 43, 97, 100, 189, 223
Gas shells, 23, 25, 39
  mustard, 36
German Army, 36, 50, 72–73, 208–9
German artillery shells, 16, 53, 175
German cemeteries, 152, 183
German graves service, 211
German graves unit, 209
German POWs, 29, 32, 37, 74
Goodland, Colonel Herbert, 133, 139–40, 142–44
Grave diggers, 170, 184
Grave exhumation units, 37
Grave markers, 117, 137, 146–47, 151–52
  improvised, 108
  official, 110
  permanent, 142
  temporary, 151
Grave registration, 113
Grave robbers, 204
Graves, 38–39, 59–61, 108–13, 116–17, 123–24, 134, 138–39, 141–42, 145–52, 154–56, 158–59, 169–71, 180–81, 183–85, 187–89, 194, 199, 201–3, 210–11
  adjacent, 146
  battlefield, 152
  duplicated, 154
  empty, 147
  family, 205
  identified, 174
  individual, 141
  invisible, 165
  known, 224
  makeshift, 119, 189
  marked, 168
  missing, 196
  original, 137, 197

potential, 111
prepared, 119
separate, 219
shallow, 22, 108
single, 210
single isolated, 109
son, 112, 126, 155, 189–90, 194
sunken, 204
unidentified, 144, 153
unknown, 154, 203
visible, 131
Graves Labour Companies, 155
Graves Registration Commission, 110–11
Graves Registrations and Enquiries, 142, 153
GRC (Graves Registration Commission), 110–11, 113, 120, 131, 172
Grieving families, 110–11, 204
Ground, 56–57, 69–70, 76, 78, 84–85, 103, 105, 126, 128–29, 132, 134, 158–59, 211, 213, 215
GRU (Grave Registration Unit) 38, 110–11, 113, 117, 122, 126–27, 133, 142, 151

H

Hague Convention, 29, 32
Hand grenades, 36, 60, 62, 65, 94, 103
Harvest time, 59, 212
HDC, 96
Headstones, 33, 199, 220
  erected IWGC, 201
Hooge, 16, 38, 47, 146, 151–52, 155
Hooge Crater Cemetery, 145–46, 150, 154, 161, 221
Hopkins, Private Grenville Carson, 189–99,

I

Identifications, 83–84, 91, 94, 118–19, 125, 128, 136, 138, 140, 147–49, 153, 155, 157–58, 217–19, 224–25
  methods of, 118
Illegal exhumations, 182, 184–89, 194, 197–99, 201–4
  alleged, 185
  successful, 204
Illegal Repatriation and Expatriation of British Bodies, 185
Imperial War Graves Commission, 59, 159, 193
Irish Farm Cemetery, 223

Isolated graves, 110, 120, 145, 157–60, 175–76
  visible, 157, 162–63
IWGC (Imperial War Graves Commission), 59, 109, 113, 121, 123, 155, 157–65, 167–68, 172–80, 182–83, 185–86, 188, 192–95, 197–99, 201, 204, 208, 211–12
  official, 211
  overworked, 178
IWGC gardeners of Tyne Cot Cemetery, 194

J

JCCC (Joint Casualty and Compassionate Centre), 219–20, 223–24, 228–29

K

King George V, 19, 23, 108–9, 124, 146, 149, 173, 224
Kortrijk, 71

L

Labour Company, 37–39, 128–45, 147, 150–55, 159
Labour Corps, 28–29, 34, 37, 39
Land, 34–35, 45–47, 51–55, 57–59, 76, 79, 105–6, 113–14, 165, 167, 169–70, 173–75, 185, 207
  foreign, 174
Landscape, 21–22, 24, 68
Lijssenthoek Cemetery, 185, 188

M

Machine guns, 14–15, 107
Manpower, 17, 26, 31–32, 40, 117, 121, 128, 157–58
Memorials, ix, 106, 208, 210–11
Messines, 25, 57, 78, 158, 169, 175
Messines Ridge, 16, 24–25, 169
Metzinger, Francois, 213
Mills bomb, 69–70
Mines, 78–79
Munitions, 37, 40, 43, 64, 72–73, 82, 84–90, 94, 96–98, 100, 103
  box of, 96
  explosive, 41, 85
  wartime, 75